WILLOW RUN

Warren Benjamin Kidder

**ALBERT KAHN
ASSOCIATES, INC.**

ARCHITECTURE
ENGINEERING
INTERIOR DESIGN
PLANNING

July 18, 1995

Dear Mr. Kidder:

Albert Kahn's unique vision of industrial architecture and background in automotive development enabled the firm to not only conceive the Willow Run plant, but to pull together the design and engineering resources to fulfill the design effort. The long personal relationship between Albert Kahn and Henry Ford, and the understanding that was developed between their respective companies over a period of 30 years were critical to achieving this monumental task -- in record time.

Sincerely,

*A Century
    of Pride
1895-1995
A Future
    of Excellence*

Gordon V. R. Holness, P.E.
President & CEO
Albert Kahn Associates, Inc

WILLOW RUN

COLOSSUS OF AMERICAN

INDUSTRY

HOME OF
HENRY FORD'S
B-24 "LIBERATOR" BOMBER

KFT
Lansing, Michigan
Order Phone
1-800-754-6830
Access Code 30
Major Credit Cards

THE B-24 "LIBERATOR" BOMBER
Dedicated to *All* the crews of the B-24

WILLOW RUN

COLOSSUS OF AMERICAN INDUSTRY

WARREN BENJAMIN KIDDER

Registered Historical Site

HOME OF
HENRY FORD'S
B-24 "LIBERATOR" BOMBER

1. Willow Run: History of the land, construction of the airport and factory. 2. Building of the B-24 "Liberator" bomber, at the rate of one an hour.

Includes Index

Excerpts from Accession 435 volumes 1-20 used by permission of the Research Center of Henry Ford Museum and Greenfield Village.

Excerpts from *THE WARTIME JOURNALS OF CHARLES A. LINDBERGH,* copyright © 1970 by Charles A. Lindbergh, reprinted by permission of Harcourt Brace & Company.

Selected quotes, illustrations and charts from *Willow Run* by Lowell J. Carr and James E. Stermer. Copyright © 1952 by Harper & Row, Publishers, Inc. Copyright renewed 1980 by Leah M. Carr. Reprinted by permission of Harper Collins Publishers, Inc.

First Edition - ISBN 0-9647205-3-1

Library of Congress Catalog Card Number: 95-94664

Printed in the United States of America. The paper in this book meets the guidelines for permanence and durability of the Committee on Production Guidelines for Book Longevity of the Council on Library Resources.

DEDICATION

This book is dedicated to Eva and Elmer Kidder who gave up their home and their land for Willow Run, and to their sons Herbert, Donald, and Warren Benjamin, who helped them build their American Dream.

It is dedicated to *ALL* of the people who helped make their sacrifice a successful operation, from B-24 bombers to automobiles; and on into the future.

Beyond those who have contributed to Willow Run, I dedicate this book to my children:

Robert Lawrence	Laura B. Elizabeth
Donald Scott	Zamie E. Ruth
Barbara	Eva P. Victoria

and to Francisca Garcia de Kidder

SPECIAL ACKNOWLEDGEMENT

This study of Willow Run began many years ago when I roamed the fields of Willow Run as a small boy. The writing, however, did not begin until recently when Linda Peckham (Professor of "Forum For Authors" at Lansing Community College and President of the Lansing Historical Society) discovered I was the last person to have lived on the land where the Willow Run Industrial Complex was built, and that I later worked there. Without her generous assistance and editing of vast amounts of material this book would never have been published.

ACKNOWLEDGEMENTS

Luke Gilliland-Swetland and the staff of the Research Center of Henry Ford Museum and Greenfield Village were especially courteous in locating material. A portion of the information in Chapters V, VI, and VIII is preserved there under Accession 435, Volumes 1 through 20, as are Reminiscences of numerous Ford employees.

Sylvia Sanders and Marsha Desert from the Library Services of Albert Kahn Associates, Detroit, were instrumental in obtaining much of the engineering and construction information provided in Chapter IV, and many of the photographs used throughout the book.

Harold Sherman receives special acknowledgment for his assistance in locating and making available information and photographs located at the Yankee Air Force library on the Beck Road side of Willow.

Information in the Appendix, found in the historical records of Eva G. (Dickson) Kidder, was complied and used by the Willow Run Plant Guide Service. Never made available to the general public, few copies, if any, of this information now exist. It is presented here to preserve for history and the interested reader one of the best sources of information during the first four years of Willow Run.

To Pat and Mel Diethelm I wish to extend a sincere word of gratitude for their years of encouragement and reading of manuscripts.

The crew of the 00 frontispiece was lost when their ship went down the day after the picture was taken. They included: Captain Thomas W. Vaughn, 27, Elyra, O., First Lt. John K. Howmiller, 25 of Lansing, Ill., C. R. Wonack Ford flight engineer, 35, Dearborn Inn, and Harvey D. Jenkins, 26, Ford flight engineer, Ann Arbor, Michigan.

CONTENTS

CONTENTS

Books By Warren Benjamin Kidder

Benjamin - His Life And His Adventures
North To Alaska
South Into Mexico
Willow Run

CORRECTIONS

Typographical

Page	Change	To
xiii	H. H. Henning	H. P. Henning
43	W. C. Thomas	C. W. Thomas
66	Kundsen	Knudsen
95	Cause & Sanders	Couse & Saunders
137	April 15, three	April 16, two
171	bomber	bombed
175	followed-up	follow-up
199	divided	divide
201	carried	carry
215	engage	engaged
231	H. H. Henning	H. P. Henning
249	Engineer in	Engineering
281	scrubs	shrubs
305	rotatoes	rotates

Page Numbers
(Illustrations)

Illustrations - Page Number Corrections (continued)

PHOTO CREDITS

ILLUSTRATIONS

ILLUSTRATIONS

ILLUSTRATIONS

WILLOW RUN IN A NUTSHELL

Area: Entire project	1,878 acres
Airport size	1,434 acre
Factory floor 80 1/4 acres -	3,503,016 sq. ft.
Including hangars	4,734,617 sq. ft.
Length of factory - east to west	3,200 feet
Width of factory	1,277 feet
Length of assembly lines	5450 feet
Runways (longest)	7,366 feet
(shortest)	6,510 feet
Cost of project	$103,000,000
Weight of B-24 on delivery	49,900 lbs.
No. rivets in B-24	313,237
Dies made as of December 1944	29,124
Fixtures in Production	10,915
No. wooden floor blocks	16,000,000
Fluorescent tubes	152,000
No. windows	28,855
Conveyors	136
Craneways	29
Monorails (all buildings)	18 miles
Power requirements approx.	13,200 KWH
Students trained in school	5 0,000
Water used daily approx.	5 ,000,000 gals.
Parking lots (capacity)	15,300 cars
Fuel capacity (gasoline)	150,000 gals.
Fire Protection (Sprinkler Heads)	5,212

Airport concrete equal to a 20 foot highway 115 miles long.

PREFACE

Willow Run is what Albert Kahn, its world renowned architect, described as "the most enormous room in the history of man." The story of Willow Run describes how Charles E. Sorensen, Ford's Director of Production during World War II, conceived the idea of manufacturing the giant B-24 bomber at the unbelievable rate of one an hour; and how the men and women from Willow Run, challenged by the opportunity, made his vision come true.

As a young boy, I lived near the banks of a small stream called Willow Run in Southeast Michigan. I saw my family evicted from their home under the rights of eminent domain to make room for the huge Willow Run bomber plant, and I felt the trauma of the war months before Japan bombed Pearl Harbor.

The first airplane ever to use the runways of the Willow Run airport came low over my head and stopped within a hundred yards from where I was standing, and I saw its pilots, H. H. Henning and C. W. Thomas, get out of the airplane. I marveled at Charles Lindbergh flight testing airplanes and remembered seeing a replica of his "Spirit of Saint Louis" hanging from the ceiling of Ford's museum in Greenfield Village.

When the first structural steel for the factory rose above the horizon I was there to see it, looking westward from where I was living on the perimeter of the airport, before my grandparent's house was moved. And before going into the military, I worked for Chicago Cafeteria Incorporated, supplying food service for the people living in the Willow Run housing project.

In later years, after World War II, I was employed at Willow Run by the Kaiser-Frazer Corporation as assistant division manager of production engineering, when Kaiser manufactured the C-119 and C-123 cargo planes during the Korean conflict. My experience in expediting the design, process, build, and tryout of all project tools, dies, jigs, fixtures and masters for both planes, along with the departmental responsibility for manufacturing the first lot of airplanes, gave me an invaluable insight into the problems that were confronted by Sorensen and the men from Ford.

It made my study of their departmental records come alive. I became a member of their group, and it provided a validity and dimension of fascination for their accomplishments.

The story of Willow Run reaches far beyond the quiet stream where the Indians camped and hunted and where people gathered in a peaceful chapel by its side; the story reaches to the thunderous rain of bombs that helped liberate Europe from the Gestapo claws of Hitler and return the South Pacific to the peaceful tranquility of its name.

Willow Run stands in honor of all the people who ever lived or worked there; from the early pioneers who settled the land to the visionaries who struggled to develop creative ideas for mass producing the bomber; and from those who built the planes that helped bring freedom back into the world, to those who came to help but could not, for lack of housing. Many of those people lived in squalid conditions to build the bombers that kept the American dream alive. To all of them, this nation and the Allied Powers during World War II owe a debt of gratitude.

Willow Run is bigger than just corporations or airplanes and automobiles. After all, Henry Ford, whose company manufactured the B-24 bombers for which the plant was originally constructed, is dead. Charles E. Sorensen, its visionary, too is dead. The Kaiser-Frazer Corporation that manufactured three different automobiles and two different kinds of airplanes under its roof all at the same time no longer exists. And should its current landlord close its doors the plant would simply await the next generation of daring entrepreneurs to come and go.

This study is offered as a contribution to the history of Willow Run, a record of its creation and the first years of its life for those who follow.

I was fourteen when the bulldozers started cutting across the fields of my father's farm, and Willow Run has been a part of my life for more than half a century. It has impacted my mind so vividly that I decided to accept a challenge from Linda Peckham, my professor of "Forum for Authors," to compile a history of Willow Run.

WARREN BENJAMIN KIDDER

DENTON, MICHIGAN
MAY 30, 1995

WILLOW RUN

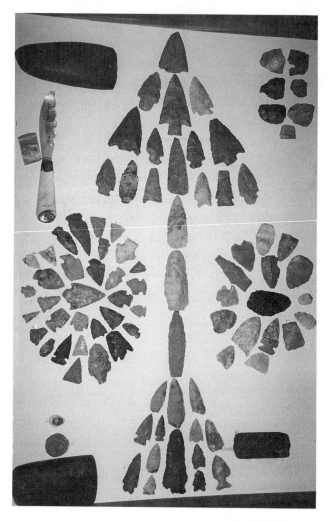

Donald E. Kidder

Out Of The Land Of Arrowheads
Came The "Liberator"

Chapter I

FROM ARROWHEADS TO B-24 BOMBERS

The Ford Motor Company was America's third largest manufacturer of military equipment during World War II. They manufactured aircraft engines, gliders, tanks, tank destroyers, troop carriers, armored cars, trucks and jeeps.[1] But the project that brought them the most notoriety was Willow Run, the world's largest industrial factory ever constructed under one roof. Built in the pastoral countryside east of Ypsilanti, Michigan, near the Village of Denton, Willow Run boasted an aircraft assembly line more than a mile long. Mass production of the 20 ton, four-engine, B-24 "liberator" bomber, at the unbelievable rate of one an hour, was the biggest challenge ever undertaken by the Ford Motor Company.

In January 1941 the project began to move quickly. The Advisory Council for National Defense needed more B-24 bombers than Consolidated Aircraft Corporation, its designer in California could supply, and invited the Ford Motor Company to submit a proposal for their production.

To mass produce the airplane required constructing a new factory and creating manufacturing methods and procedures of assembly never before thought possible in the aircraft industry. To Charles E. Sorensen, Ford's Director of

1

Production, it became the challenge of his career.

Willow Run derives its appellation from a small stream of the same name that flows through the cultivated fields and woodlands to the Huron River which empties into Lake Erie. During construction of the Willow Run bomber plant, as it was first called, Henry Ford had the stream preserved, routing it underneath the floor of the factory.

In the early 1800's and before, the Potawatomi Indians used the banks of this stream for a camp site and hunting lodge. In the heavily forested countryside, they hunted for food and trapped the fur-bearing animals for pelts to trade, including the wolf that lived in the area at that time. When Alexis de Tocqueville, a French explorer, visited the Michigan territory in 1831, he was in search of the rough, untamed frontier of the continent. Traveling from the cities of the East Coast he was in search of "the utmost limits of European civilisation,"[2] where the primitive Indians lived. He wanted to find the place where no man could tell him, "I cut down the first tree of the forest."[3]

In the wilderness of Michigan he found what he was looking for. It began only a mile from the Detroit River. Beyond Pontiac, which took him a day to reach by horseback, "settlements became infinitely rare... cultivated fields seemed to stop all at once."[4] Except for the rare sound of a cowbell or growl of a bear, used as a watchdog, affirming a settler's clearing, de Tocqueville saw nothing but darkened forests through which he traveled until reaching Flint, a settlement of "only two or three cabins;"[5] and in Saginaw, where he turned back, he found what he had been searching for, the absolute end of European civilization.

Beneath the trees on his way to Flint, de Tocqueville discovered in the pioneers the future greatness of America. "A nation of conquerors," he said.[6]

Traveling west brought the same wilderness. Jonathan Morton, in 1824, traveled by foot from Detroit to Ypsilanti. He used an Indian trail going through Flat Rock, and in a paper for the Washtenaw County Pioneer Society, Morton wrote, "Where the city of Ypsilanti now stands there were two shanties constructed of poles and occupied by George Hall and John Stewart."[7]

The federal government settled with the Indian tribes for the land in this part of Michigan in 1807, and Michigan Governor Lewis Cass's Treaty of Saginaw opened the area to pioneer settlement in 1819. In 1827, the first federal land grant in the Willow Run area was sold by the government for a fee of $1.25 per acre.[8]

The first grant was purchased by Jacob Larzelere, in section six of Van Buren Township on the north side of the airport. He granted 360 acres for a total of $459 on August 14, 1827, but he lived four miles to the west, in Ypsilanti, named two years earlier after Demetrius Ypsilanti, a Greek general whose heroism was sung in a patriotic ballad. Larzelere's land lay idle and uninhabited.

In December of 1831 brothers Robert and John Geddes purchased 87 acres from the government. Their land was heavily timbered and Robert Geddes constructed a saw mill. But they too resided elsewhere.

In 1837, Michigan became a state, and in February of

the following year the state-built Michigan Central Railroad extended its service from Dearborn to Ypsilanti, passing through what would become the Village of Denton, reaching Chicago 13 years later. The railroad opened up territory to more settlers and farmers who cleared the forests and expanded the farmland. By 1840, the two counties in which the Willow Run industrial complex would be built ranked first and third in Michigan's invested manufacturing capital, Washtenaw with $315,000 and Wayne with $275,000.[9]

Samuel Youngs Denton and his wife Maria came from Ypsilanti in 1847. They purchased the Geddes saw mill, and 10 acres adjacent to the north side of the railroad. The mill operated 24 hours a day, six days a week, while the land was being cleared, and the timber shipped to Detroit via the new rail system. Samuel Denton became an agent for the Michigan Central Railroad, built a rail siding which also provided service for Belleville and Rawsonville, operated a general store, and arranged for the post office to be relocated from South Plymouth. Denton registered the village plat that bears his name on June 21, 1866, and that same year he sold two lots to the District Seven school board for erection of a school.

February three years later, the Dentons sold two more of their village lots to the trustees of the First Methodist Church of Denton for the sum of one hundred dollars. The church, having a seating capacity of 250 people, cost $3000 and was dedicated in December 1869.

According to Cathy Horst and Diane Wilson in *Water Under The Bridge,*

The last to take up land in this section was the first to bring his family and actually put down roots in Van Buren Township. Jesse N. Horner...purchased the last 80 acres available by grant on June 1, 1832. He sent word back to his... brothers in New York and they too made the journey to Van Buren.

Clark and Hannah (Freeman) Horner came to Van Buren in 1832.... Upon their arrival, they erected a small log cabin near [actually on] the area of what is now Willow Run Airport. It was in this cabin that the township's first religious society was formed in 1835.... Clark and Hannah soon added a second room to their home to accommodate the attendance at the "Horner Mission," as it became known.

Mr. Horner served as steward of the Methodist-Episcopal Church of Denton for over 40 years prior to his death in November 1886 at age 77. His wife Hannah remained a member of the... church for the rest of her life.[10]

It was in this heavily forested country just outside of Dearborn, Michigan, that Henry Ford's grandfather, John, arrived with his family of seven in 1848. He had traveled through Canada from his farm in Clonakilty in the County of Cork, Ireland. His wife, Thomasina, had died en route leaving the family burden to John and his eldest son, William, Henry's father. They cut and cleared the land for farming, and in April of 1861, at the age of 35, William married Mary Litogot (O'Hern, was her adopted name).

On this farm, in de Tocqueville's land of conquerors, Henry Ford was born on July 30, 1863.

WILLOW RUN

Long before Henry Ford's Model-T began frightening horses off the dirt streets of Detroit, the interurban trolley system played an important role in developing rural America. Public transportation in and around Detroit began in August of 1863, the year of Ford's birth, when horses were first used to pull streetcars from the Michigan Central Depot to the eastern edge of the city limits. By 1895, the last horse-car was replaced by steam engines and electric trolleys, and a number of outlying communities already owned their own trolleys. Inter-connecting those towns established the electrified rural and interurban rail system.

Detroit was the center of interurban transportation with six lines reaching out 20 to 75 miles, and by 1900 it boasted more mileage than any other city in the United States. The passenger business exploded, and electrified interurban freight commerce, with overnight service, expanded between Michigan, Ohio, Indiana, and parts of Illinois.

Ypsilanti and Ann Arbor had pioneered the interurban in 1890 with the "Ypsi-Ann" route running parallel to Packard Road. They ran scheduled round trips every half hour between the two college towns for a one-way fare of ten cents, and carried 600 passengers a day. In eight years that figure increased to 4000. In 1896, the company electrified the line and retired the original steam engine, called a steam dummy, because it was camouflaged as a regular passenger car to avoid scaring the horses. A year later, the line was extended to Denton, Dearborn and Detroit by adding a power house in Ypsilanti and Dearborn to compensate for the severe loss of amperage encountered in transmitting the electric current more than twenty miles. The early success of the "Ypsi-Ann" was attributed, largely, to the University of Michigan in Ann Arbor which had "three thousand boys and not enough girls,"

"WHY THE TROLLEY!"

ABOVE: Gratiot and City Limits (Harper) May 9, 1908. The Rapid Railway track was on the right.

and [the Normal College in Ypsilanti which had] "a thousand girls and not enough boys."[11] The interurban helped to restore the balance, especially on the weekends.

Interestingly, the "Ypsi-Ann" did not develop outwardly from Detroit, but as an enterprising local service between the two communities. In 1899 a branch of the line was installed from Ypsilanti to Saline. Two years later, the main line was pushed from Ann Arbor to Jackson, and passengers wanting to travel further west could transfer to another line for Kalamazoo.[12]

In 1900, Detroit had grown to 285,704, and the trip by interurban north to Pontiac, that took de Tocqueville a

An 1890's rush hour in the streets of downtown Detroit shows both the horse drawn street car and the electric rail system.
(Burton Historical Collection, Detroit Public Library)

day to travel by horseback, was now completed in an hour. The interurban carried nearly a million passengers to Pontiac in luxury cars with ornate paneling, comfortable seats, smoking compartments, lavatories with brass fixtures, and dining cars providing the finest in cuisine. By 1904 they were carrying more than four million passengers at an average fare of a penny a mile and at speeds of up to 50 miles an hour, luxuries far beyond the imagination of de Tocqueville when he traveled on foot through that part of Michigan. After World War I, the automobile became the more popular form of transportation and commerce. In 1925, motor buses replaced the trolley in Ann Arbor and Ypsilanti, in September the line to Saline was abandoned.

By 1940, the population of Detroit (2,222 during de Tocqueville's visit) had grown to 1,623,452; Ypsilanti had 12,121 residents, with an additional 4,153 living in the township outside of the city limits.

As the railroad had opened the frontier to the early pioneers after 1838, the interurban opened the land to early settlers. But the electric system that developed so quickly to serve the needs of the people, before Henry Ford developed the Model T, died as quickly as it began. The Ford Motor Company became the fastest growing private corporation in the world.

Late in the 1920's, Henry Ford started buying large parcels of land throughout the State of Michigan for what became known as the Ford Farms. In both the Van Buren and Ypsilanti Townships, surrounding Willow Run, he

Year	Population				
	Michigan	Detroit	Washtenaw County	Ypsilanti City	Ypsilanti Township
1820	8,896	1,442	a	a	a
1830	31,639	2,222	4,042	b	971[b]
1840	212,267	9,124	23,571	b	2,419[b]
1850	397,654	21,019	28,567	b	3,051[b]
1860	749,113	45,619	35,686	3,955	1,327
1870	1,184,059	79,577	41,434	5,471	1,561[c]
1880	1,636,937	116,340	41,848	4,984	1,459
1890	2,093,890	205,876	42,210	6,129	1,236
1900	2,420,982	285,704	47,761	7,378	1,233
1910	2,810,173	465,766	44,714	6,230	1,082
1920	3,668,412	993,618	49,520	7,413	1,083
1930	4,842,325	1,568,662	65,530	10,143	2,618
1940	5,256,106	1,623,452	80,810	12,121	4,153

a First white settlement in Washtenaw county came in what is now Ypsilanti city in 1823.
b Ypsilanti city incorporated in 1858. Not separated from Ypsilanti township in preceding censuses
c 1870 marked peak of open country population in Ypsilanti township.

Population Changes In Michigan, Detroit, And The Willow Run Area
From 1820 to 1940

purchased thousands of acres. On some of that land Mr. Ford maintained two camps to help sons of World War I veterans. He felt that if they could experience the rural atmosphere of working and living off the land they would become more self-sufficient and better citizens. When he started the camps, many of the boys were out of work and walking the streets of Detroit. The first "Camp Legion" started near Dearborn in 1938. The second camp, near the Willow Run stream, was started in 1939 and called Camp Legion II or "Camp Willow Run." Marion Wilson, in *The Story Of Willow Run,* describes the camp:

> The boys at Camp Willow Run lived in army tents. There was a mess hall and a chapel. The sixty-five boys came to camp in April and stayed until early in November. They farmed the three hundred and twenty acres next to the camp, working eight hours a day for twenty-five cents an hour. Mr. Ford provided the use of the land, tents, tractors and equipment; the boys did the work. They raised the vegetables and sold them at a stand at one end of the farm, on Ecorse Road. At the end of the season, after the expenses of seed and fertilizer had been paid, plus the cost of the food they did not raise, the profit was divided among the boys.

> William Coons was one of the boys in Camp Willow Run in 1941. "That was a wonderful summer.... Of course, it was sort of like being in the army with lots of rules, but we all really loved the work. We were healthy and gained weight. Besides the two dollars a day which I earned---and that was good pay

in those days---there was enough profit at the end of the summer which, when divided, gave each of us a hundred and sixty-eight dollars. With what I had saved from my two dollars a day and my season's profits, I bought my first car."[13]

Boys Working The Fields At Camp Willow Run

The Ford farms, on which Mr. Ford raised mostly soy beans supplied raw material for his plastics experimental laboratory in Dearborn. They also provided a wonderful hiding place for pheasants, but he kept the land posted and we could not hunt there. The Ford farms provided summer work for local school boys, like my brothers, who hoed and pulled weeds to keep the fields clean for the same $2.00 a day received by the boys at Camp Willow Run.

Several times a week, between eight o'clock and ten-thirty in the morning, Mr. Ford would pass our farm on his way to and from the Willow Run Camp. All summer long whenever I was working in the fields, he would wave to me, and I would wave back to him.

When school started in the fall, I missed the relation-ship I had established with Mr. Ford. Then one day, hitch-hiking to the Belleville school, I held out my thumb to an approaching car and Mr. Henry Ford, in his chauffeured black Ford sedan, stopped to give me a ride. I could hardly carry on a conversation with him I was so nervous, my voice cracking and all. When he asked me if the hay cutter setting along side the barn was a McCormick, it was obvi-ous he had observed the details of our farm quite well. When I replied that I wasn't sure, he asked me to check its manufacturer, and if it were a McCormick to let him know. He would buy it from my father for his museum in Greenfield Village. It turned out to be manufactured by Brown & Co.

When we got to Belleville Road, two miles down the highway, I thanked him for the ride and told him I would get out there and get another ride on to school.

"No," he said. "I'll take you into Belleville," and he gave his chauffeur, Mr Wilson, the instructions. He let me off right in front of the schoolhouse.

Several weeks later, I was attending a school fair at the Edison Institute of Technology in Greenfield Village, Mr. Ford's private college, where my brother Donald was a student. Mr. Ford spotted me in a crowd of spectators observing a demonstration at a pottery wheel, and came over to ask me how I was enjoying the program. I introduced him to my mother and Uncle George Knapp, the postmaster at Royal Oak, and his wife May. Uncle George never got over telling people about the night his nephew introduced him to Henry Ford.

In 1940, a white colonial chapel with an eight-sided steeple towering above the trees was erected on the site of Camp Willow Run (now located on the northern outskirts of Belleville), and every morning before heading into the fields the boys would attend service. "The organ was played by Ted Winters (one of the boys living and working in the camp), who three years later was killed in action over the English Channel while serving as a radio operator on one of the B-24 "Liberator" bombers, built on the site where he had played the organ."[14]

In January 1941, Charles Sorensen visualized using the land under cultivation by the Ford Farms east of Ypsilanti as the location for the Willow Run factory. While he negotiated for production of the B-24 bomber, architects put together construction plans for the huge plant, and conscription of the land began taking place under rights of eminent domain. In the spring, land owners were evicted from their homes and quickly moved off the land to meet Sorensen's schedule for completion of the airport and bomber plant.

Ford's Chapel On The Banks Of Willow Run

Fortunately, Ford owned large parcels of the land in both Wayne and Washtenaw Counties, on which the airport and factory were built, reducing the number of families to be relocated. The two counties were separated by Rawsonville Road. In Wayne County, the airport for the airplanes as they came off the assembly line was built on the flat open land in Van Buren Township near the Village of Denton. In Washtenaw County, the manufacturing plant was constructed in

15

Ypsilanti Township where Ypsilanti served as the major population area of both townships. The airport, more than a mile wide by two miles long, was bordered by Ecorse, Beck, Chase and Rawsonville roads on its north, east, south, and west sides respectively. This area encompassed four square miles of land. The two gravel roads that crossed in the middle, Denton and Tyler, were closed at the perimeter, and families living on them were required to move.

South of Ecorse Road on Denton Road, seven families had to move. They included:

The Norwood family, where the first airplane beacon west of Detroit was located for guiding the pilots on the first U.S. airmail service between Detroit and Chicago (lack of an emergency landing strip was indicated by the red light on the tower);[15]

The Elmer Conant family with two houses, one for Mary Conant and their son, Herbert, who made maple syrup in the woods during the springtime;

Mrs. Clarabelle (Horner) Avery, daughter of William K. Horner the son of Clark and Hannah, and grandmother to the children of Edna and William Alton Smith;

The Neubert family, who originally came from Mankato, Minnesota, lived in the Edward Forgarty house.

The Elmer W. Kidder family, living on the original Clark Horner land grant located on the southeast corner of Ecorse and Denton Roads; and across from the Kidders, the Spurr house.

To the East, between Denton and Beck Roads were the Dicks and Gerich farms. West, between Denton and Rawsonville Roads, there were the Parks and Dolby farms with homes to be removed.

At Rawsonville Road at Ecorse, near the edge of the airport perimeter but not obstructing construction, were the homes of Howard and Scott Colby. These farms had been purchased by the Ford Farms a number of years before construction and were used, during the war, to house military officers. After the war, the property reverted to Ford and was sold to private individuals. Today, both homes remain on their original location.

The Schlossstein family and others living on the north side of Ecorse Road were not required to relocate.

The socio-economic changes that had taken place in Europe and Asia since our pioneers first settled around Denton had begun to show their devastating effect. They had brought about two World Wars, including the one to which we were about to become committed, and now huge portions of this Denton land would become part of Sorensen's vision to mass produce the B-24 bomber.

Clark and Hannah Horner and the Scott Colby family could never have dreamed that a hundred years later their land, granted to them by the government for $1.25 an acre, would be used to build flying mechanical birds or a factory estimated to cost $200,000,000.

END NOTES

1. GM's contracts totaled 13.8 billion between 1940 and 1944, Curtiss-Wright's $7.09 billion, and Ford's 5.26 billion. Chrysler ranked eighth in the table of defense contractors with $3.39 billion. During World War II, the Ford Motor Company built 8600 B-24 bombers, 57,000 aircraft engines, 250,000 jeeps, 93,217 military trucks, 26,954 tank engines, 4291 gliders, 1,718 tanks and tank destroyers, 13,000 amphibians, 12,500 armored cars, and other pieces of other equipment." Robert L. Shook. *Turnaround.* New York: Prentice Hall, 1990: 44.
2. Alexis de Tocqueville. *Journey To America.* New Haven: Yale Press, 1960: 335.
3. de Tocqueville, 351.
4. de Tocqueville, 360.
5. de Tocqueville, 362.
6. de Tocqueville, 364.
7. Pioneer Society of Michigan. *Historical Collections:* 399.
8. Lowell Carr and James Stermer. *Willow Run: A Study of Industrialization and Cultural Inadequacy.* New York: Harper and Brothers, 1952: 22.
9. Carr and Stermer, 23.
10. Cathy Horst and Diane Wilson. *Water Under the Bridge.* Belleville, Michigan: Van Buren Township Bicentennial Commission, 1972: 195. Photos by David Carlson.
11. Jack Schramm and William Henning. *Detroit Street Railways Vol. I: City Lines 1863-1922.* Chicago, Illinois: Central Electric Railfans' Association, 1978: 87.
12. William H. Henning. *Detroit Its Trolleys and Interurbans.* Fraser, Michigan: Michigan Transit Museum, 1978: 26.
13. Marion Wilson. *The Story of Willow Run.* Ann Arbor: The University of Michigan Press, 1956: 19.
14. Research Center of Henry Ford Museum and Greenfield Village, Dearborn, Michigan: Accession 435, Box 15, Vol. 1: 7.
15. Donald E. Kidder. Reminiscence.

Eva and Elmer Kidder spent their twenty-fifth wedding anniversary on Belleville Road, May 12, 1942. Later, they moved into a new home on Packard Road west of Ypsilanti.

The homes of Eva and Elmer Kidder before they were moved. The large house was moved two miles east and relocated on the east side of Belleville Road, north of Ecorse. The small house was relocated west of Ypsilanti on Gulfside at Packard Road. It traveled a distance of nine miles. Taken by author Spring 1940.

Doctor Bion Arnold - Denton's Country Doctor

An 1889 graduated from the University of Michigan Medical School, he made his rounds on foot; carried his own scales and powdered medicines which he dispensed onto strips of newspaper and folded into individual packets; and he accepted chickens, eggs, asparagus and strawberries in exchange for his medical services.

Myrtle and Louis Schlossstein, our neighbors to the north of Ecorse Road. He saved their beautiful family home by working for 25 cents an hour during the great depression. Later, General Motors purchased the property. Today, their home is gone and the land again grows wild. When your author was a small child, Mrs. Schlossstein taught him how to use the knife and the fork. When he grew older, Mr. Schlossstein taught him to sing in the Denton church.

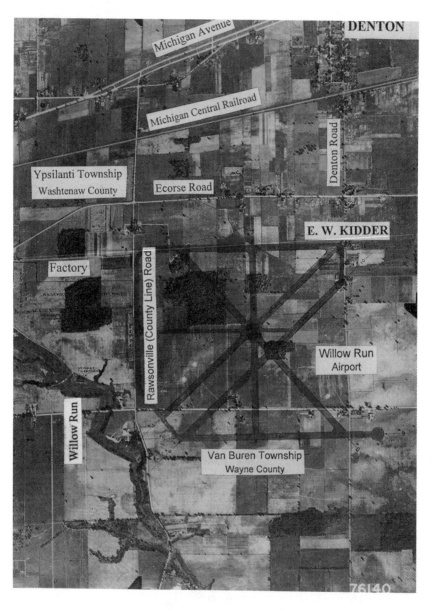

Van Buren Township - Denton - Willow Run Airport

Chapter II

THE LAST WILLOW RUN PIONEERS

Before Sorensen could build Willow Run and the B-24 bombers, he first had to displace the early pioneers and a way of life that had taken them generations of hard work to build.

Mrs. Clarabelle (Horner) Avery, daughter of the first settler in the Willow Run area, was one of those pioneers. The picture on the following page illustrates Sorensen's workmen cutting down trees and clearing the land around Mrs. Avery's home, even before she was able to relocate. The truck backed up to the house belonged to her grandson, Robert Smith, who was removing her household furnishings. Ester Smith, his sister, said that the house was not moved from the location. It was demolished by the bulldozers and set afire.

The Elmer Kidder family, of which I am the youngest, was the last of the pioneer families to leave what is now the Willow Run airport. My father settled there in 1921, before I was born, and when the bulldozers began moving through the countryside uprooting trees and leveling everything in sight for construction, it etched an image in my mind that even now, after more than fifty years, is as vivid as when I lived there.

When I cultivated the fields, I collected sea shells deposited there when the Great Lakes receded after the last glacial period, some ten thousand years ago. I found arrowheads, made of stone, lost by the Indians who hunted our land, and as a small child, not yet old enough for school, I walked behind my father in the fields looking for cutworms while our horses pulled a single bladed plow turning furrow upon furrow across acres of farm land.

Sorensen's Schedule At Work: Mrs. Avery's House
(Taken by Author Spring 1941)

I treasure how my family toiled for years to turn a barren piece of Michigan countryside into a beautiful farm, until Adolph Hitler, in some far off country, started World War II.

In 1921, my grandfather, Leonard Henry Dickson, a harness-maker who migrated from Ontario, Canada before the time of automobiles, loaned my parents the money to make a down payment on the farm, providing that my father would build him a home where he and my grandmother could live out the rest of their lives. The land Dad purchased was the original land granted to Clark and Hannah Horner located on the southeast corner of Denton and Ecorse Roads a half mile south of Denton. With the help of their friends they built a four-room house, and on November 20, 1921, they moved from a tent into the house.

From then on Mother said, "Our work, our troubles, and our pleasures combined kept us very busy."

In April of every year, my mother, Eva, received baby chickens and worked with them in heated brooder coops with rounded corners to keep them from huddling together and suffocating. One year, in an hour while attending the Denton church, she had lost an entire shipment of them. When the days got warmer and the asparagus was in full growth, she helped me cut bushels of it by hand before I went to school and after I came home. In June and July, she worked in the open heat of the strawberry patches with Dora Plonte and the rest of the Denton pickers, working barebacked and in sunbonnets for two or three cents a quart to help fight against the worst depression in history that started in October of 1929.

The hot summer sun blistered our skin until it peeled off in sheets, leaving the body sore and tender to the new red-skin below. When my father hand mixed the cement and poured the floors in the chicken houses, his blisters were as big as my hand. They covered his entire back and hurt him so much he would go to church without even wearing his shirt. When they broke you could see the water running out from under them, and in the mornings Mother would complain how wet the bed sheets were because of the blisters that had broken during the night.

Hard Work And The Model T Ford Built The American Dream

In the winter, Michigan's sub-zero temperatures froze the breath of the farm animals on their faces giving them a ghostly appearance, and I carried fresh warm water from the house to replace the ice in their watering tub so they could drink. The northwest winds piled snow drifts as high as the fences and all winter long we dug ourselves out of the snow that blocked access to the outbuildings and the driveway. And Jack Frost would leave his etchings on the bedroom windows in the attic where there was no heat.

At the age of five, all bundled up in warm clothes and with blustering snow blowing in my face, I would trudge north down the country road to the Denton school. For my little feet, it seemed like miles. Not until years later, when I survived a miracle rescue in the fierce cold near the Arctic Circle in Canada, did I feel the bravery that compared to walking the winter road to the Denton school.

Our entire family helped in working the farm. We specialized in chickens, eggs, strawberries and asparagus. We had a small orchard and grape vineyard, and we planted acres of corn, alfalfa and cabbage. Our cow was named Bess and we had two horses, Jim and Jess, who pulled the plow and helped us cultivate the fields. They pulled the big scoop when we dug out the dirt for our driveway system and filled it full of concrete. The concrete was purchased from the Michigan Highway Department for a dollar a truck load, when old Michigan Avenue was made into a four-lane divided highway as far west as Ypsilanti in the early 1930's.

But when I learned how to milk, which my older brothers eagerly taught me, it became more of a one man job, except for the help my mother would give me. In the winter, I ran a trap line to harvest muskrat, skunk and mink, in the same streams as the Potawatomi Indians, which meant I got out of bed a couple of hours earlier in the morning, between three-thirty and four.

Everyone helped prepare for the market. Chickens were plucked and placed in tubs of ice to keep them fresh; asparagus was bunched and stored in the cool basement, as were the strawberries; eggs were candled throughout the week and butter was churned by hand. The flowers I grew to help pay for my clothes and school books were cut after the heat of the day and placed in buckets of water to keep them fresh. In the fall, Grandma Dickson gathered orange bittersweet and dried flowers to help pay for her sewing materials.

Mother would leave for the Detroit Western Market at three-thirty on Saturday mornings to sell our produce. In the cold weather she carried a kerosene heater and an old army blanket that her brother, Herbert, had given her from his European tour of duty during World War I. They helped to protect her from the chill winds that blew through the open stalls of the market place.

Even with all of her responsibilities, Mother still found the time to bake bread, oatmeal cookies filled with date sauce, and fruit cake and plum pudding for the holidays; she preserved tomatoes, peaches, pears and vegetables for the cold Michigan winters; and she prepared the finest venison buffets when one of the family was fortunate enough to bring home a deer from the hunt.

I will never forget the delicious taste of strawberry shortcake topped with pure whipped cream made from the milk of our own cow, a treat Mother often had ready late at night when my two older brothers and I would return from a three mile bicycle ride to the Huron River where we would swim and cool off after long hot days in the fields.

It was Mother who worked right along side of my hard-working disciplinarian father, who expected us to see the work to be done and to do it without being asked. And it was Mother who added the warm touch that turned a hard working Michigan farm into a warm and loving home.

How beautiful had been the patch of violets half hidden beneath Mr. Fogarty's centenarian maple trees that lined Denton Road before the bulldozers came ripping through the countryside. Blue as the Concord grapes in the vineyard beyond the creek, beyond the cattails where the muskrats played, were those bouquets I gathered for years on Mother's Day until my grandmother, Phoebe, passed away. Then it was lilacs, white ones for Mother and lavender ones for me and the rest of the family.

Fresh and clear as a crystal of morning dew, the first Sunday I cut those white lilacs. Walking back across the lawn from where the white bush grew, out near the chicken coops, between the bee hives and the snowball bush, I can still remember my thoughts: "How will mother feel today when she wears the white lilacs and I wear the lavender? What of her sadness at the loss of her mother? "

She sensed my feelings as I pinned on her corsage and her embrace reassured me her love was forever, a gift to be passed from one generation to another. That Sunday in church when I looked around, I could tell by the color of flowers all the people who had mothers and those who did not. Now, it is my turn to wear the white flowers and pass on her gift of love.

The spring of 1926, when she was pregnant with me, was especially hectic for Mother. On February 10th her mother went to the hospital with cancer; Mrs. Schlossstein, our neighbor, gave her a baby shower and my oldest brother, Herbert, came down with the measles. Following the measles, he developed whooping cough, and so did my other brother, Donald. After the whooping cough they both developed the three-day measles. Herbert did not return to school until six weeks before the start of summer vacation.

When I started walking back and forth to the Denton school, I remember seeing the different colored quarantine signs nailed to houses. The house with the bright red sign was the one to really stay away from. Someone there had scarlet fever. There were other quarantine signs for measles, mumps, chicken pox, and other diseases that had not been brought under control by the school vaccination programs. Each disease had its own sign and distinctive color.

When my brothers and I finished elementary school in Denton, we traveled the five miles to the Belleville High School by bus. The driver, Mr. McMullen, was never late. His bus was high centered with double rear wheels to help him get through the heavy mud and the snow of the back country roads. One day, snow had drifted so high across Tyler Road it was completely blocked, and he backed his bus half-a-mile through the deep snow to Rawsonville Road, the county line between Wayne and Washtenaw counties, and continued his run to Denton.

By the time we got on the bus every morning at 8:15, we had fed and watered our livestock, cleaned out their stables and put down fresh straw. We had milked the cow, separated the milk, cleaned and reassembled the 32 metal cones of the separator. The chickens had been fed and watered and the eggs gathered. When the asparagus was growing, several bushels would have been cut by hand and bunched ready to sell at the roadside stand. And we had changed our clothes, washed and eaten breakfast.

My father took the interurban train to and from his work at Ford's in Highland Park until it stopped running in 1925. Then he drove the twenty-five miles each way until he was laid off during the depression of 1929. Then he found work at the Magee Machine Shop a mile-and-a-half away on Rawsonville Road near the Michigan Central Railroad tracks. In 1931, he was rehired at Ford's River Rouge plant and in 1932 transferred to the Ypsilanti Starter and Generator plant. He served there as general foreman of their Tool and Die Department until he retired in 1956 with 42 years of service.

In 1932, Dad purchased a two-story house from the Ford plant in Ypsilanti. It was in the center of an expansion area and he bought it for $5.00, agreeing that it would be dismantled and the ground left bare. Piece by piece the house came down and we hauled it to the farm and reused the material. I had just turned six and my job was to straighten every nail that came out of the house and to sort them by size.

Grandpa Dickson used several of the windows to make a hot-house on the south side of his house. Sheltered from the cold north wind of early spring, he slanted the windows to get the best effect of the sun, and his seeds were always the first to be ready for transplanting. Grandpa took great pride in his garden, particularly in a new brand of large red beefsteak tomatoes that were so heavy the plants had to be supported with stakes.

When he went hunting, Grandpa always carried his double-barreled 12-gauge shotgun, and he would let me follow him through the fields. We first walked through the small corn patch near the house, then cross the small creek where my father had made a bridge out of 50 gallon drums. They had been purchased full of buttermilk from the Ypsilanti Farm Bureau, located near the route of the old underground railroad used to smuggle black slaves from the south into Canada during the Civil War. The buttermilk was used to feed the chickens. After crossing the creek we would walk through the orchard looking for a rabbit. Rarely would he get a pheasant out of the corn patch, or a rabbit in the orchard. But Grandpa enjoyed the short walks through the fields on a warm fall day, and I am sure that they brought him closer to God.

I know he was happy to have me with him because he taught me the difference between the good eating mushrooms and the poison ones; he pointed out the fruit of the quince with all of its seeds, and showed me the difference between the leaves of the peach and the apple tree; and we gathered the fallen apples to exchange for cider at Wiard's Orchard. One bushel of apples, regardless of condition, for one gallon of cider.

Walter Wiard later said of his own orchard, "It took me twenty-nine years to plant, cultivate, and make that a fine orchard. It took those tractors and bulldozers just twenty-nine minutes to tear it down."

There were no nursing homes in those days and when Grandpa suffered a stroke he lay in bed for nearly nine months, in the home my father built for him, before he died. I was too young then to realize the tragedy of what was happening. But the day of his funeral, with the undertaker flipping coins up his coat sleeve and pulling them out of the children's ears and the speeding car that nearly crashed into the funeral procession, is vividly engraved in my mind.

During the winter of 1933, when I was seven years old, I got sick with the measles and my grandma Dickson taught me how to sew to keep me from scratching the sores. I sewed colored squares of the animals and flowers around the farm and one of the Methodist church in Denton until I had enough to make a full-sized quilt. Grandma pieced it together and quilted it for me. Her quilting stitches were so small and uniform they were unexcelled anywhere and she was always setting up the quilting frame in her dining room to do work for someone. I entered the quilt in the county fair at the Belleville High School and received the white ribbon for third place prize.

The depression years from 1929 to 1932 were tough years, the years we nearly lost the farm. I never knew how difficult until 40 years later when swapping stories with my father over a cup of coffee at Agnes Fuller's, a friend of ours at Littlefield Lake. I told him about the time I had worked for our neighbor, Louis Schlossstein, ten laborious hours pushing tanks of insecticide, nearly as tall as I was, the full length of his half-mile long orchard while he walked along side spraying the fruit trees. At the end of the day he gave me 50 cents for pay. I told my father that that was the day I learned the value of money.

31

But he said, "Son, when Mr. Schlossstein paid you that 50 cents things were tough. During the depression he was working right along side of me on a drafting board at Magee's Machine Shop for 25 cents an hour, and he had the mortgage on his home to pay, food and clothes to provide for his family. And we carried our lunch and walked to work because we didn't have money to spend for gasoline."

For the first time, I understood how terribly bad things must have been during those days of the depression, and my whole opinion of Mr. Schlossstein changed. Had I known at the time, I would have helped him for nothing.

Every year my father would make an improvement to the farm. He built three brooder coops, three long chicken houses, two barns, the small house where my grandparents lived, and of course, the main house where we lived. He did all of his own work, including plumbing and electrical, and he installed the tub and a toilet when we changed from the outhouse to the inside bathroom.

I remember the large jacks used to raise the house off its foundation when the basement was hand dug. My father laid the cement blocks to support the house and poured a cement floor. He installed a coal furnace, piping and radiators for steam heat.

I filled the glass jar of the cook stove with kerosene until Dad bought Mother an electric stove. Then she set the timer to start our Sunday meal while we were in church. My father rigged it to turn on the lights in the chicken houses to get the chickens up earlier for more egg production.

One year, we enclosed the front porch. The extra space

Living In A Tent

The First House, 1921

Right to Left: Eva holding Donald, Kitty Dickson behind Herbert,
Phoebe (O'Bryan) Dickson, her sister Emma Lempki, and Hazel
Cowell, Emma's daughter.

Spring, 1926: Herbert, Donald and the family Essex.
Before lawns and flower gardens.

Building The American Dream
Beautiful in full foliage and flowers. Father's Day, 1936:
Donald, Warren, Elmer, and Herbert Kidder.

provided a den with a wood burning fireplace and French doors to close it off from the living room when not in use. It provided a study for my brother, Donald, when he went to the Edison Institute of Technology, Ford's college at Green-field Village.

Another year, using blocks of wood filled with nails protruding out of one side, we scraped through layer after layer of wallpaper to the plaster and lath that had been used in the original construction. We scraped the side walls and ceilings, and Mother recalled the years that the different papers had been installed by their patterns.

Dad wired the dining room for a chandelier and the side walls for sea shell lighting fixtures. Then came Mr. Gorham with his soft cream colored plaster and expert tear drop design to finish off the rooms.

One year we installed the linoleum for the kitchen floor, another year the wall-to-wall carpet. I wrote a note to the person who would someday take it up, put it right by the doorway leading to the kitchen. I told him how nice it was going to be now that I didn't have to mop and polish the floor around the throw rugs. Then came the Hoover sales-man demonstrating the power of his vacuum cleaner by vibrating kernels of rice on the carpet.

The outside beautification was coming along at the same time. It cost less in dollars but a lot more in labor. That we could afford! My father didn't like the shallow ditch at the edge of the road and because the property line extended to the center of the highway he filled it in and ran the main lawn to the edge of the roadway. We planted beds of flowers and small pine trees, seeded for the lawn, and got compliments from people who stopped to buy produce at our roadside stand.

Mother was happy. After all the years of hard work and sacrifice their American dream was becoming a reality.

Then came Adolph Hitler, and Eva and Elmer's dream went up in smoke. Throughout the spring and summer of 1941 tremendous scarring of their land was taking place, Sorensen was building Willow Run. And every year for more than quarter of a century, no matter where I lived or what I did, nightmares came to haunt me.

In my nightmares, the roar of bulldozers echoed through in my mind. Working together two of them rooted out the maple trees that lined our farm along Denton Road. Then they ripped through the countryside with the rest of the bulldozers leveling everything in sight.

The ashes of our largest barn still glowed red and hot on the ground. The workmen had put a torch to it Saturday afternoon. My father's mover had scheduled Monday morning to move it. He was too late. It had taken our entire family a whole summer of hard work on dangerous scaffolding to build. Now it was gone.

Herbert Conant's buckets shone brightly, hanging from the sugar maple trees in the woods catching the sap, ever so slowly, drop by drop so it could be distilled into maple syrup for hot pancakes. The fragrance of my flowers drifted across on the wind.

My hands were blistered from pushing the lawn mower, cutting the lush green grass around the homes of my parents and grandparents. Before the time of power mowers, it took a week to cut them by hand, then it was time to start over again.

The bulldozers were running in high gear again, ripping out our main lawn. Off they ran like maniacs, side by side through the soft Michigan soil. They made their turn, tearing out my flowers and headed back, their blades set deeper this time.

When they hit the truck loads of concrete Father had purchased from the Michigan Highway Department and buried as a foundation for our driveway, one of the operators was thrown clear of his machine and knocked unconscious. The driverless bulldozer just kept on going. When it got to the road it turned with the rest of the machines ripping out the violets and started back. It crushed its driver and continued on. Blood was everywhere. They made their next turn together, tearing out the rest of the flowers, and headed off in another direction.

The big truck came with its huge "I" beams and dragged the main house off its foundation. The open hole of the basement, that took us a summer to dig by hand after jacking up the house, was ugly in its bareness.

My golden collie, Flash, who Aunt Orpha gave me as a tiny puppy the Christmas I was 17 months old, and my first memory in life, came to lick my face. His tongue was cold against my cheek. The steps where I had shelled lima beans were standing all by themselves with no house attached and he was telling me it was time to leave.

I could see myself huddled tightly against the wooden

WILLOW RUN

Bulldozers Digging Shade Trees Out Of Our Lawn

Herbert, Elmer and Donald Building The Big Barn.
It was leveled to the ground and burned.

riser of the third step. My eyes closed, I looked into the April sun. Hues of red and white filled my retinas. Secure on the steps of my father's home I dreamed of times to come.

My little toy trucks in the sand pile called me to come and play with them. But I was comfortable on the steps, playing my game between the cool chill of the northwest wind blowing over the steps and the warmth of the April sun that penetrated my body.

Tomorrow I would play with the trucks. But the bull-dozers roared. And tomorrow never came.

The lawns and flower gardens were rutted from the truck moving the house away. The American flag that had always waved so gently in the breeze every day from atop its mast in the center of the main lawn was gone. My brother, Donald, had saluted it the day before when he had taken it down for the last time.

I was glad my oldest brother, Herbert, had gotten safe-ly through the battle of the Coral Sea to Australia before going on to New Guinea. He had his hands full fighting Japanese soldiers and he didn't need to see any of this. After all what was he fighting for?

The loud roar of the bulldozers came back, closer this time. The dirt and the dust blew in my face as they filled in the ugly hole of the basement and smoothed out the ground.

Now for a stranger passing by, the barren earth would appear to be calm and tranquil. But the horrors of what was happening to me and to my family left huge scars and hid-den forces below the surface of the land and in my mind

WILLOW RUN

THE AMERICAN DREAM - SPRING 1941

UGLY IN ITS BARENESS

Left: The barn was burned. Right: My grandparents house where I lived during the fall and winter of 1941-1942 while the airport and factory were being constructed. From here, I saw Major Jimmy Doolittle make the first official landing at the Willow Run airport, October 22, 1941.

that even time would never erase.

Government conscription of our land that forced us off the farm, even before the United States had entered World War II, came under rights of eminent domain to provide B-24 bombers to help England in her war against Hitler. The Ford Motor Company made the schedule come true. The Elmer Kidder family sacrificed their home and their land.

END NOTE

1. Marion Wilson. *The Story of Willow Run.* Ann Arbor, Michigan: University of Michigan Press, 1956: 48.

Fall 1941: Constructing north lane of two-lane divided highway between Belleville Road and Willow Run factory. It ran parallel to Ecorse Road, M-17, far right center. **Top View:** Visible in the background, looking west, are the farm house, barns and long low chicken houses of Eva and Elmer Kidder. My grandparents' house and three brooder coups are hidden by the large barn. **Bottom View:** Looking east from Denton Road driveway.

THE LAST WILLOW RUN PIONEERS

The first airplane to land on what became the Willow Run Airport, then the Kidder farm. It was flown by William G. Spurr who in 1939 came to visit his grandmother Phoebe Dickson and his aunt Eva Kidder, my mother. Spurr went on to work with Charles A. Lindbergh at Willow Run, before serving as a World War II fighter pilot and instructor.

William G. Spurr - The First To Land An Airplane

H. P. Henning and W. C. Thomas - First To Land On Willow Run's Unfinished Airport (Both taken by author).

43

Charles E. Sorensen
1934

Chapter III

CHARLES E. SORENSEN

When the unit production method of the aircraft industry could not provide sufficient airplanes to meet the needs of President Roosevelt's "arsenal of democracy" and England's war against Germany, the U.S. Army Air Corps (later to become the U.S. Army Air Force) looked to the mass production methods of the Ford Motor Company.

At that time, Henry Ford was approaching eighty years of age and his health was beginning to fail. He had recovered from a stroke in 1938, but another later in 1941 was to leave him with lapses of memory and unpredictable decision-making. Once Mr. Ford gave Charles E. Sorensen the approval for Willow Run there was little more the aging master of mass production could do, except provide the forceful power of his name.

Hired personally by Mr. Ford in 1905 as a $3.00 an hour pattern maker, Sorensen had fought his way through the rough competition of the Ford organization to become a member of its board of directors. In July of 1941 he became the Company's Executive Vice-President. As Henry Ford had been the visionary for mass production of the automobile, Sorensen was the visionary for mass production of large aircraft.

Sorensen had migrated from Denmark with his parents in 1885 at the age of four. He received a grade school education, entered an apprenticeship in foundry pattern making at the age of sixteen, and studied drafting at night school.

In 1907 Ford promoted him to assistant superintendent of production, and for his work in the foundry gave him the name of "Cast-Iron Charlie." Later, Sorensen developed the moving assembly line for the Model N automobile (not the Model T as normally assumed). During World War I, he went to England to develop factory and machinery specifications for production of British farm tractors. However, due to a daylight attack by the German airplanes while he was there the British asked him to manufacture the tractors in the United States. In October 1940, Sorensen directed the manufacture of 4236 Pratt-Whitney eighteen-cylinder, air-cooled aircraft engines, which made Ford the largest manufacturer of aircraft engines in the nation.[1] Sorensen was also active in the planning, construction, and manufacturing operations of Ford's huge River Rouge production facility.

The genesis of the idea to mass produce the B-24 bomber and to build the Willow Run Production Facility belongs to Charles E. Sorensen. He conceived the idea during the night of January 8, 1941, in San Diego, California, and from that moment until he left Ford, he orchestrated the phenomenal accomplishments of the B-24 production at Willow Run, an accomplishment that in 1944 alone produced 4611 bombers. "Even then," Sorensen said, "we had not reached capacity production which would have been 650 a month."[2]

CHARLES E. SORENSEN

In December 1940, Dr. George J. Mead, Director of Procurement for the Aeronautical Section of the Advisory Council for National Defense, and Major Jimmy Doolittle of the U.S. Army Air Corps visited Mr. Ford in Dearborn to determine his willingness to manufacture airplanes for the U. S. defense program. Mr. Ford earlier had refused to build 9000 English Rolls-Royce aircraft engines, after accepting the order, because of a statement in England implying that Ford was now supporting British war efforts and because of his negative feelings about the war and President Roosevelt.

Mr. Ford raised no opposition to building the airplanes as he had with the engines, and it was agreed that on the morning of January 8, 1941, Sorensen and Dr. Mead would fly to San Diego to visit Consolidated Aircraft, the company that had developed the B-24 bomber. Consolidated's goal was "to produce one B-24 bomber a day or 350 planes a year,"[3] but Sorensen quickly realized that Consolidated did not have the factory, equipment or procedures to reach their goal. They were producing airplanes as a job shop would custom make them, which was far short of the quantity needed by Dr. Mead.

If Consolidated was to supply the thousands of airplanes needed for the defense program, their plant would have to be enlarged and modernized for mass production, a move which the U.S. Army Air Corps opposed because of the plant's location and accessibility to attack from the sea. Improving the factory's efficiency would require its closing, resulting in a costly loss of production. In addition, Consolidated's final assembly operation was completed out-of-doors on a steel tubing fixture where expansion and contraction from temperature changes would create distortions and production difficulties unsuitable for mass production.

In San Diego, Sorensen met with Edsel Ford and his two sons, Henry II and Benson, who had left for San Diego on January 4. Sorensen was also joined by several of Ford's finest specialists: Logan Miller, one of the best sheet metal men in the country; William Pioch, Ford's master of tool and die; Harry Hanson, responsible for factory construction; Edward Scott, automobile body engineer; Rosco Smith, Ford's manager of outlying factories; and Ernie Walters, who for years had been in charge of Ford's production and engineering departments.

The group spent the day analyzing Consolidated's production facility, their methods and procedures of operations. At the end of the day Sorensen said, "I liked neither what I saw nor what I heard."[4] Sorensen told Dr. Mead and Major Reuben H. Fleet, President and General Manager of Consolidated Aircraft, that his evaluation of the plant's production capacity was very discouraging. When they asked him how he would manufacture the airplane, he told them he would have something for them in the morning.

The knowledge Sorensen had acquired throughout his 35 years of production experience served him well for the Herculean task he undertook that night in his room at the Coronado Hotel, but the story of that night is best expressed in his own words.

> I really did have something in mind. To compare a Ford V-8 with a four engine Liberator bomber

was like matching a garage with a skyscraper, but despite their great differences I knew the same fundamentals applied to high volume production of both.... First break the plane's design into essential units and make a separate production layout for each unit. Next build as many units as are required, then deliver each unit in its proper sequence to the assembly line to make a whole unit... a finished plane. To house all this and provide for efficient operation there should be a new plant especially designed to accommodate the progressive layout. I saw no impossibility in such an idea even though mass production of anything approaching the size and complexity of a B-24 never had been attempted before. But who would accept such a wild notion? Instead of one bomber a day by prevailing methods I saw the possibility of one B-24 an hour by mass production assembly lines. How could the aviation people take that estimate seriously?

As soon as I returned to my room at the Coronado Hotel I began figuring how to adapt Ford assembly methods to airplane construction and turn out one four-engine bomber an hour. Throughout the day I had made copious notes. I listed all major units of the plane and the sub-units and fractional units required for their assembly, and I had gathered figures on Consolidated's labor force and job performance. From these I computed each unit operation, its timing, and required floor space as I saw them, and paper began to fly. Figures for each unit I kept together in a separate pile, and soon there were little stacks of paper all over the floor of my room. I was back at my old game of sketching a series of manufacturing and sub-as-

sembly operations and their orderly progression to-
ward becoming major units... a game I had played
many times since that morning in 1908 at the Piquette
Avenue plant when we first experimented with a
moving assembly line....

As I look back now upon that night, this was the
biggest challenge of my production career... bigger
than any Model T assembly line sequence for Highland Park, more momentous than the layout and construction of the great River Rouge plant in which I'd
had a part. It took eight years to develop Ford's mass
production system, and eight more years before we
worked up to a production of 10,000 cars a day. Now,
in one night, I was applying thirty-five years of production experience to planning the layout for building
not only something I had never put together before,
but the largest and most complicated of all air transportation and in a number and at a rate never before
thought possible.

Once again I was going on the principle I had
enunciated many times at Ford: "The only thing we
can't make is something we can't think about."

Throughout the night I set down figures and
revised them. I arranged and rearranged the stacks of
paper as it became plainer to me which unit came
after the other in moving to final assembly and how
much floor space was involved. At length the whole
picture became clear and simple. I knew I had the
solution, and I was elated by the certainty that the
Germans had neither the facilities nor the conception
for greater bomber mass production. Along towards
four o'clock, I was satisfied that my piles of paper

were arranged in proper order and represented the most logical progress of units to the main assembly line; and I knew I could prove a construction rate of one big bomber an hour. Now I had something to talk about.

Standing over the papers, I roughed out on Coronado Hotel note paper a pencil sketch of the floor plan of a bomber plant. It would be a mile long and a quarter mile wide, the single biggest industrial building ever. I still have that sketch, initialed by Edsel Ford, his two sons and others, and I still get a kick out of it. The result of one night's work, it is a true outline of Willow Run, which took two years to build and came through on schedule with one four-engine Liberator an hour, 18 bombers a day, and by the end of the war a total of 8,800 big planes [came] off the assembly lines and into the air.

When I finished my sketch I went to bed, but was so carried away by enthusiasm for the project that I couldn't sleep. I was building planes the rest of the night.[5]

The following morning, Sorensen outlined his bomber-an-hour idea to Edsel Ford who agreed with his proposal and assured him "that the Ford Motor Company would be willing to build such a plant," a plant they estimated would cost "two hundred million dollars."[6]

Later that day, Edsel Ford, President of the Ford Motor Company, announced that Ford would begin immediately with plans to construct an entirely new type of plant to manufacture B-24 bomber parts.

At their meeting with Dr. Mead in Major Fleet's office,

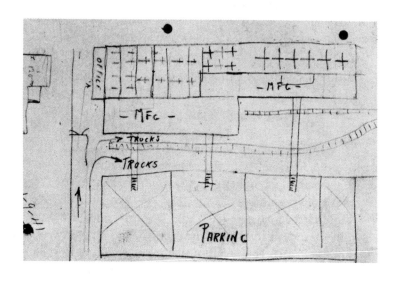

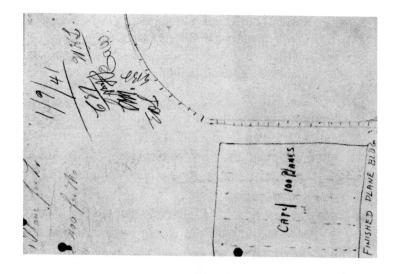

Sorensen's Original Sketch of His Mile Long Factory

And right, as built. "The biggest challenge of my life," Sorensen said,
was Willow Run and building a four engine B-24 bomber every hour.

Sorensen told Dr. Mead the Ford Motor Company was prepared to manufacture the B-24 bomber. Sorensen said,

> We are not interested in building assemblies.... We'll make the complete plane or nothing. If the Air Force will give Ford Motor Company a contract and will spend up to two hundred million dollars, we will build and equip a plant capable of turning out one Liberator bomber an hour. With that I tossed him the sketch I had made the night before. The offer and the estimate took Mead and his Air Force associates by surprise. They did not question our ability to go through with an undertaking of such magnitude, and the Ford group was all smiles when Mead said this plan was just what he wanted. Instead of perhaps 520 planes a year, it would give him 540 planes a month. "Develop the idea as much as you can, and I'll call you to Washington in a few days."[7]

Before leaving San Diego Sorensen requested a complete set of blueprints and was surprised to learn that Consolidated, for lack of draftsmen and procedures for making engineering changes, did not have up-to-date drawings for their own airplane that was already in production. Sorensen promised to send engineers and draftsmen from Dearborn to make a complete and detailed set of working drawings.

Back in Dearborn, Sorensen put the architects to work designing a cross section of the factory for his up-coming trip to Washington. The plant was high enough for a full plane sitting on the floor, with an overhead crane capable of covering the whole area. He put Pioch and Hanson to work dividing the plane into its sub-assemblies for manufacture, and analyzing its metal and electrical components.

He discussed with Henry Ford his ideas for mass producing the airplane, showed him the sketch for the mile long production facility needed to manufacture a bomber an hour, and told him about his ultimatum to Dr. Mead that Ford was not interested in building assemblies.

Mr. Ford, impressed by the grandeur of the idea, told Sorensen, "Make a complete plane only."[8] That statement from Henry Ford was Sorensen's authorization to proceed with the Ford Motor Company's and the world's largest single industrial factory.

After Pearl Harbor, it was Willow Run that excited the nation. Willow Run and Henry Ford became a rallying point of hope against the Japanese. Across the spectrum of national publications Ford was portrayed as a national hero. "When Ford tools up he tools up," declared the *Manchester Leader and Evening Union*. "It is a promise of revenge for Pearl Harbor," enthused the *Detroit Free Press*."[9] Charles Lindbergh, employed at Willow Run, said that the factory was like the Grand Canyon of American industry.

Regardless of what Henry Ford did or said privately during peace time, he never failed to make his company and factories available to his country in the time of war. He was always there when his country needed him. In his early years, his feelings about President Roosevelt and other power players in industry taking over his business merited his vigilance. Now those feelings were perceived as an old man's paranoia. His lapses of memory and pulling up of construction stakes for starting Willow Run, saying, "We're going to raise soybeans here," was only a nuisance of senility. It was easily remedied by his son, Edsel Ford, and Sorensen who had the bulldozers move in and start grading.

Edsel Ford, sick with undulant fever and stomach cancer, struggled, under heavy painkillers and medication, with the problems of Willow Run. Just three months before his death on May 26, 1943, at the age of 49, Edsel faced a grueling session from Senator Harry Truman's Special Committee Investigating the National Defense Program for what they presumed was a slippage in Willow Run's B-24 production schedule. Still, it was Edsel Ford who came up with the idea to decentralize production of numerous sub-assemblies which, as much as any single factor, assisted Willow Run in reaching its goal of a bomber an hour, a goal reached in March of 1944.

Harry Bennett, Ford's pistol-packing director of personnel and head of the service department, had for years been purging Ford's top executives to gain control over the company and Mr. Ford himself. The trepidation he created within the organization left it short of top management personnel, and the vacuum created left the company highly vulnerable. The Ford Motor Company was losing millions of dollars a month throughout much of the late 1930's and according to Robert Shook in *Turnaround,* "Had there been no World War II and the defense contract work Ford received, it is likely that the company would not have survived as an automaker."[10] In the opinion of Jack Davis, a Ford sales manager, the company was not dying: "It was already dead... and rigor mortis was setting in,"[11] a fact later discovered by the "Ford Whiz Kids" Henry Ford II hired to revitalize the company in 1945. Bennett's personnel policies and practice of controlling key men strategically placed throughout the company created Willow Run labor problems that challenged the very core of the UAW-CIO "No Strike Agreement," during war time. Changing of a shift schedule and hours of work, in the middle of the night, that disrupted worker's transportation to and from their homes was a classic example of UAW strength in keeping thousands of their union members from walking out on a strike.

The seriousness of the morale problem became so great the 90th B-24 Bomb Group was stationed in the hangars at Willow Run to provide a military appearance in an effort to build the moral of the workers. Again, showing the strength of Walter Reuther in maintaining control over his 40,000 union membership.

During a discussion in Bennett's office with Sorensen and Rosco Smith, Willow Run's first Director of Production, Bennett, an ex-Navy fighter, threw a fist that blackened the eye of Smith. The reins of Willow Run were then taken over by Mead Bricker, Ford's highly skilled and experienced Production Manager, but the seriousness of the problems eventually required replacement of Bennett's hand picked director of personnel.

It was only after Henry Ford II had been discharged from the Navy in August 1943, and took over Presidency of the Ford Motor Company on September 20, 1945, that Harry Bennett was fired. It was young Henry's first official act as Chief Executive Officer after taking over control of the company from his grandfather. But it came too late to help Sorensen.

It is little wonder, from the seriousness of the problems surrounding the Ford Motor Company and Willow Run, that after Edsel Ford died the government considered the possibility of taking over the company. The idea of a major American supplier of war material being run by a senile old man under control of Harry Bennett and his collection of Purple Gang mobsters and political fixers was not to be considered lightly.

In 1941, Charles E. Sorensen, Ford's Director of Production, was the only remaining person in the dying Ford empire with the power to control the company and the expertise to build the Willow Run Production Facility. Responsible for Ford's total civilian and military output, Sorensen had 35 years of Ford experience. He had developed Ford's moving assembly lines, directed production of the huge River Rouge complex, and was hardened in the ways of success. Even so, under the burden of responsibility for the entire manufacturing output of the Ford Motor Company as well as the start-up of Willow Run, he collapsed twice inside of the plant and was hospitalized.

The lack of a planned governmental housing project for the tens of thousands of employees Sorensen was to hire created untold problems at Willow Run, and deserved the national scandal it created. It is impossible to estimate the loss and delays in production brought about by demoralized employees living in squalid conditions said by some Washington officials to have been the worst mess in the whole United States.

Design changes, for lack of current drawings and engineering information from Consolidated, and demands for changes by the Army Air Force, doubled the amount of Ford engineering, the amount of tooling and its cost, and the time for production start-up.

In spite of this atrocious background, and using a work force of 40,000 employees without any previous aircraft experience whatsoever, Sorensen and the men and women from Willow Run went on to produce the giant four-engine, 20 ton airplane at the rate of one an hour.

Sorensen left the man and the company to which he had hitched his life for its ride to the stars in January 1944, after completing nearly 40 years of work with the Ford Motor Company. He had extended his time with Ford because of Willow Run, the company's wartime commitments, and his desire to see Henry Ford II return from the Navy and take over leadership of the company. Now, "taking advantage of a retirement plan that had been agreed upon for 1941.... There was only one other thing left for me to do: see that Henry II stayed on [with the company], making it impossible for him to leave by passing the responsibility to him."[13]

Sensationalism sells a lot of newspapers, and Sorensen leaving the Ford Motor Company certainly was big news. So it was that on March 3, 1944, the very month Willow Run production reached Sorensen's unbelievable goal of a bomber an hour, Detroit newspapers proclaimed in bold, three inch headlines: Ford Fires Sorensen.

Lindbergh eulogized:

> It has been coming for a long time, but it seems an unnecessary crude way to handle such a situation. There was no need for such headlines. Still, it is true to the character of the Ford organization, and there is a certain justice in them. Sorensen has shown little or no consideration for the men under him, and he has fired many a workman in a flash of temper and for no reasonable cause.
>
> Sorensen was born for another era, an era which is rapidly passing even in the industries of Detroit. His production genius lay to a large extent in this driving ability exercised in a day when engineering was less important in industry than it is at present.... Probably it is unfair to judge the man on the standards of the present generation. He lived in the "two-gun" days of American industry and "shot it out with the best of them." He was a hard-boiled, hard-fisted fighter and probably would prefer to be known as such.[14]

Whether Sorensen was fired by Henry Ford, whose health was failing at the time, or left of his own accord in January, what difference does it really make?

Working together nearly 40 years, the two of them had built a giant empire.

CHARLES E. SORENSEN

Together They Built A Giant Empire
Ford River Rouge - From Iron Ore To Finished Automobiles

CHARLES A. LINDBERGH
A Great American Hero

In addition to his responsibilities as Ford's Engineering Consultant, Lindbergh flight tested many of the B-24 bombers that came off the Willow Run assembly line. He also performed high altitude tests on Republic's P-47 Thunderbolt ignition system, and was the only pilot to achieve an altitude of over 42,000 feet.[15]

Born a year before the Wright Brothers developed the airplane at Kitty Hawk, Lindbergh purchased his first airplane from World War I army surplus. Four years later, on May, 20 1927, he left Long Island, N. Y. on the first solo flight across the Atlantic to Paris, a 33 ½ hour flight that catapulted him into immediate and lasting world recognition.

His pioneer flights, after marrying Anne Morrow, opened up mail routes around the Caribbean for Transcontinental Air Transportation. Together, they surveyed the Pacific for future airlines to Alaska, Japan, and China, and they flew the North Atlantic to Greenland, Iceland and Ireland, and crossed back over the Atlantic to Brazil for Pan American.

Upon request of the U.S. Military attache in Berlin, before W. W. II, and a U. S. "instigated invitation" from Marshall Hermann Goring, of the German Air Force, Lindbergh obtained for U. S. Intelligence what Air Force director, General H. H. Arnold, described as " the most accurate picture of the Luftwaffe, its equipment, leaders, apparent plans, training methods, and defects [he had] received up to that time."[16]

Politically ostracized by President Roosevelt, Lindbergh served in World War II by flying active combat for General MacArthur in the South Pacific as a civilian. After the war, the United States Senate made him a Brigadier General in the United States Air Force Reserve.

END NOTES

1. Bryan R. Ford. H*enry's Lieutenants.* Detroit: Wayne State University Press, 1993: 271.
2. Charles E. Sorensen. *My Forty Years With Ford.* New York: W. W. Norton, 1956: 290.
3. Sorensen, 279.
4. Sorensen, 279.
5. Sorensen, 281.
6. Sorensen, 283.
7. Sorensen, 284.
8. Sorensen, 286.
9. Robert Lace. *Ford, The Man and The Machine.* Boston, Toronto: Little, Brown Company, 1986: 392.
10. Robert L. Shook. *Turnaround: The New Ford Motor Company.* New York: Prentice Hall Press, 1990: 44.
11. Lace, 420.
12. Sorensen, 329.
13. Sorensen, 329.
14. Charles A. Lindbergh. *The Wartime Journals of Charles A. Lindbergh.* New York: Harcourt Brace Jovanovich, Inc., 1970: 768.
15. William G., Spurr. Reminiscence.
16. Anne Morrow Lindbergh. *War Within And Without.* New York: Harcourt Brace Jovanovich, Inc., 1980: xv.

July 22 to December 3, 1941, Contractors drain, grade, and pave 1434 acre airport - Seven month schedule set for factory.

Chapter IV

BULLDOZERS AND HOT STEEL RIVETS

Years of planning and construction went into Ford's River Rouge plant for the mass production of automobiles. According to Sorensen, "It took eight years to develop Ford's mass production system, and eight more years before we worked up to production of 10,000 cars a day."[1] Now under the pressures of national defense the schedule for completion of the airport and factory for mass producing the B-24 bombers at Willow Run was compressed into months and days. A list of events shows the speed at which things were happening:

January 9, 1941: Sorensen submits Ford's proposal to Dr. Mead in San Diego.

January 12: Ford officials visit Wright Field and notify the Air Corps that Ford could start as soon as ordered by the Government.

January 31: General Oliver P. Echols, Chief Procurement Officer, U.S. Army Air Corps, arrives in Dearborn suggesting that Ford draw up a letter of intent outlining their proposal for:

    1. Manufacturing an "educational order" to acquaint Ford with the aircraft.

    2. Making parts for Consolidated and Douglas Aircraft to assemble in plants

to be constructed in Tulsa, Oklahoma and Fort Worth, Texas.

3. Manufacturing the complete airplane.

February   4:   Four days later, Echols announces approval of steps one and two of Ford's proposal. [Verbal consent from the government authorizing Ford to manufacture complete airplanes came on May 1.]

February 19:   William Kundsen, Director of the War Department, announces that the Ford Motor Company will erect a bomber plant at Ypsilanti to manufacture assemblies for Consolidated and Douglas.

February 21:   Ford receives letter of intent covering airframes for 1,200 bombers to be shipped to Tulsa and Fort Worth for assembly.

February 25:   Project approved in Washington.

March 11:   Two hundred Ford engineers and draftsmen arrive in San Diego to begin work.

March 13:   Ford receives educational contract on B-24 in amount of $3,418,000.

March 24:   Work Order request filed for first tooling.

March 28:   Clearing started on five square miles of land by hundreds of workmen and countless pieces of construction equipment to make room for the airfield and factory.

April 18:   Ground-breaking started for the factory.

BULLDOZERS AND HOT STEEL RIVETS

April 20:	First concrete poured in foundation footings.
May 1:	Ford plans factory enlargement on the government's verbal assurance of building the complete bomber.
May 3:	Spur from New York central Railroad reaches bomber plant construction site.
May 5:	Factory's structural steel frame work seen rising above the ground.
June 5:	U.S. Army Air Corps sends Ford letter of intent for 800 complete planes.
August 13:	First sewers laid in the airfield.
September 1:	First machinery arrives at Willow Run.
October 15:	First bomber part produced in River Rouge press shop.
December 3:	Airport sewer completed.
December 4:	Last concrete runway poured.
December 8:	First horizontal milling machine is put in to operation, and the first Willow Run part is manufactured.
December 24:	Started setting up first Center Wing fixture.
April 16, 1942:	**First center wing completed.**
May 15:	Ford's first assembled bomber, the educational aircraft .01 completed and turned over to Flight Department.
September 10:	First Ford-built B-24 completed.

WILLOW RUN

June, 1943:   Manpower peak reaches daily average of
                  42,331 employees.

March 1944:   Production peak (monthly), 462 bombers,
                  62 over Sorensen's original schedule.

April 1944:   455 airplanes in 450 hours. An airplane every
                  59.34 minutes.

June 28, 1945:   Production ceases; last bomber No. 8685.

From the time Sorensen presented his $200,000,000 proposal and hand-drawn sketch of Willow Run to Dr. Mead in San Diego on January 9, 1941, until the government, in Washington, D.C., issued final approval of the project on February 25 was only 47 days.

From authorization to completion of the world's largest manufacturing structure, and acceptance of the first B-24 bomber completely assembled at Willow Run in September of 1942, took only nineteen months. From ground breaking to completion of the first center wing took two days less than a year in a factory that was still under construction.

Once final approval was received, additional land was procured under rights of eminent domain and on March 28, 1941, ground leveling operations got underway. Bulldozers and a crew of three hundred men with saws and axes ripped through the Michigan countryside uprooting trees and knocking down buildings. They leveled four square miles of farms and woodlands for the airport in Wayne county, and another square mile in Washtenaw county for the factory.

The woodlands, still plentiful with large oak, elm and

sugar-maple trees left over from the pioneer days, were cut and hauled to a saw mill that Mr. Ford had dismantled at Greenfield Village and sent to Willow Run for cutting the logs into lumber. There was logging at a rate far exceeding that of Samuel Denton when his village mill ran 24 hours a day. Smaller trees, brush, and buildings, including the Horner cabin, were demolished and burned.

The peaceful countryside surrounding the quiet Willow Run stream was gone.

Unprecedented Logging Cleared The Land Of Woodlots

WILLOW RUN

Albert Kahn
Associated Architects & Engineers

The Willow Run complex was designed by Albert Kahn, considered the greatest industrial architect in the world. Born in Germany in 1869 of Jewish heritage, Kahn had designed Henry Ford's buildings for 30 years. His first Ford design was the Highland Park factory, where the Model T automobile was manufactured, in 1910. From then until he completed the design of Willow Run in 1942, Albert Kahn Associates designed hundreds of buildings for the Ford Motor Company, and in 1926 Kahn designed Edsel B. Ford's personal residence on Lakeshore Drive in Grosse Pointe. Bryan Ford writes about Kahn and his work for Ford in *Henry's Lieutenants*:

> Kahn designed the famous River Rouge plant and numerous production facilities throughout the United States and Canada. The majority of the buildings in the Rouge... main power house, openhearth, glass plant, tire manufacturing plant, pressed steel building, auto assembly plant, foundry, cement plant, coke ovens... were Kahn designed. Kahn designed the Ford Rotunda and exposition buildings for the Chicago World's Fair in 1934, and five years later, in 1939, he designed Ford's Pavilion for the New York World's Fair.[2]

When Sorensen came back from San Diego in January 1941 and needed preliminary plans of Willow Run for his upcoming meeting with Dr. Mead in Washington, it was Kahn and Associates who rushed them out for him. Later, they designed and supervised construction of the complete

Willow Run complex, and by February 22, 1941, plans and drawings for the plant were virtually completed.

Albert Kahn, Founder of Albert Kahn Associates

His architects and engineers designed and supervised construction of the largest industrial factory in the world. He died, on December 8, 1942, after completing the design of Willow Run, the factory he described as the most enormous room in the history of mankind.

CONSTRUCTION OF THE AIRPORT[3]

Airport Drainage System

By June the engineers realized the land selected by Sorensen did not have the perfect drainage essential for constructing the Willow Run airport as he had believed. The site consisted of four to five feet of coarse sand interposed between a thin layer of topsoil and a layer of clay. Under this first layer of clay was a four foot stratum of fine water-bearing sand and silt which in turn rested on hard clay encountered at 15 to 18 feet below the surface. A high groundwater level of two to three feet and poor drainage to the northeast, where there was no outlet, made it necessary to install an artificial drainage system for the entire airfield. Combined with the pressure of time to complete the airport, draining of the airfield created a major undertaking. It was finally decided to drain the entire airport back into the Willow Run creek on the west side of the property.

The land sloped gently downward to the east away from the creek, and was graded to government airport specifications not to exceed three inches of slope in every hundred feet. The sub-grade soil was humus and spongy from a mixture of farming and woodlots, and there was muck and vegetation from the Horner Ditch that ran across two sections of land. It was removed and a firm foundation of sand and gravel prepared for the runways and taxi strips.

Julius Porath & Son Company of Detroit, began grading the airport site on July 22 when one of their tractor-scrapers took the first bite out of 650,000 cubic yards of earth to be moved. The first drainage crew began digging trenches for the sewer lines on August 13. Others quickly followed to complete the job scheduled for October 15.

The experienced management and astute coordination of the Porath company unified a number of accomplished construction companies into an efficient and fast moving organization. They put into the field hundreds of pieces of equipment, including 33 cranes, 24 systems of well points for draining the sub-soil, and four complete paving units each headed by a 34E dual-drum mixer. The combined management teams carefully planned and coordinated operations scattered across four square miles of open fields to meet the rigorous schedules set by Albert Kahn. The pouring of concrete and the airport needed to be completed before onset of frost and Michigan's cold winters. The deadline set was November 6.

Working against the natural slope of the site the contractors set to work on a 74 mile drainage system that included sixteen miles of sewer and fifty-eight miles of drain tile before laying 153 acres of concrete for the runways. The main sewer line, ranging in size from two to seven feet in diameter, ran diagonally from the northeast to southwest down to a depth of thirty-six feet to accommodate the outfall to Willow Run creek. Connecting to the main sewer lines were concrete and vitrified feeder lines ranging in size from 15 to 48 inches in diameter.

The trunk sewers and outfall were the most difficult problems overcome by the Porath company in the race against the 65 days allowed for completing the drainage system. The toughest job was excavating and encasing, in steel pilings, the first 100 feet of the 36 foot deep cut away from the bank of the Willow Run creek. The remaining 800 feet for the seven foot concrete pipe used for the outfall was laid in an open trench. The cuts, having an average depth of 26 feet, were pre-drained by well points and excavated to a depth of 15 feet by tractor-scrapers. The remaining lower depth, 10 to 21 feet, was of hard blue clay and was excavated by dragline. During this operation the contractor averaged only 60 feet of sewer a day.

To assist in other portions of the trunk sewer system Porath employed the experienced and well-equipped companies of Drainage Contractors, headed by John Ventral, and the Gargaro Company, with Chris Nelsen heading up the operation. This group of contractors was able, in spite of an exceptionally wet October, to complete the work on schedule. Installation of field drains was completed later.

Outstanding among the equipment used by the sewer constructors were the well points which pulled water out from the fine sand just above the bottom layer of clay. To dewater the ground for excavation by draglines and ladder-type trenching machines, the various sewer crews operated 24 well-point outfits, consisting mostly of Moretrench units; some were Griffin and Jaeger. To dig the relatively shallow trenches for field drains, the contractors used eight wheel-type ditchers. Four ladder-type trenchers, two Buckeye and two Parsons also worked on the trenches, as did draglines and a few clamshell cranes.

It took eleven teams of workmen using drag-lines and numerous trenching machines 107 days to dig the main trunk line with all of its tributaries, install the sewer lines, and complete the drainage system. They started excavation on August 13, and the job was completed December 3.

The airport's concrete runways, aprons and taxiways were placed on drained subgrade of coarse sand and small gravel. Sewer trenches under the runway slabs were back-filled in 6 inch layers and thoroughly compacted, and a 56 pound steel mesh reinforcement was used wherever the runway slabs were laid on top of them. In the area between the runways, averaging 30 inches below the surface, field drains of four inch pipe were laid in parallel lines spaced on 33, 66, and 100 foot centers as indicated on the Plan of Airfield Drainage. Along the edges of the runways and along their center lines, where the clay came within a few feet of the surface, drain pipe of 6, 8, and 10 inches was installed. Both field drains and runway drains were connected into laterals of the main trunk collection system. The 4 to 10 inch drains, totaling 330,000 feet, were made of plain end, double-strength vitrified clay tile, and were laid with open joints in trenches and covered with gravel.

Pipe for the entire sewer system was bell-and-spigot laid with tight joints. Double-strength vitrified clay tile pipe was used for sizes up to 36 inches. All sewer pipe more than 36 inches in diameter was precast concrete. Sewers lying twelve feet or more below finished grade were bedded and backpacked with lean-mix concrete.

Airport Grading

While ditches were being dug for the drainage system, grading for the runways and leveling of the airfield was done by the Cheney Wright Company of Williamston, Michigan. They operated eleven LeTourneau scrapers, three of 18-yard capacity and eight of 12-yards. They were pulled by 96-horsepower Caterpillar diesel crawler tractors and used to cut off high areas and haul excavated material to lower portions of the field. In October, three 12-yard pneumatic-tire Tournapull tractor scraper units were added to speed the hauling of 2,750,000 cubic yards of overhaul. A six-yard tractor-scraper was used for miscellaneous work.

Three to seven tractor-scrapers normally operated out of each cut with a 96-horsepower diesel pusher tractor to assist in the loading. When several scrapers hauled out of the same pit, they frequently loaded in tandem with as many as four or five units. Each tractor was equipped with a large pusher-plate which allowed it to act as a booster behind the scraper immediately ahead of it. When lined up like a train at the pit, all of the tractors in back of the unit engaged in loading contributed their combined traction to speed up the loading operation.

A cut of 700 to 800 feet provided sufficient distance for tandem loading of four to five units on a straight push, and loading was synchronized to get a maximum load in minimum distance. While the first scraper was being filled the second unit made a shallow, level cut, plunging for a deeper bite as soon as the forward scoop raised its cutting edge to start its haul to the dump. Loading always started at the end farthest from the dump which allowed the loaded scraper the shortest haul to the unloading area. The return trip by the pushing tractor to the starting end of the cut was considered less interference with production than a longer loaded haul to the dump by the tractor-scraper.

Loading with the help of the pushers allowed the 18-yard scrapers to consistently scooped up 20 yards per load and the 12-yard scrapers to load 14 yards. On 2,000 foot hauls the 18-yard scoops moved 80 yards of loose material on four trips per hour. On a haul averaging 1,000 feet from the cut to the dump, each 12-yard scraper made better than seven trips and moved 100 bulk yards an hour.

Runway Design And Paving

The airport's six runways were 160 feet wide, and ranged in length from 6,363 to 7,232 feet. Two parallel runways, on 750 foot centers, crossed the field diagonally in the direction of the prevailing winds. At their intersection with the three 6,000 foot runways was a large central area of concrete ten acres in size. Each runway was made up of eight 20 foot concrete lanes having an 8-6-8 inch cross-section. Each lane was laid with a 3/4" expansion joint every 120 feet, and traverse contraction joint every 20-feet. A doweled longitudinal center-line contraction joint was included in each 20-foot lane, and a keyed construction joint was used between adjacent lanes.

Paving units, the largest of their kind in the world,

began placing and finishing concrete on August 12. They worked a tight schedule, laying concrete 16 hours a day, six days a week, for a period of 77 days. The runways were scheduled to have been completed by November 6, but due to unusually heavy rains during the month of October the last concrete slab did not get poured until December 4.

Each paving unit had dual mixing drums to avoid any time loss in mixing cement. They were preceded by fine graders, running on rails, that prepared the ground for pouring, and followed by jointing machines and floaters that cut the slabs, inserted asphalt expansion strips, and gave a smooth finish to the runway.

Each paver started construction on their own 160 foot wide runway by first placing a 20-foot lane next to the center line. The outfit then completed the 80-foot half width out to the edge of the pavement by adding successive adjacent lanes on the next three trips. To reduce lost time in moving equipment, the contractors followed a plan which kept a paver traveling continuously forward around the sides of a triangle formed by three runways. A sled resembling an oversized stone boat was equipped with rails, the same width as the equipment allowing them to be easily transported from the end of one lane to the next.

The equipment used by the four duplicate paving outfits included four Buckeye R B fine graders, three Ransome pavers and one Koehring 34E dual-drum paver, four Jaeger finishing machines, four Flex-Plane joint machines and four Koehring longitudinal floats.

It was impossible to pipe water to the paving units

laying the runways because of the open trenches used for the installation of the drainage system. The water was supplied by tank trucks of 2,000 and 3,000 gallon capacity that hauled 240,000 gallons a day to the paving outfits for mixing and for wetting of subgrade ahead of the pavers.

No water was required on the finished slabs, as the concrete was cured under a cover of waterproofed, reinforced four-ply kraft paper. For curing the pavement, 800 rolls of Sisalkraft, measuring 22 1/2 feet wide and 60 feet long, were used and reused an average of six times. While weather remained hot, the Sisalkraft cover was kept on the slab for seven days; after September 15 the period of curing under paper was reduced to four days.

Batch Plants

To deliver dry mix to its pavers Julius Porath set up a batch plant just off the newly constructed siding of the Michigan Central Railroad. It consisted of two Blaw-Knox bins and one Blaw-Knox bulk cement plant arranged for straight through loading of trucks that supplied their dual-drum pavers. Complete charging of a two-batch truck in three stops under the three bins could be accomplished in 15 seconds, according to time studies made by Edward W. Porath, secretary-treasurer of their company.

Aggregate delivered by rail was unloaded from gondola cars to stockpiles by two Koehring cranes equipped with clamshells of one (1) and 1 1/4-yard capacity. A 1 1/2-yard Northwest crane charged the 100-ton sand bin and the 200-ton gravel bin from the stockpiles. Cement was hauled to Willow Run from Ford's River Rouge plant by George F. Alger, and Hess Cartage Companies in tank trailers equipped with unloading screws. The trailers carried approximately 75 barrels of cement per trip and were unloaded at the foot of a bucket type elevator that fed the cement to a 350-barrel bulk plant.

At the batch plant of Lewis & Frisinger and E. B. Schwaderer companies, both the aggregates and cement were delivered by truck. Separate sand and gravel bins, set up some distance apart, were equipped with double hoppers for one stop charging of the two-batch trucks. Two bulk cement plants, a Butler and a Blaw-Knox, were located side by side at an intermediate point between the gravel and sand bins, and each truck made two stops under the hoppers to take on the two batches of cement.

Ten two-batch trucks served each of the four 34E paving units which worked a continuous two shift schedule. This required a continuous line of 80 trucks to be operating during those shifts, and to supplement the contractors' hauling fleets many of those trucks were rented. Due to the limited capacity of most trucks the batch size was set at 31.5 cubic feet, considerably less than the 37.4 cubic foot capacity of the 34E pavers.

Concrete specifications called for six sacks of cement per cubic yard to produce test cylinders with a minimum compression strength of 3,500 pounds per square inch at 28 days. The gravel aggregate was graded to 1 1/2 inch maximum size, and the volume of water was regulated to hold the concrete slump within a specified maximum of 2 inches. The normal range being between 1 1/2 to 2 inches.

On the basis of a two percent average overrun, a 31.5 cubic foot batch paved 2.94 linear feet of the 20-foot slab. This provided a normal daily run of 1.5 miles with the four pavers turning out 2,700 batches. This meant an overall average of 42 batches per hour for each mixer throughout the 16 hours of a two-shift day. Specifications required 60 seconds mixing of each batch, and batchmeters were set for 32 seconds of mixing in each dual drum compartment.

On a typical day when the pavers were laying 1.5 miles of concrete, the two batching plants weighed out about 5,200 tons of sand and gravel and 900 tons of cement. The tank trucks, in the course of such a day, delivered 240,000 gallons of water to the paving outfits for mixing and wetting subgrade. The total amount hauled, during the 94 working days required to pour the runways, was 470,000 tons of sand and gravel and 84,600 tons of cement.

The airport covered 1,434 acres of land and had six runways. Including the runway for the Army Air Base that was 4,817 feet long, there were 7.7 miles, or 40,647 feet of runway poured. Within the Bomber Plant Airport there were 2.3 miles of 80 foot wide taxiway and the area of the aprons covered 320,000 square yards. The apron for the Army Air Base was 3325 feet long by 416 feet wide, and fifty foot taxiways connected the apron to runways 27R and 27L (See Appendix A; Air Base, Army, and Airport).

In addition to the above construction, lighting of the airport required its own electrical sub-station. Miles of electrical wire and hundreds of lights were installed to mark the runways and boundaries. Control and range lights were installed, rotating beacons, search lights, and numerous pieces of traffic control equipment. Never had such an elaborate array of equipment or drainage system been used to build an airport. (See Appendix A, Lighting Airfield.)

Albert Kahn's engineering drawing below details the elaborate drainage system needed for the Airport. Sub-surface and runway edge drains provide quick discharge of storm water, and prevent frost heave damage in the winter.

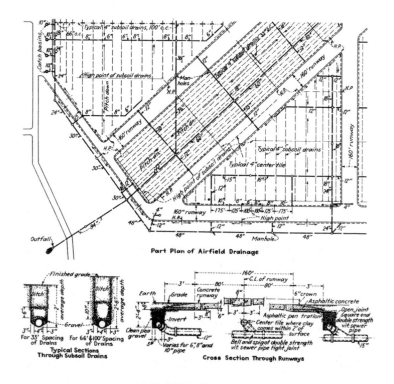

Airfield Drainage System

82

Lines of Moretrench well points pre-drains soil before excavation.

Running sand in the trench for the 84 inch sewer pipe.

Steel hammers hung from crane booms drive protective steel
sheeting at site of 36-foot deep trench for the 84-inch outfall sewer.
Excavation by Porath & Sons Co.

Gargaro Co. employed Jaeger well points to dry 19 foot deep trench
for laying 1800 feet of 84 inch sanitary drain from the factory.

Julius Porath & Son management. Left: Simpson Albion, job engineer.
Center: Edward W. Porath. Left: William E. Duffy, general manager.

Airport Supervision: came under the direction of: (1) Glenn Guther, Mgr of concrete supply, (2) Glenn Cargill, Gen Supt., and (3) William. E. Duffy, Gen. Mgr, Julis Porath & Son Co; (4) Manley Stegeman, Supt. Engineering, Albert Kahn Associated Architects & Engineering, Inc; (5) William Dorrance, Project Engr. Ford Motor Co.; (6) Charles V. Patridge, Chief Time Keeper, and (7) A. Zak, Chief Clerk, Julius Porath.

7   6   5   4   3   2   1

Winch-propelled finegrader travels on steel forms and previously completed pavement, cuts subgrade to cross-section profile, depositing excess dirt outside of forms.

24,000 gallons of mixing water delivered daily and transferred by portable pump to tank on pavers.

Two bulk cement plants serve batch trucks hauling from Lewis & Frisinger Co. and E. B. Schwaderer.

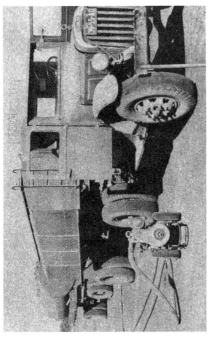

800 rolls of waterproof Sisalkraftm - 60 feet by 22.5 feet protected concrete slabs while curing.

PORTABLE LIGHT PLANTS moved by farm tractors furnish illumination for paving and finishing work after dark. Rolls of waterproof paper for curing concrete slab are piled on carrier for reuse.

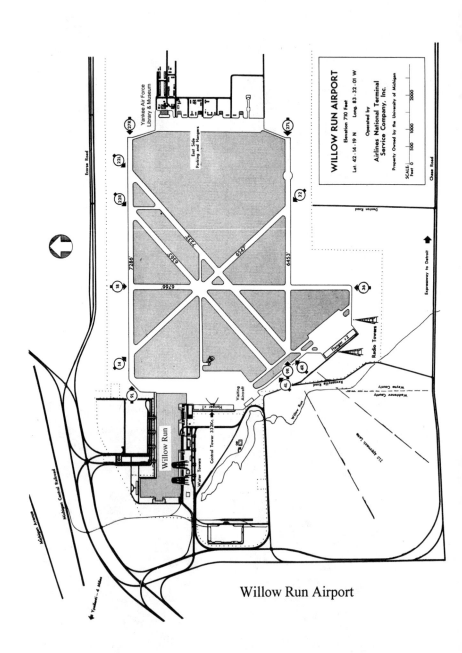

WILLOW RUN AIRPORT

Elevation 710 Feet

Lat. 42-14-19 N   Long. 83-32-01 W

Operated by

Airlines National Terminal
Service Company, Inc.

Property Owned by the University of Michigan

SCALE:
Feet 0   500   1000   2000

Willow Run Airport

Finishing machine follows the giant 34E dual-drum paver.

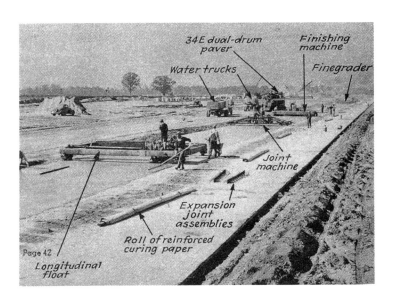

Equipment used in laying the 740,000 sq. yards of concrete.

89

WILLOW RUN

Aerial View Of The Willow Run Industrial Complex
Under Construction - October 1941.

CONSTRUCTION OF THE FACTORY[4]

Planning and construction for Willow Run was carried on by the Ford Motor Company until June 25, 1941. At that time, they established the Defense Plant Corporation which assumed ownership and responsibility for the Willow Run project. Ford then entered into a lease arrangement with the newly formed corporation to manage construction and factory operations on their behalf.

Construction of the entire Willow Run bomber plant, including the airport, came under the direction of Robert H. Daily, supervising engineer for the Defense Plant Corporation. Supervision of all construction for the Ford Motor Company was carried out under the direction of H. B. Hanson, who for years had been Ford's head of power and construction. During airport construction Ford's project engineer was William Dorrance.

Excavation for the manufacturing and assembly areas of the factory was started on April 18, 1941, by J. A. Utley Company of Detroit. Construction was concentrated in the smaller factory design until the Government gave Ford the final go ahead to manufacture the complete bomber in May. In that design, the longer leg of the "L" was only 1720 feet and the shorter leg 880 feet as compared to 3200 and 1279 feet in the final design. The order to start construction had come from the Ford Motor Company, but Utley's official contract was not dated until July 20, and came from the Defense Plant Corporation.

Utley's contract for $600,000 covered nearly 2,500 concrete footings for columns, 120,000 lineal feet of grade beams, or foundation walls, between footings, and more than 5250 lineal feet of reinforced-concrete box tunnels to carry steam lines from the power house to various parts of the building. The inside dimension of the tunnels were, 6 ½ feet high by 8 feet wide, with 10 inch walls and 9 inch roof and floor. The walls and roof were protected by membrane waterproofing covered with a one-inch coat of cement plaster.

Construction was rapid. Foundations and footings were poured, and on May 3 the first structural steel was erected. Within days the steel skeleton of the factory could be seen rising above the horizon. The total area of the factory floor was 3,503,016 square feet, or 80.4 acres. This included 2,764,836 square feet on the first floor, 297,380 sq. ft. on the mezzanine, and 440,800 square feet on the second floor. The area of the factory roof was 63.5 acres, and the total floor area including the hangars was 4,734,617 square feet, or 109 acres.

As imposing as it was, the manufacturing and assembly building was only the center of a larger industrial complex created on a square mile of land bordering the west side of the airport. Facing the airport, on the south side of the factory, were two hangars with a total of 503,744 sq. ft. and a winter hangar with 38,822 square feet.

Other independent structures were the administration building and garage, personnel building, airplane school, sewage disposal, oil storage, transportation garage, dope and paint storage, commissary, gas house, incinerator, a 47,407 sq. ft. power house, and a new materials building of 577,120 sq. ft. These all totaled 1,345,471 sq. ft. (See Appendix B, Area.) In addition to these structures, there were two electrical sub-stations and two water towers.

A "Compass Rose," used for swinging and calibrating the compass of each bomber was constructed at ground level of non-metallic material. The only one of its kind in the country, it was 52' 2" in diameter, weighed 85 tons, and was powered by a 30 hp motor.

The pre-production intention of Ford to employ 60,000 people on two shifts gives a further indication as to the size of the factory. Parking areas for 15,000 automobiles were included in the original layout, and the Michigan Highway Department, aided by defense road funds, constructed a divided multi-lane highway from Detroit to Willow Run.

The Bryant & Detwiler Company of Detroit headed the list of companies as general contractor because of its low bid and agreement with the Ford Motor Company to act as coordinator of all inter-related trades. They worked under a fixed-fee contract of $5,000,000, which included general masonry and architectural work performed by its own employees. Their contract was later increased by inclusion of work on the power house, hangar buildings and installation of permanent machinery.

Under urgent demands for rapid construction and the insistence of an importunate War Department, Albert Kahn executives established a rigorous schedule to be met by the contractors. Preliminary sketches and drawings were made and approved. Structural steel drawings were expedited with great speed while, simultaneously, additional architectural drawings were being developed by a large staff of engineers. Steel bids were taken and contracts let while excavation plans were being completed. Trade contracts were awarded while steel was still being fabricated and while foundations were being dug and made ready for erection of the steel when it arrived on the job site.

Despite inescapable complications, the architects, engineers and contractors managed the job so skillfully that the entire work force and equipment units were delivered close to capacity production during the seven months required for plant construction.

On the basis of a competitive price per pound for fabrication and erection, Whitehead & Kales, Detroit, received a contract valued at about $3,000,000 for 27,000 tons of structural steel to be erected in the main building, 4,400 tons in hangar buildings, and 710 tons in the power house. Structural members and trusses were shop-fabricated in large units and delivered to the job on truck-trailers for unloading and erection by crane. An industrial 60-ton steam locomotive crane unloaded and stocked the fabricated steel. Six Industrial gasoline crawler cranes, five of 15-ton capacity and one of 25-ton capacity, and two Universal heavy truck-cranes with long booms erected the heavy trusses.

Concrete requirements under the Bryant & Detwiler contract totaled 95,000 cubic yards, of which 65,000 were in the 8-inch ground floor of the manufacturing and assembly building. This slab called for reinforcement with two layers of six-inch welded wire mesh of which more than 5,000,000 sq. ft. were used. In addition to the ground floor, the building included 800,000 sq. ft. of mezzanine and locker floors which consisted of concrete slab reinforced with bar steel and supported on I-beam joists. An agreement with Julius Porath & Son who had contracted to supply all of the concrete on the job, not just that for the airport, called for delivery of 1,000 cu. yds. in an 8-hour shift, or 2,000 cu. yds. during a two shift schedule.

Sewage and water facilities for the entire project were designed by the Detroit consulting engineering firm of Hubbell, Rosh & Clark, Inc. Then the firm of Cause & Sanders, also from Detroit, built a $260,000 sewage disposal plant of activated sludge south of the main factory near the banks of Willow Run. Again the impermeable clay compacted by years of glaciation created problems, but the engineers put the clay to work for themselves as well. To trap seepage of ground water, they installed drain tile in gravel-filled trenches cut into clay benches around their work, and proceeded building their sewer plant under dryer conditions.

Electric power was supplied by the Detroit Edison Co., which installed two electric substations for stepping down 120-kv. power to 24,000 volts. Eleven secondary transformer stations installed below the floor level in the manufacturing and assembly building made further reductions in voltage to supply the 110 and 220 volt outlets established by plant layout. Power usage by the factory at peak periods was estimated to be 50,000,000 kwh. per year.

The extensive electrical work covered in a $6,500,000 contract to John Miller Electric Company, Detroit, is reflected in the use of more than 300 tons of copper cable, 130 car loads of ½ to 6 inch steel conduit, and 30 carloads (293,000 ft.) of fiber duct.

Steam for power and heating the plant was supplied by four oil-fired boilers located in the power house. They were installed by Wicks Boiler Company, Detroit, under a $249,000 contract, and each unit had a capacity of 60,000 pounds of steam per hour at 175-lb pressure.

The $3,000,000 plumbing and heating contract was carried out by Donald Miller Company, Detroit. The installation included 100 miles of pipe for water and steam, and 88 central heating units in the manufacturing and assembly building. Each unit was capable of heating six good-sized-houses and was equipped with steam coils, air filters and blower fans to force the air through the duct system. Steam radiators were used for heating offices, toilets and lunch areas. The equipment installed included 5,000 plumbing fixtures.

To cover the 63.5 acres of roof, the design called for using a U. S. Gypsum steel rib deck of 16-gauge sheet metal dipped in enamel. The Capital Erection & Welding Co., Lansing, Michigan erected the steel roof deck and welded each of the interlocking ribbed metal planks to the steel roof purlins. The 27,800 squares roof deck was covered with insulation and composition roofing.

Arrow Roofing & Sheet Metal Company, Detroit, held a $650,000 bid to lay 1 ½ inch J-M Rock Cork vermiculite insulating sheets covered with bonded Barrett built-up roofing of four plies of asphaltic felt membrane, mopped on and topped with a layer of hot pitch and slag. The latter, applied at the rate of 400 pounds per square, required a total of 5,175 tons to cover the area. Pitch for the roofing crews was delivered hot by Barrett Company in Travia tank trailers at the rate of nearly 20 tons per day.

Creosoted wood block flooring, 2 ½ inches thick with a 16 pound treatment, was used to cover the concrete floor throughout the factory. The bid, valued at $550,000, went to Jennison-Wright Company, Detroit, who installed sixteen million of the blocks.

Each of the 150 foot wide aisles of the assembly building was equipped at the outer end with a vestibule 120 feet deep through which assembled bombers could be moved without exposing the rest of the factory to drafts. The vestibules were fitted with canopy doors 143 feet 9 inches wide which folded upward to provide a vertical clearance of 33 feet. Manufactured and installed by Byrne Doors, Inc., Detroit, for a bid of $260,000, each weighed 35 tons.

Mullions between the steel sash, fitted with clips into which wooden blackout shutters could be installed in the case of wartime necessity, were the responsibility of Detroit Steel Products Company under an $85,000 contract.

The Armand Cassill Co., Detroit, under an $85,000 contract, received after competitive bidding, laid three miles of railroad track by the middle of September 1941 to expedite service to the contractors and to the factory.

Under a competitive-bid contract Taylor and Gaskin,

Detroit, provided $232,000 worth of miscellaneous iron-work, and the Cyclone Fence Co. erected $65,000 worth of 7-foot high woven wire fence.

Bids for all trade divisions except plumbing, heating, ventilating, electrical, and fire protection were taken by Ford Motor Company in the spring of 1941, but the earliest date of formal contract signing was July 20, 25 days after the Defense Plant Corporation took over the project.

On September 17, 1941, the payroll for the entire project, including the airport, was 2909 employees, of which nearly 2,200 were engaged in construction of the factory. The Bryant & Detwiler Co. had 690 on its own payroll and 130 more on payrolls of sub-contractors. Two hundred of those men worked for Whitehead & Kale in steel erection and riveting; other contractors employed the remainder of the work force.

The following chart shows contractors' manpower from January 1, 1941 to January 1, 1945.

January 1,	1941	0
July 1,	1941	183
January 1,	1942	3762
January 30,	1942	4500
July 1,	1942	3163
January 1,	1943	614
July 1,	1943	181
January 1,	1944	646
July 1,	1944	885
January 1,	1945	43

Supervision

As previously mentioned, construction of the entire Willow Run bomber plant, including the airport, was under the direction of Robert H. Daily, supervising engineer for the Defense Plant Corporation. Supervision of all construction for the Ford Motor Company, which operated the plant and managed construction on behalf of the Defense Plant Corporation, was carried out under the direction of H. B. Hanson, Ford's head of power and construction. William Dorrance was Ford's project engineer responsible for airport construction.

George Scrymgeour was delegated executive in charge of operations for Albert Kahn Associated Architects and Engineers, Inc., who designed and supervised construction of the entire project. Raymond C. Bernardi was Kahn's superintendent for the Willow Run factory, and M. Stegeman was engineering superintendent on the airport.

The Bryant & Detwiler Company was represented by Charles M. Reik, with John G. Campbell as General Superintendent of operations and J. K. Calder directing and coordinating all of the trades.

Operations of Julius Porath & Son Company, contractor for all phases of airport construction, was under the leadership of Edward W. Porath, secretary-treasurer, and William E. Duffy, its general manager. Glen Cargill, their on-site general superintendent, was assisted by Simpson Albion, estimating engineer; M. M. Martens, was grading superintendent; J. Gothard, paving superintendent; and L.

Rhodes, drainage superintendent.

The paving work done by the Lewis & Frisinger and E. B. Schwaderer companies was directed by Curtis R. Hunt, veteran Schwaderer superintendent.

During construction of the giant Willow Run factory, contractors used 38,000 thousand tons of steel, 2,400 tons of sheet metal, and ten million brick. They also used 200,000 gallons of paint, 2,000 miles of electric wire and cable, 580 miles of steel and 110 miles of fiber conduits. Six miles of conductor pipe, and six miles of roof sumps went into the building, along with 12 miles of monorail in the manufacturing area and an additional six miles in the rest of the buildings. There were 28,855 panes of 30 different types of glass and 11 miles of fence installed. Seven copper expansion joints were run across the width of the building, and two lengthwise. (See Appendix B.)

The longer leg of the "L" shaped construction, running east and west, was 3200 feet, and the shorter leg, at the base was 1279 feet. The assembly lines inside of the building, however, were 5460 feet, 180 feet longer than Sorensen's original mile-long estimate.[5]

END NOTES

1. Charles A. Sorensen. *My Forty Years With Ford.* New York: Norton & Co., 1956: 282.
2. Bryan R. Ford. *Henry's Lieutenants.* Wayne State University Press, 1993: 141.
3. "In 100 days Contractor Grades, Drains and Paves $3,900,000 Airport." *Construction Methods*, March 1942.
4. "Seven Months Schedule Completes 62-Acre Building for Ford Bomber Plant." *Constructions Methods*, January, 1942.
5. *Willow Run Reference Book,* 1945 (Appendix B).

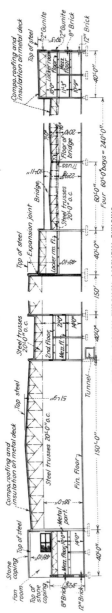

TYPICAL SECTION THROUGH ASSEMBLY BUILDING

TWO 150-FT. BAYS for major assembly and final assembly and four 60-ft. bays for sub-assembly make up bulk of 700-ft. width of assembly area 2,800 ft. long. Overhead bridges provide employee access between locker rooms on upper floors and parking fields on south side of building.

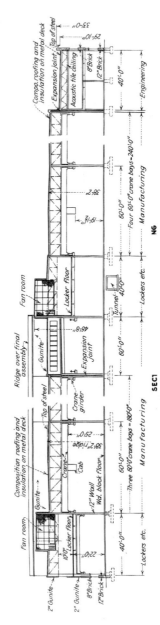

Section Through Manufacturing Wing

Ten craneways in 60 and 40 foot bays facilitate handling of parts between manufacturing machinery. A 40x1,200 foot bay along west wall is for engineering, laboratory, hospital, lunch rooms and toilets.

Construction Sections For Progress Schedule
Willow Run Manufacturing Area - Ford Motor Company Bomber Plant

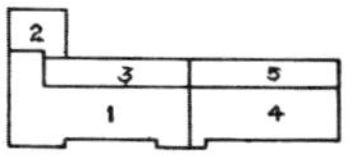

KEY PLAN	2	3	5
	1	4	

TRADE DIVISION	QUOTATIONS		SECTION-1		SECTION-2		SECTION-3		SECTION-4		SECTION-5	
	BIDS ASKED	AWARDED	START	COMPLETE	START	COMPLETE	START	COMPLETE	START	COMPLETE	START	COMPLETE
EXCAVATION	JULY 20	JULY 20	APRIL 18	AUG. 8	JULY 21	AUG. 10	AUG. 4	AUG. 29	SEPT. 2	OCT. 8	SEPT. 15	OCT. 15
FOOTINGS	"	"	" 25	" 15	" 23	" 24	" 4	SEPT. 12	" 9	" 22	" 17	NOV. 1
WALLS BELOW GRADE	"	" 20	" 25	" 15	" 23	" 24	" 6	" 12	" 9	" 22	" 17	" 1
ELECTRICAL/TEMP CONST.	AUG. 5	AUG. 5	AUG. 5	" 15								
STRUCTURAL STEEL			SEPT. 1	SEPT. 1	SEPT 1	SEPT. 21	SEPT 15	OCT. 10	OCT. 1	NOV. 1	NOV. 3	DEC. 15
ROOF DECK	AUG. 5			" 8	" 7	" 28	" 22	" 18	" 7	" 8	" 21	" 22
ROOFING - SHEET METAL	AUG. 5	JULY 30		" 14	" 7	OCT. 5	" 29	" 24	" 14	" 15	" 28	" 29
STEEL SASH	AUG. 8	AUG. 5	SEPT 8	" 15	" 14	" 12	" 22	NOV. 3	" 7	" 22	" 21	JAN. 5
GLASS & GLAZING		AUG. 8	"	" 22		" 30	" 29	OCT. 7	" 14	" 22	" 28	" 7
EXTERIOR BRICK WORK	JULY 20	AUG. 5	AUG. 5	" 22			" 29	OCT. 31	" 7	" 22	" 7	"
GUNITE	AUG. 5	AUG. 5	" 8	" 22			" 22		" 7	" 22	" 2	" 5
FLOOR ON GROUND	JULY 20	JULY 20		OCT. 1	SEPT 2	OCT. 26	OCT. 6	NOV. 14	" 21	DEC. 6	DEC. 5	" 6
CREOSOTED WOOD BLOCK FLOOR	AUG. 8	AUG. 8	SEPT. 1	" 8	" 28	NOV. 5	" 13	" 21	" 28	" 15	" 12	" 26
MEZZANINE - 2ND FLOOR SLAB	JULY 20	AUG. 21	AUG. 21			" 5	SEPT 29	OCT. 24	" 7	NOV. 18	NOV. 21	" 29
MISCELLANEOUS IRON WORK	AUG. 5	AUG. 5	SEPT 7	" 15	" 2	NOV. 6	" 15	" 25	" 7	DEC. 15	DEC. 5	FEB. 1
METAL TOILET PARTITIONS		AUG. 8		" 15		" 6	OCT. 1	" 25	" 21	" 15	DEC. 5	" 1
METAL OFFICE PARTITIONS		" 8	SEPT. 1	" 15	" 2	" 6	"	" 25	" 7	" 15	DEC. 5	" 1
PAINTING		" 8	AUG. 7	" 15	" 7	OCT. 25	SEPT 22	" 28	" 7	" 15	NOV. 21	JAN. 19
ACOUSTICAL WORK		" 15	SEPT 21	" 6	OCT. 5	" 25	OCT. 20	" 14	NOV. 5	" 6	DEC. 20	" 19
MARBLE		" 15	" 21	" 6	" 5	" 26	" 20	" 14	" 5	" 6	NOV. 20	" 19
CARPENTER WORK		" 1	AUG. 1	" 15	SEPT 7	" 26	SEPT 22	" 14	OCT. 7	" 6	NOV. 21	FEB. 1
HARDWARE		" 15	" 15	" 15	"	NOV. 6	OCT. 13	" 25	" 28	" 15	DEC. 12	" 1
COMPOSITION TILE		" 15	SEPT 21	" 15	" 28	" 6	" 13	" 25	" 28	" 15	NOV. 21	" 1
QUARRY TILE		" 15	" 21	SEPT 29	" 14	OCT. 20	SEPT 29	" 7	" 14	NOV. 29	NOV. 28	JAN. 12
HANGAR DOORS		" 15	"	" 29	" 14	" 14	"	"	" 14	" 28	" 28	" 12
FOLDING DOORS		" 15	"	" 29	" 28	" 20	" 29	" 7	" 28	" 29	DEC. 12	" 12
HOLLOW METAL WORK	JULY 20	" 15	"	" 29	" 28	" 20	OCT. 15	" 7	" 28	" 29	" 12	" 12
INTERIOR MASONRY		JULY 20	OCT. 6	OCT. 15	OCT. 19	NOV. 6	NOV. 3	" 25	NOV. 18	DEC. 15	JAN. 3	FEB. 1
CLEAN UP												
UNDERGROUND PLUMBING	AUG. 10	AUG. 15	AUG. 18	SEPT. 22	SEPT. 7	OCT. 12	SEPT. 22	OCT. 31	OCT. 8	NOV. 22	NOV. 10	JAN. 5
" HEATING	" 10	" 15	" 18	" 22	" 7	" 12	" 22	" 31	" 8	" 22	" 10	" 5
" ELECTRICAL WORK	" 10	" 18	" 18	" 22	" 7	" 12	" 22	" 31	" 8	" 22	" 10	" 5
" FIRE PROTECTION		" 25	" 28	" 22								
ELECTRICAL WORK	AUG. 21	AUG. 15	SEPT. 1	OCT. 15	SEPT. 14	NOV. 6	SEPT. 29	NOV. 25	OCT. 14	DEC. 15	NOV. 28	FEB. 1
PLUMBING WORK	" 21	" 15	" 1	" 15	" 14	" 6	" 29	" 25	" 14	" 15	" 28	" 1
HEATING & VENTILATING WORK												

(Left margin note spanning the QUOTATIONS columns: "BIDS IN COMPETITION IN ORIGINAL")

Albert Kahn's stiff construction schedule demanded maximum speed - Completion dates determined rates of construction for all contractors

SHOP-FABRICATED TRUSS for 150-ft. final assembly bay is erected in two parts. Steam locomotive crane of 60-ton capacity, ordinarily used in yard service, swings half of truss into position to be handled by two gasoline-powered crawler-type erection cranes.

Incoming steel is sorted and stocked by 60-ton locomotive crane.
Whitehead & Kales Co.

Electrical conduits being laid under the floor - John Miller Co.

Ransome cement mixer pours reinforced tunnel floor in trench pre-
drained with Moretrench well points - J. A. Utley Co.

Deep excavation being made under garage for transformer room
Bryant & Detwiler Co.

Brick Spandrels and steel sash for continuous windows close
exterior wall of engineering area - west end of factory.

Sand-lime backup brick are tiled with headers in every fourth
course. Stone sill is laid on top of 8" brick spandrel.

Metal rib panels of 16-gage enamel-dipped steel being welded in
place by crew of Capital Erection & Welding Co.

Four-ply build-up roofing being applied over 1 1/2 x 18 x 36 inch
panels of vermiculite insulation - Arrow Roofing & Sheet Metal Co.

Heated tank trailer supplied nearly 20 ton of hot pitch per day to the
roofing crews.

Fifteen columns picked up on needle beams for underpinning to depth below bottom of press pits required after government approved expansion to build complete B-24s. Browning crane handles air-powered hammer driving corrugated steel sheeting. Below: Night shift driving corrugated sheets. **A big job.**

With ground seepage trapped by title drains in gravel-filled trenches on clay bench of the excavation banks, construction of Cause and Sanders' sewage plant job proceeds under dry conditions.

WILLOW RUN

Prefabricated expansion joint with copper flashing being lowered into a concrete mud mat in tunnel trench - A. Utley Co.

Sewer plant construction Superintendent, John C. Westphal (left) talks to office manager

Etor Gargaro, General Superintendent, storm sewers - Gargago Co.

BULLDOZERS AND HOT STEEL RIVETS

BOMBER PLANT SUPERVISION: (Left to Right) JOHN G. CAMPBELL, general superintendent, Bryant & Detwiler Co.; RAYMOND C. BERNADI, superintendent, Albert Kahn Associated Architects & engineers, Inc.; EMORY HORST, assistant superintendent; FERDINAND J. OTTO, job engineer; and JACK K. CALDER superintendent of trades. The last three men were supervisors of Bryant & Detwiler.

B-24 "Liberators" Waiting For Shipment
Left: Hangar One. Right: Vestibule To Final Assembly Line.

Chapter V

OVERCOMING PRODUCTION INERTIA

During July of 1908, Charles Sorensen, using a rope, had pulled a Model N automobile chassis along the floor of Ford's Piquette Avenue plant until the wheels were installed and it could be pushed by hand. Now, 33 years later, the man who had developed Ford's first moving assembly line for mass production of automobiles would develop the aircraft industry's first assembly line for mass production of large airplanes.

Ford had acquired years of experience in mass-producing automobiles and developing unique ways of solving difficult problems. The employees, steeped in those principles, had mass produced numerous pieces of military equipment, from artillery shells to 18-cylinder aircraft engines, and from tanks to gliders capable of carrying troops and heavy military equipment. But never before had their methods of mass production been used in the aircraft industry.

Now, the Ford Motor Company was being asked to apply their expertise to manufacture the B-24 bomber, a four-engine airplane weighing 37,205 pounds. It was so much larger than an automobile that Sorensen had compared it to "building a skyscraper instead of a garage," and he himself had set the goal of a bomber an hour.

When the government accepted Ford's proposal, it

introduced into the aircraft manufacturing industry two discordant systems of production, the unit production of the aircraft industry and the mass production methods of the automobile industry. The aircraft industry provided their design and mastery of aerodynamic principles and experience in handling aluminum alloys on the basis of unit or job shop production. Ford would have to prove they could mass produce the airplane in a way heretofore unknown and untried in the assembly of airplanes.

The men from Ford went to work. They designed and built a colossal tooling program. Considered to be the largest in the world, it challenged the wildest imaginations of their finest engineering minds. They worked through growing pains of designing and installing equipment, manufacturing parts and building up assemblies while, at the same time, the factory was being constructed around them. In so doing, they reduced production lead time to a minimum, and provided parts for shipment to plants at Fort Worth and Tulsa for assembly into complete bombers before Willow Run was ready for full production.

From the moment the U.S. Air Corps accepted Ford's proposal, it set into motion a series of events more powerful than the men who had created and approved the idea. It is doubtful if anyone, including Sorensen, fully realized the magnitude and complexities of the entire process leading to the accomplishments of Willow Run, and the planes they built that helped bring an end to World War II.

On March 4, 1941, 45 days before ground breaking for the Willow Run factory, a group of Ford officials, responsible for the success of Willow Run and the B-24 program, left for San Diego to study the complexities of assembling a product totally unfamiliar to them.

They rented office space in the Freckles building for 200 Ford engineers and production experts who arrived in San Diego a week later, on March 11, and for the draftsmen who prepared the engineering drawings that Consolidated could not provide. Among this group of 200 were tool designers, electricians, factory layout men, and laboratory technicians who created ideas for tooling and production and developed the flow of parts and assemblies throughout Willow Run. A tool room was set up at the Consolidated plant where Ford tool and die makers could start building tools for Willow Run.

In the group of Ford officials who left for San Diego on March 4 were some of Ford's finest men. All of them had been in the entourage studying Consolidated's production with Sorensen in January.

Logan Miller, Willow Run factory superintendent, was in charge of the engineers, tool designers and production personnel who developed the methods and tooling for Willow Run. He was assigned the job of planning for B-24 production late in 1940, after Ford and Sorensen had met with Dr. Mead in Dearborn the week before Christmas.

Miller, one of the best sheet metal fabricating men in the country, was largely responsible for the decision to use hard dies in stamping out parts, and for the tooling, production, and many of the shortcuts which enabled Willow Run workers to establish numerous records.

WILLOW RUN

H. B. Hanson, Director of Ford's Power and Construction, was in charge of all of Willow Run building projects, which included construction of the factory, airport, power house, and numerous other buildings. Hanson had started working at Ford in 1914 as a molder in the foundry and later, after taking a course in engineering, he became plant engineer. As a Ford employee, Hanson had worked with Albert Kahn designing the floor plan and buildings for a new Ford foundry, and in building the intricate River Rouge production facility.

Edward Scott worked as Ford's chief body engineer at the Engineering Laboratory in Dearborn until he was assigned to the B-24 project in January 1941. He set up Ford's engineering department in San Diego for the engineers arriving from Dearborn, and later took engineering information from San Diego to another group of Ford engineers set up in Dearborn to help overcome the extra-heavy burden of engineering. He was in charge of Willow Run's engineering department until after production got underway. Then he was assigned to San Diego, as coordinator between Consolidated and Willow Run.

William F. Pioch, in charge of Ford's tooling for many years, directed the design of B-24 tools and fixtures from Ford's San Diego office. Later, he was placed in charge of both engineering and tool design at Willow Run. He was in charge of the engineering change on the nose turret assembly and development of the new single tail assembly to replace the twin tails on the original B-24. He also established a system for handling the massive numbers of engi-

116

neering changes ordered by the U.S. Army Air Force.

Roscoe Smith, who was in charge of Ford's outlying factories, became Willow Run's first plant manager until the fist fight with Bennett; he was replaced by Ford's long experienced production manager, Mead Bricker.

Ernie Walters, was an old time Ford employee with years of experience gained in the company's early days of rapid growth. Now he was applying his experience as Superintendent of the Press Steel Division to help Willow Run reach the magic goal of a bomber an hour.

These were the men with Sorensen the night the decision was made to build the giant airplane at the rate of one an hour. They were the men who developed innovative equipment and procedures never before used in the manufacture of airplanes. They developed the layout of the giant presses that stamped out huge pieces of aluminum, decided the flow of parts from manufacturing to assembly areas, and developed the layout and sequencing of the final assembly line. For these men, responsible for the ultimate success of the B-24 at Willow Run, this was the crowning challenge of their careers.

Factory Layout

While construction of the Willow Run factory was taking place, Ford's layout men were at Consolidated's plant in San Diego making man-hour studies to aid them in laying out Willow Run machinery and facilities. The chief tools used by the Layout Department were 36x48 inch layout boards made of a fiber material. Each board was painted black and contained approximately 20,000 square feet of the plant drawn to a scale of one-quarter inch to the foot. For expediency, a model of the entire plant was built and divided into bays representing 40x60 feet in the manufacturing area and 40x150 feet in the assembly area. Nine manufacturing bays or three assembly bays were shown on each layout board. One hundred and fifty-seven boards comprised the main floor layout, 23 were used for the mezzanine and balconies, 11 for the hangar, seven for the school, and one for the Personnel Building.

When machinery or other facilities were to be located, white paper templates, made to the same scale were moved about on the layout board to determine the most advantageous location. The templates, then stapled to the board allowed for numerous changes without constant erasures or need to remake layout drawings. In addition to machinery, the layout boards showed permanent installations of items such as sewer drains, tunnels, electric cables, cranes, columns, hospital and partitions needed by the architect.

After all the templates were spotted, the layout board was photostated, which reversed the color scheme and provided details of black equipment on a white background. These photographic copies were sent along with a work order to the men installing the machinery at Willow Run and became their authorization to proceed with work.

The first items to be located were the acid tanks which required permanent connections with water, air and special

To plan for arrangement of machinery in the new Willow Run Bomber Plant, Ford engineers constructed a scale model of the factory. C. E. Sorensen second from right, discusses the model with Ford Engineers at Dearborn.

drains, all of which had to be installed with the foundations. Before locating machinery, fixtures or benches, layout personnel needed to know the size and weight of each item, whether water or a drain were required, and if so what type. Would gas or compressed air be used, and how many men would work at the equipment? On columns throughout the plant they located master controls for electrical power. Some areas were supplied with 110-volt current while others needed 220 volts or higher. Machines requiring these voltages were placed in their respective area, reducing power losses from the sub-stations as individual lines were not required for each machine.

The size and weight of material to be used in a machine were important factors in determining location. Bulky, unwieldy materials required space around the machine to facilitate operation. If materials were heavy, room had to be allowed for crane and truck handling. Unnecessary movement of stock was costly in both time and money and it was desirable to eliminate long intra-plant hauls.

Allied with material handling was the conveyor system. This inter-departmental form of transportation was an over-head endless chain secured by rollers on a six-inch steel mono-rail. Determining the location and speed of the ordinary conveyor was accomplished through experience gained at the River Rouge plant. But a new type of trolley conveyor, never before used in manufacturing, was designed especially for use in the assembly of the wing and presented its own development problems.

Employee safety and comfort were other concerns of

the Layout Department. Operations that created fumes, smoke, or dust were fitted with suction ducts for their elimination. Adequate toilet facilities for both men and women, locker rooms handy to the worker's department, and large lunchrooms close to the employees' work station all added to their comfort. In event of an air attack, the factory was divided into nine zones. Each zone chart showed the location of the first-aid station, gasoline and acid tanks, fire extinguishers of various types, graphite and sand supplies, and other emergency equipment.

First-aid stations required considerable research. They were not located according to floor space, but were concentrated in departments where experience indicated there would be a higher rate of accident. In addition to 25 paramedics working in six first aid stations, the plant had its own hospital with eight doctors, a dentist, and 44 registered nurses. In 1943 the hospital handled 819,779 cases.[1] (For location of First Aid Stations, see Appendix B - Hospital.)

Production Tooling

In the aircraft industry the basic material was aluminum instead of steel, and considerable discussion went into the final decision of which dies to use. The aircraft people advocated the use of soft kirksite dies made of 92% zinc and 7% aluminum and copper, instead of the hard metal dies used in stamping out automobile parts. They pointed out that aluminum, used in aircraft manufacturing, stretched a third more than the sheet metal used in automobiles, and that parts formed by using kirksite dies received less molecular shock than parts formed by hard steel dies. They contended that parts made on metal dies would set up stresses causing the aluminum to become brittle and lose strength. They felt that engineering changes would create serious production delays and expense in reworking metal dies.

The Ford men objected to the use of these soft dies because they would lose their precision in high volume production. Under the tremendous pressure of hydraulic presses, soft dies would become dull and disfigured. The parts they produced, after the first runs of pieces were made, would no longer be interchangeable and could not be used in mass production. Maintenance costs and time lost in production to repair and service the soft dies would be greater than with hard metal dies.

Tests proved that the strength of the aluminum was not significantly impaired by the use of hard dies, and Logan Miller decided to use the hard metal dies that for over 35 years had become so familiar to the men from Ford.

To complicate Ford's problem, it was discovered that Consolidated's engineering department had not maintained an accurate set of drawings; numerous changes, left to the discretion of shop foremen to facilitate production, had not been recorded; and, with continual changes being made to the plane, Consolidated's engineering was six months behind the model being produced. Lack of good engineering information on a plane already in production, combined with Ford's totally different concept of manufacturing, necessitated a larger than anticipated engineering staff.

OVERCOMING PRODUCTION INERTIA

To meet the growing demand of engineering to detail thousands of drawings not supplied by Consolidated, an additional group was established in the Airframe Building at Ford's Dearborn location. Over 900 men worked night and day, seven days a week, for several months. They designed and processed tooling and fixtures, allowing the airplane to be manufactured by the fastest possible methods of mass production. By midsummer 1941, most of the engineers had returned from the west coast and the Airframe Building was busy with activity. Every effort was made to get drawings into the hands of tool makers, and their work began to show results when tools were ordered and dies and fixtures began arriving at Willow Run.

The decision to use hard dies opened up innumerable opportunities to the engineers, even though they were severely criticized by the aircraft industry and others for using them. It allowed them to create improvements that led to many production records being established by Willow Run employees. The savings in man-hours of labor by using hard dies became enormous and it was demonstrated in thousands of cost-saving ideas developed by the Ford engineers. The ideas and tooling were not only used at Willow Run, but they were also used by Consolidated and Douglas Aircraft in their assembly plants in Fort Worth and Tulsa.

Design engineers developed not just blanking dies to form parts, but blank and piercing dies that, while forming the part, also punched the holes for riveting. Consolidated made those same holes in a separate operation by stacking and drilling the parts after they had been formed, an operation that produced elongated holes if the drill were to travel as it went through the stack of parts.

At Willow Run, "781 individual punches were built into one die to pierce, in just a single operation, a row of rivet holes in the flange of an elliptically shaped piece.... The holes maintained an accuracy of .002.... [In another operation] 2160 holes were punched at one time in a piece of aluminum instead of having to be drilled after the part was formed."[2]

Never before in the history of production had such an extensive tooling program been undertaken. Over 13,000 tools were built in shops throughout the country. According to the Willow Run Reference Book, compiled by members of the Plant Guide Service, dated February 1, 1945, the work order request was filed for the first die on March 24, 1941.[3] (That was four days before the first trees were cut down to make room for the airport, and 25 days before ground breaking for the factory.) It was assigned "tool number 690B-101" and was called a "Punch and Die to flange experimental bomber wing part."[4] By April 1, 1945, there had been 30,739 dies manufactured, of which 15,659 were still being used, 8,357 at Willow Run and 7,302 at vendor sources. The remaining 15,080 were in salvage or storage.

William Pioch's conception of the center wing, and machining fixtures provided unbelievable savings in man-hours, and assisted greatly in reaching Sorensen's schedule of a bomber an hour. When Pioch went to San Diego in March of 1941, he spent nearly a week timing and observing the wing section, and described his observations of

OVERCOMING PRODUCTION INERTIA

Consolidated's production operation in his reminiscence:

They had a very poor condition there at San Diego because the tides would change their floor levels and their fuselage fixtures were made of pipe. The tide would come in every day and go out and it would just raise that floor and let it down. They never knew where they were. That was a very poor condition which we noticed when we took a look at the job [in January 1941].

Their major problem was to get their wings to line up with their fuselage and then drop them on. They would line the end of wings up on a transit and put them on. They used shims to make up the difference in their joints. When they joined the wings to the fuselage they used shims for that.

They never made two wings alike. They never made two fuselages alike. They used to machine the ends of their wings to get them so they would be somewhere near right.

I came to the conclusion that in order to make a good wing and make it accurate, make them identical and one right after another, we would have to make it like we do an automobile part; that is put it in a machine, machine it up, take it out, and put it on the assembly line.

Everyone thought I was nuts, I couldn't even sell it to Logan Miller.... They told me the machine cost too much.

I said, "It does cost a lot of money, that's right, but look at the money they are spending down there. They're spending 550 man hours for doing these operations and we're not going to get enough people out to this Willow Run plant if we're going to build a bomb-er an hour," which we were planning on. I said, "You are not going to get enough people to do 550 hours on one wing. You've got two wings, so that's over 1,000 man hours on each plane."[5]

Pioch assigned John Mistele to continue designing the machine, never showing it to anyone until Sorensen came to San Diego and approved an estimated $250,000 expenditure for building the largest machining fixture ever used in the aircraft industry. It was 70 feet long, 18 feet high and 13 feet wide, and it needed only six men working an average of 35 minutes to machine the entire center wing section. The final cost of the machine, built by Ingersoll Milling Com-pany, was $168,500. Originally two machines had been ordered, but the first machine was so efficient that the order for the second one was canceled. (See Appendix B: Center Wing Milling Machine.)

When Ford finished building bombers, the patented center wing machining fixture had saved approximately $10,000,000 over Consolidated's method of manufacturing.

Shipping Sub-Assemblies

Before the plant and assembly lines were completed at Willow Run, Sorensen was manufacturing parts for ship-ment to Consolidated and Douglas Aircraft where they were assembled into completed bombers. During 1942, parts were shipped over the road in 114 truck trailers, 75 feet long, specially designed to carry the largest assemblies.

They were pulled by dual-engine Ford V-8 trucks guarded by an Army escort. In comparison, it would have taken four railroad cars to transport the parts carried by two-and-a-half trailers.

The trucks were so large that Sorensen needed special permission for their use, and when President Roosevelt visited Willow Run he asked Sorensen, "Are those the trucks I am getting complaints about blocking the highways?"[6]

Shipment of the sub-assemblies began on March 31, 1942, less than eleven months after the first structural steel had been set in place for construction of the factory. They made possible Consolidated's production of 1,140 B-24s during 1942, and are one of the reasons that Ford manufactured only a few bombers that year.

A propaganda statement in May 1942 by Sir Oliver Lyttleton, Britain's Production Chief, claiming that Willow Run was then producing a bomber an hour, may have provided hope for the people of England and Europe, but in this country it produced skepticism and statements of "Will It Run"[7] when no announcements of completed bombers were being made. What critics overlooked was that Willow Run was manufacturing knock-down parts of the airplanes to be assembled elsewhere, which was in accordance with the War Department's original objective announced by William Knudsen, its director.

It was not until production at Consolidated was up to schedule and could meet the demands of their own assembly lines that Willow Run was given the go-ahead to build

Breakdown Of B-24 For Transport via Trailers

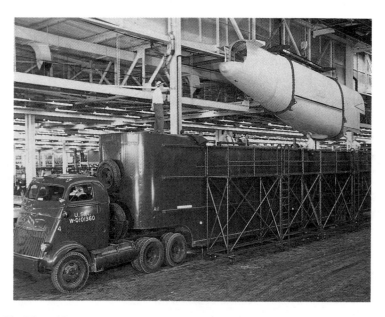

The First shipment of sub-assemblies to Douglas left the factory March 3, 1942. First knock-down shipment of the bomber left on July 12, 1942.

its first lot of 15 full airplanes. That go-ahead was received in August 1942.[8] The trailers, that had served so well in getting production going at Consolidated and Douglas, were then taken off the highway.

In 1943, Consolidated manufactured 2960 B-24s, while Willow Run's output was 2184. In 1944, before cutbacks were ordered, Consolidated's yearly output was 3817 bombers. Willow Run's output in 1944 was 4611, with capacity production set at 9000 bombers a year.

Lack of Experienced Workers

Sorensen's most troublesome problem in getting production started was, by far, a workforce lacking in aircraft production experience. Lack of experienced personnel increased the lead time for quality production, disrupted schedules, and accounted for the majority of criticism directed at Willow Run's early production output.

Until this problem could be solved, the speed at which Willow Run was readied for production, and the expertise of the Ford engineers in creating world class assembly fixtures, only served to amplify the poor quality of workmanship and slow start-up that plagued Willow Run throughout 1942.

When the government failed to re-allocate the nation's 300,000 experienced aircraft workers, Ford, with only 400 experienced employees, had to train tens of thousands of unskilled laborers.

S. D. Mullikin, experienced instructor at the Henry

Ford Trade and Apprentice Schools was selected to head up the training schools at Willow Run. In 1941, he studied Consolidated's methods and procedures in San Diego before selecting a faculty for Willow Run's educational program. Mullikin also organized the Air Base Training program that was carried out in conjunction with Willow Run, and under his leadership the Willow Run Schools trained over 50,000 civilian workers and 20,000 enlisted men in less than three-and-a-half years.

The need was urgent for employee training not only to overcome the lack of aircraft experience, but the total lack of industrial experience in the employees entering the work force for the first time, mainly the women replacing the men inducted into the armed forces. Some months hundreds of men left for the military. In January 1943 alone 888 employees left the production lines for the military. In 1943, 15.2% of the total quits were employees entering the military, and Edsel Ford made an unsuccessful personal plea to Washington for deferments.

Willow Run's desperate need for employees experienced in trades of the aircraft industry is nowhere better described than in the *Wartime Journals of Charles A. Lindbergh.* In his journal entries from May through October 1942, Lindbergh, employed at Willow Run as Ford's Engineering Consultant from March 1942 to March 1944, describes Willow Run's bleakest days, days when production quality was its worst, and self-esteem and morale at their very lowest.

On May 15, 1942, Lindbergh arrived at the Douglas B-24 assembly factory in Tulsa to check on a fuselage section passed by Ford and Army inspection at Willow Run, but which both the Air Force inspector and Douglas refused to accept. "I found the workmanship to be fully as bad as reported,"[9] Lindbergh said.

Willow Run, now in the spotlight, had made their first delivery of assemblies in worse condition than even the aircraft industry had predicted. When Lindbergh inspected the shipment at Douglas he found more than just a few problems:

> ... rivets missing, rivets badly put in, rivet holes started and forgotten, whole lines of rivets left entirely out, wrong sized rivets, lopsided rivets, badly formed skin, corner cuts improperly made, cracks already started, soft metal used where hard metal is essential, control holes left out, pilot's escape hatch incredibly badly constructed, rubber de-icers installed on an angle and with an inch-high wrinkle where they should be smooth, frame tab to stringer flanges broken off and not replaced, grommets left out of flippers and inspection holes forgotten, wrong name plates on oil tanks and other parts, metal edges bitten rather than cut out, round-head rivets in bomb-door tracks where flush rivets must be used, sharp and protruding corners on skin plates, etc., etc., etc....
>
> It was the worst piece of metal aircraft construction I have ever seen; yet it was passed by both the Ford Company and the Army inspectors at Willow Run.
>
> After supper I called a conference between Henning, Mr (Logan) Miller, Ford Company inspector at Willow Run, Captain Rooney, Army inspector at Wil-

low Run [all of these men had traveled to Tulsa with Lindbergh] and myself.... What has happened is clear enough: under the pressure, and encouraged by the desire to get production under way at Willow Run, and more than a little due to lack of experience, both the Army and Ford inspection passed material that should have been rejected (and which was rejected by the more experienced and impartial inspectors at Tulsa).[10]

On July 8, Lindbergh reported telling Mead Bricker, (who replaced Roscoe Smith as director of Willow Run in May 1942), "I doubted we would get No. 1 bomber out of the factory before August, and possibly not before September! (It was originally scheduled to be out in May.) ...On June 19, Ford's chief test pilot, Henning, flew the educational training ship 'O-1' for the first time. It was scheduled for completion by May 1, but had been rushed out of the factory, far from complete, on May 15.... the test flight shows much is still to be done."[11]

On August 31, 1942 Lindbergh wrote:

Arrived at Willow Run at 8:45. Morning on routine. Lunch at flight department with Stanley Gerding, flight superintendent at Willow Run.... Then through the factory with Gardner. The workmanship is still poor, inexperience shows everywhere. But there is a gradual improvement, and bombers are beginning to flow up the final assembly line.

On September 4 Lindbergh described a day with Henry Ford, Bennett and Sorensen:

OVERCOMING PRODUCTION INERTIA

Mr. Ford opened the door to my office and walked in about 9:30---no advance notice, as usual. Harry Bennett arrived about ten minutes later. Half hour with them discussing the war, labor problems, etc. Then all to the airport, Bennett driving. Looked over turntable [the Compass Rose] for swinging B-24 compasses. Then picked up Sorensen and the four of us drove around the area east of Willow Run airport to select a location for a permanent Army base [eventually located on Beck Road] and considered the possibility of lengthening the runways. Then, Bennett still driving, we went on to the engineering laboratory at Dearborn.

Sorensen brought up the question of our production schedule and the quality of workmanship at Willow Run - said we were ahead of schedule and that our workmanship was just as good as that of other companies. He tried to get me to agree with him and put me in a corner where I had to say bluntly that we were not making schedule and that the workmanship on the first bombers that went through Willow Run was the worst I had ever seen. Sorensen is not used to having anyone oppose him, and I have seen him bluff his way through difficult situations time and time again. He tries to get a man to agree with him either out of fear or courtesy, and then constantly reminds him of the fact that he once agreed. The only way to handle Sorensen is to say exactly what you believe when he asks a question, and I did. Henry Ford listened quietly and apparently enjoyed the situation very much. We went into the electrical department to see the reversible spark ignition developed by Emily

WILLOW RUN

Zoerlin [Ford electrical engineer].

Monday, October 12, 1942:

Walked through the plant with Henry Ford and
Harry Bennett. The final assembly line is beginning
to fill up, and the plant is now really on production
not large production yet, but it will increase rapidly
from now on, and workmanship is improving constantly.[12]

A conference held in Mead Bricker's office at Willow
Run on the morning of October 26, 1942, could well have
been the most powerful meeting ever held on Willow Run
and included many of Ford's board of directors. In attendance were Henry Ford, Edsel Ford, Harry Bennett, C. E.
Sorensen, Mead Bricker, Roscoe Smith, Arnold Miller
(Ford's personnel director), Logan Miller, C. A. Lindbergh
and several other Ford officers. They were gathered to discuss the main concerns and problems surrounding Willow
Run: the employment of more men, the housing problem,
the lagging schedule, and the quality of workmanship on
the B-24. They were well aware of the problems at Willow
Run.

But as Sorensen had once told Meigs, there was only
one thing that Willow Run needed that Meigs in Washington, D.C., could not give them. When Meigs asked him
what that was, Sorensen replied,"Time."[13]

Lindbergh's October 26, 1942 journal entry describes
this conference, and shows the concern and recognition of
Willow Run's internal problems by all the Ford officials:

134

OVERCOMING PRODUCTION INERTIA

Edsel Ford took the stand we should employ more men at once. Bricker felt we would progress faster if we refrained from employing more until our present personnel is better trained. (We have more than 30,000 employees at Willow Run now, and less than 400 of them had experience in aircraft manufacture before they came here.) I sided mostly with Bricker and told Edsel Ford that the quality of the planes now being put out is poor, and that Ford is getting a reputation in the industry for turning out poor quality of workmanship. I mentioned the B-24 that Skocdopole [Ford's test pilot] refused to fly until the fuselage tail section had been strengthened, and other instances. I said that if we took on too many additional untrained men now, the poor quality of workmanship would continue.

I told Mr. Ford (Edsel) that on the other hand our quality would improve rapidly if we gave our men a chance to learn their jobs thoroughly, and that after our present personnel had gained experience it would then be possible to expand quickly. I outlined to him the difficulty of producing so complicated a plane as the B-24 without a highly trained nucleus to build around and the handicap we started with in comparison to the aviation companies, who had such a nucleus at the time their wartime expansion began. I said I felt the government made a great mistake originally in not dividing the experienced aviation workers up among the various concerns who were given war contracts for aviation products. Edsel Ford countered with the statement that nevertheless we were just up against it and would fall still farther behind on our schedule unless we took on many thousand more workers. I replied that it was a question of balance between production and quality, both now and in the future.

Bricker brought out the fact that some of the assemblies we recently sent to the Consolidated plant at Fort Worth have been turned down and sent back because of unsatisfactory quality. (He also) reported that Consolidated Aircraft Corporation in San Diego is now turning out B-24's in less than 30,000 man-hours per ship. We have over 30,000 workmen here at Willow Run, and, as yet, our production is no where near a ship per day.[14]

The next day, October 27, 1942, after discussing various defects found by inspection in planes turned over to the Flight Department by the factory, Lindbergh made the following entry in his journal:

We are faced with inexperience, indifference, and resentment at interference on the part of the workmen. However, there is encouragement to be found in the fact that morale is better than it was a few weeks ago, and that bombers now on the final assembly line are much superior to those which have been delivered to Flight.[15]

In March of 1944, before leaving Willow Run for the South Pacific where, as a civilian, he flew more than 50 combat missions with our pilots, showing them how to increase their combat range by using proper engine settings, and where as a civilian, he is also credited with shooting down at least one Japanese Zero, Lindbergh noted,

Took a bomber up for initial shakedown flight late in the afternoon. Plane in excellent condition so ran Army acceptance flight also. Gave my Co-pilot two landings and take-offs while we were passing time. (A bomber must have at least two and a half hours in the air before the Army will accept it.)

On March 27, 1944, just two days before leaving Willow Run, Lindbergh said,

We have been ahead of schedule for several months now, and produced over 400 B-24s in February (including the knock-downs shipped to Douglas, Consolidated, and North American).[16]

The task of setting up production at Willow Run was like the factory itself - the largest in the world.

First came the huge drainage system for the airport; then building the factory with its mile-long assembly line to house the creative tooling and fixtures; then the enormous task of developing engineering information not available from the aircraft's designer; and then the training of 50,000 employees without any aircraft experience.

On December 24, 1941, setup of the first 30-ton center wing assembly fixture started in the still unfinished factory. On January 15, 1942, the fixture was ready for production, and the first of 6,439 parts, excluding 78,606 rivets and 1000 bolts, were placed in the fixture. On April 15, three days short of a year from ground breaking for the factory, the first Center Wing was completed and taken out of the fixture.

The enormous accomplishment of the men and women

from Willow Run and of Ford's methods of mass production can only be appreciated when one fully realizes that in 1941, before Ford entered the aircraft industry, it required *201,826 man-hours* to manufacture a single B-24 bomber. In March 1944, Ford's hard-tooling and procedures of mass production had reduced those man-hours to *only 17,357.*[17]

During the month of March 1944, there was a record 462 B-24 bombers manufactured.[18] That was 62 more than Sorensen's original goal.

The average rate of production during that month of March was a bomber every 63 minutes.

Later, even that record would be broken.

END NOTES

1. *Willow Run Reference Book.* Appendix B: Hospital.
2. Research Center of Henry Ford Museum and Greenfield Village, Accessions 435, Box 15, Vol I: 53.
3. *Willow Run Reference Book.* Appendix A: March 24, 1941.
4. Research Center. Acc. 435 Box, 15, Vol I: 50.
5. Research Center. W. F. Pioch, *Reminiscences*: 64.
6. Charles Sorensen. *My Forty Years With Ford.* New York: W. W. Norton and Company, 1956: 289.
7. "Will It Run?" *Flying Magazine,* May 1943.
8. Charles A. Lindbergh. *The Wartime Journals of Charles A. Lindbergh.* New York: Harcourt Brace Jovanovich, 1970: 697.
9. Lindbergh, 642.

10. Lindbergh, 642.
11. Lindbergh, 642.
12. Lindbergh, 732.
13. Sorensen, 290.
14. Lindbergh, 737.
15. Lindbergh, 738.
16. Lindbergh, 772.
17. Lowell Carr and James Stermer. *Willow Run: A Study of Industrialization and Cultural Inadequacy.* New York: Harper and Brothers, 1952: 173.
18. *Willow Run Reference Book.* Appendix A

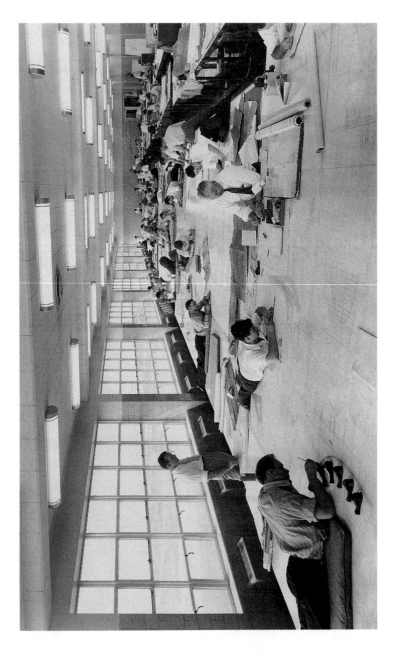

Master Loft Where Engineering Changes Were Made
And Tens Of Thousands of Design Errors Were Discovered.

Chapter VI

ENGINEERING CHANGES

In addition to an untrained work force, large numbers of engineering changes created a massive production problem in the new plant at Willow Run. Engineering changes, required because of erroneous or outdated engineering information supplied by Consolidated and change orders from the Air Force, obsoleted over fifty percent of the project tooling, doubled its cost, and significantly delayed Willow Run's bomber production. The magnitude of the engineering changes placed in jeopardy the entire Willow Run program and required special attention from the highest levels of Willow Run and U.S. Army Air Force management.

The problem created can be seen readily in the 80,000 templates that had to be scrapped because of omissions on Consolidated's original Master Templates.

An old engineering procedure, going back to the early days of shipbuilding, is to make a complete and accurate set of templates. With the advent of the automobile and mass production, the use of templates became extensive, highly developed, and exact; in the aircraft industry it became a tool for production and a means of preserving the original development information. At Willow Run, where automobile and aircraft techniques were combined on an unprecedented scale, template making was given primary consideration.

Among the engineers and craftsmen sent to San Diego in March 1941 were twelve of Ford's most experienced template makers. They reproduced more than 7000 Master Templates for what was then an airplane well into production. Steel copies were made of all of Consolidated's templates for the major parts of the B-24; these became the Master Templates for Willow Run and were preserved for reference. In July, the group returned to the Ford Airframe Building in Dearborn, Michigan, where they made duplicates of the templates, and sent them out to the tool and die shops to have tools built.

However, it was later discovered by the Willow Run Loft Engineering Department that many changes in Consolidated's original design had not been recorded on their templates. This required not only remaking the entire set of Willow Run Master Templates, but a major reworking of all tooling that had been built from them. According to their records, "This drastic move was necessary because 90 percent of the copies made at San Diego were useless."[1]

To get some idea of the amount of rework involved, the Willow Run Tool Shop had originally processed more than 29,000 work orders for templates. Each order required an average of three templates. Later, several thousand more Re-work Orders were processed to keep these tools up-to-date with additional changes.[2]

On July 18, 1942, Lindbergh recorded in *The War Time Journals of Charles A. Lindbergh* that Consolidated had not supplied Willow Run with accurate, up-to-date engineering information. In his Journal entry of that date Lindbergh noted,

> Spent part of the morning in conference with Raymond Boyer, a general foreman with Ford, in regard to the delay in production being caused by improper die design and the necessity of changing a large percent of the 11,000-odd dies which are required to build the B-24 on Ford methods. One difficulty, and one of the major causes of delay, lies in the fact the Consolidated Company was unable to furnish a complete set of up-to-date blueprints for the B-24.[3]

On July 23, 1942, Lindbergh addressed the issue again:

> Lunch with Boyer. Afterward we drove to the Rouge where he showed me the method of constructing and repairing hard dies. Most of the dies for the B-24 were improperly designed and have had to be changed.[4]

After the employees had been trained, the most difficult problem encountered at Willow Run was engineering changes. These changes that could affect the lives of the fighting men at the front would also reduce or stop production of the airplanes critically needed by them as well. A decision would be made to freeze a design so that desperately needed airplanes could be manufactured, but then a designer would put through an engineering change order calling for immediate incorporation, with little or no consideration for production of the aircraft.

Even after Sorensen had established new procedures for handling engineering changes with the Air Force Subcommittee on Engineering, he received a change order from some Wright Field officer advising him that "delivery of ships from Willow Run would not be accepted until certain changes were made."[5]

"I never had much trouble putting changes into effect after they had been finally decided upon and passed," Sorensen said, "but what discouraged our organization was the need to halt or slow down production while waiting for Air Force decisions regarding proposed changes."[6] Merrill Meigs, who succeeded Dr. Mead as chief of the Aviation section of the War Production Board, and William Knudsen, the Board's Director, "were howling for airplanes, yet tolerated changes that held back Willow Run production."[7]

Eventually, Sorensen was able to get the U.S. Air Force committee on bomber design to come to Willow Run to develop a faster procedure for implementing engineering changes. William Pioch developed a system for handling the large numbers of changes ordered by Wright Field, and General Arnold, head of the U.S. Army Air Force, "built fires under officers charged with design changes and got quick action."[8]

The plan basically allowed for changes to be incorporated only at certain intervals, and it was agreed that planes without those changes would be accepted by the Air Force until those time periods came due. The first ship in each new design group was designated the Master Change Ship and the groups varied in size from 200 to 400 airplanes.

ENGINEERING CHANGES

Willow Run records show that on November 16, 1942, there was a meeting of the B-24 Engineering Sub-committee at Willow Run, but it was not until nearly a year later, on October 20, 1943, that "engineering changes in B-24 [were] halted except those authorized by prior approval of Chief Material Command, Wright Field."[9] (See Appendix A.)

Willow Run's material conservation program, started by Pioch on June 28, 1943, to reclaim material obsoleted by engineering changes, provides information about the number of changes going into the B-24. (See Appendix A.)

Month	Engineering Changes	Reclaimed	Total	Men
July	63,894	13,450	77,344	35
Aug.	107,545	4,048	111,593	42
Sept.	114,588	7,882	12 2,470	45
Oct.	58,306	24,539	82,845	48
Nov.	78,360	8,726	87,086	49
Dec.	145,253	14,510	159,763	53

Efforts To Improve Armor Plating

One particular engineering problem of considerable consequence which Ford and Willow Run were helpless to do anything about is noted in Lindbergh's *Journal.* It describes his efforts to enlist the services of Wright Field in the development of armor plating for the B-24.

On August 11, 1942, General Arnold discussed with Lindbergh the Air Force's concern over armor plating on the

145

B-24. Lindbergh's *Journal* of that date records that he

> spent twenty minutes with General Arnold discussing
> Ford production... defects of the B-24, lack of arma-
> ment, etc. Arnold says the combat squadrons greatly
> prefer the B-17 (Boeing four-engine bomber), be-
> cause "when we send the 17's out on a mission, most
> of them return. But when we send the 24's out, a good
> many of them don't." Arnold says the B-17's "can
> take terrific punishment" and often land "full of bullet
> holes"--members of the crew dead and wounded, but
> still they get back.[10]

After his discussion with General Arnold, Lindbergh
went into action. He arranged a conference with Henry
Ford, Sorensen, Bennett, and Ford's test pilot, Henning,
with regards to armor plating for the B-24; he examined the
installation of armor plating on a B-17 newly arrived at
Wayne County Airport from Seattle; and he flew to Wright
Field in one of the B-24's to discuss with their chief armament officer the problem of armor plating. Lindbergh's
impressions of Wright Field are expressed in his journal
entry of September 15, 1942:

> The chief armament officer is Frank Wolfe, who
> was a classmate of mine at Brooks and Kelly--now a
> full Colonel. Spent half an hour with Wolfe; then
> went over to the new armament laboratory for a con-
> ference with Captain Robert G. Evans and Thayer E.
> Bartlett and a number of other armament officers.
> Wright Field is in a chaotic state. One gains the
> impression of immaturity, sloppiness, and indiffer-

ence, with here and there an efficient officer or department as sort of an island with waves of disorganization lapping around at the shores. There are rooms full of commissioned officers in uniform slouching about in shirt sleeves on desks and chairs, hands full of papers from the piles of papers overflowing the file boxes in front of them. Smoke from cigarettes, cigars, and pipes is everywhere. Young stenographers in bright and varicolored dresses move tiredly about in the narrow spaces between desks and chairs.... The corridors are full of people moving back and forth, from generals to messenger girls.

I spent an hour in conference with the armament officers. Told them, to start with, that Mr. Ford wanted to improve the armor plate on the B-24 and that the facilities of the Rouge plant and the Ford engineering organization would be available for this purpose. The officers seemed uninterested. They were, of course, courteous, but kept emphasizing their feelings that it would be inadvisable for the Ford Company to do anything about armor plating the B-24 except in the closest co-operation with the Wright Field armament division. I told them that I had come to Wright Field because we desired just the type of co-operation they suggested.

I then asked what they thought we should start on. They had no suggestion to offer except to say again that whatever we did should be "in close co-operation" with the armament division. I asked if they could furnish us any data in regard to the penetrating power of enemy bullets or the direction from which most hits came. They said the data they had was not in a form that would be of value to us. One of the officers said that there were too many ideas about armor plate anyway. I could see what I have seen so often before at Wright Field and at Army stations - that their primary desire was to be left alone to carry on their own experiments and work out their own solutions, and that outside assistance was really unwanted. I thanked them all, told them to let us know if we could be of any help in the future, and left. [11]

Efforts To Improve Nose Armament

Another major engineering problem involved the nose armament of the B-24. From the very onset of the Liberator, it was known that the front end of the bomber was vulnerable to enemy frontal attacks, and the Japanese kamikaze pilots put it to good use.

The long range of the B-24 made it difficult for our smaller fighter planes to provide them with adequate protection on long missions, and many of the planes were being shot down. The need to improve the defensive fire power in the nose of the B-24, where initially there had been none, was urgent.

Lindbergh's inspection report of May 4, 1942 revealed that the small angle of movement in Consolidated's new .50 caliber machine-gun installation for the B-24C rendered the gun virtually useless. That afternoon, in a meeting with Sorensen, an engineering department was established to re-design the B-24 nose to permit an adequate machine-gun installation.[12]

In the first hundred bombers manufactured at Willow Run a single swivel gun was mounted in the center of its plexiglas nose. In bombers 101-400 a second gun was added, and in bombers 401 to 800 still a third gun was added. The long breeches of these individually operated guns, located in the bombardier's compartment, were too cumbersome to maneuver against speedy enemy fighter planes, and interfered with the duties of the bombardier.

The Army Air Corps, from General Arnold down through the field commanders, was well aware of the problem. Brigadier General E. L. Eubank was working on a new and improved turret for the B-24 in 1942. Major General Willis H. Hale, Commander of the Seventh Air Force stationed in Honolulu, wrote in October 1942, "Certain features of this airplane were comparatively unsatisfactory... the forward gun installation and congestion in the nose.... A nose turret similar to the tail turret would be the best solution."[13]

Colonel Mussett, Commanding Officer of the 90th Bombardment Group H, which was billeted at Willow Run in 1942 said, "The B-24 without a nose turret was extremely vulnerable to head on attacks."[14]

The War Time Journals of Charles A. Lindbergh offers a personal insight into two of Mussett's officers, Colonels Arthur Rogers and Marion Unruh who developed their own field versions of a nose turret before production units became available.

Starting August 6, 1942, Lindbergh wrote,

WILLOW RUN

Went with Colonel McDuffee to see Major Rogers and officers of the B-24 squadron [90th Bomb Group], which is to train on the airport here for the next three weeks.... Major Rogers is a young man in his early thirties--alert, able, active.... He has had a great difficulty in training his squadron, has much still to do, and is scheduled to be sent overseas in the next few weeks. Many of his pilots have been out of school for less than six months. The last field where he was sent for training had uncompleted runways - cement still being poured. And his gunners have been given no machine-gun ammunition with which to train. (I learned from one of the other officiers that the last [B-24] bomber squadron to be sent overseas had been given only twenty-five rounds per gunner for training before they left.) In order to train his gunners Major Rogers had removed a top Martin turret from one of his bombers, removed the .50-cal. machine guns, and installed a twelve-gauge shotgun in place of the right-hand machine gun. With this arrangement his gunners shoot clay pigeons for practice and they break twenty out of twenty-five birds when experienced! Rogers said he ran into great opposition from his higher officers when he applied for permission to mount a shotgun in a turret and finally had to go ahead on his own authority at risk of being court-martialed. He is now trying to put a tail turret in the nose of the B-24 and again being discouraged and told it is no use.

The officers of this squadron are not B-24 enthusiasts. They say the Bendix bottom turret is no good, the nose gun no good, the armor plate inadequate, the take off run too long, and that it is impossible to fly a close formation at altitude. Morale is extremely low, and both officers and men tired.... I told Major Rogers I would try to get some help for him on the turret. He has been revising a tail turret from one of his planes; but has had to do the work somewhere it would not be noticed by his higher-ranking officers, who say that such things should be done at experimental stations. (They should, but they aren't--at least in time.)

Friday, August 7:

Conference with DeGroat [supervisor of Ford Developmental Engineering] in regards to helping Major Rogers and (Marion D.) Unruh with their nose turret project. Took DeGroat over to see them and their mock-up and to discuss the tail failure on one of their B-24's, which occurred shortly before they came to Willow Run. We all went to see the clay-pigeon shooting with the Martin turret: amazing accuracy.

Monday, August 10:

Phoned Sorensen to get his O.K. on assigning man to help Major Rogers with his B-24 nose-turret mock-up. It is exactly the type of thing that Sorensen likes - the short-circuiting of red tape, engineering and sequence of authority. "Give 'em all the help they want," he said. "Those boys know how to get things done." (And in this instance I think he is right.) I told Sorensen I had already cleared the project unofficially with Colonel McDuffee and Major Saunders. Sorensen said, "To hell with Army authorization! Go ahead anyway."

WILLOW RUN

Lunch with Colonel Acheson, Lieutenant Colonel Mussett, Major Rogers, and Major Unruh. Completed preliminary details in regard to turret mock-up .... We arranged for the mock-up to be removed from the squadron's quarters in the flight department and set up in the Development Engineering Department in the factory building.

Thursday, August 13:

[Went] to development engineering department to see what progress had been made on the B-24 nose-turret mock-up. When I arrived, I found one of the engineers in the nose-gun mock-up, puttering around in an attempt to find some way of following out the last order that has come through, demanding the installation of three .50- cal. pivot guns in the nose. (A "four star general" is reported to have given the order, so--good or bad--it must be carried out.) He was terribly discouraged when I talked to him; said the two side guns would spoil the effectiveness of the nose-gun we have about completed [this was the single gun unit that went into the first 100 bombers made at Willow Run] and so crowd the bomber's compartment that it would interfere with bombing while the guns themselves would get so much in each others way they would be practically useless. Just one more impractical and little-thought-about idea, he felt, and more valuable time lost.

Monday, August 17:

Conference with Major Unruh in regards to the nose turret and about the B-24 which crashed Friday

near Battle Creek with the loss of the entire crew of
nine. I found the pilot had been out of flying school
for only a few months and had less than 500 hours
total flying time; yet he was captain of a four engine
bomber and sent out through a stormy night to carry
on a practice mission! What possible good can come
from pushing men so fast?

First, this B-24 squadron is organized of young
and inexperienced officers; then it is sent for training
to a field with the concrete runways uncompleted;
then it is ordered to be ready for the combat zone "in
one month," unequipped, and without having had a
single round of .50-cal. ammunition with which to
train its gunners.[15]

After Lieutenant Colonel Rogers and Major Unruh left
Willow Run they continued to personally modify the B-24
nose turret. Lieutenant Colonel Rogers continued on with
the 90th Bomb Group, and arranged modification of his
airplane at the Air Service Command in Brisbane, Australia
where the repair and maintenance group was under Brigadier General Carl Connell, one of his prior commanders.

General Kenney, whom General Hap Arnold placed in
charge of the South Pacific Air Command under General
MacArthur, sheds some light on the early fire power in the
nose of the B-24. In January - February, 1943, he reported:

The forward gun protection in the B-24 turned
out to be quite unsatisfactory. The Jap fighters found
out about it and we were getting the airplanes shot up
badly every time we got intercepted. There were four
fifty-caliber guns in the nose of the B-24, but, as they

shot through individual "Eyeball" sockets, only one could be fired at a time. It was a clumsy arrangement and didn't give the protection we needed, so I started Lieutenant Colonel Art Rogers of the 90th Bombardment Group installing a turret, which we took off the tail of a wrecked B-24, in the nose. This would give us a pair of power-operated fifty-calibers and should surprise the Nip the next time he tried a head-on attack against a B-24 so equipped. Rogers said the Air Depot in Hawaii had been working out something along this line when he left here a month previously and he knew how to do it.... I gave him a go-ahead and told Connell to give him all the help he needed to expedite the job.[16]

The ship was christened the "Connell's Special" and after a series of flying and firing tests Rogers returned to his command post at Moresby. On April 10, 1943 he arranged for the ships first combat duty, a solo mission to Wewak, but encountered no Japanese fighter planes on which to try out his new turret. On returning, the nose wheel of his plane collapsed due to a burst of flak which had damaged a hydraulic line, and the "Connell's Special" came sliding home, tearing out the under side of its nose. It was repaired and flight tested again on May 3, 1943.

After Willow Run, Unruh was reassigned from the 90th bomb group to the 7th Air Force in Hawaii where he became the first person to install a nose turret in the B-24. The plane was lost on its initial flight while on a search mission before it could prove its combat readiness, and Major Unruh, promoted to Lieutenant Colonel, went on to

ENGINEERING CHANGES

Harry Clay

The "Connell's Special" Before Its Maiden Mission on April 10, 1943

F Woodling

After Its Landing Gear Collasped
A Very Disheartened Colonel Rogers - Second From The Left

develop and install an improved version of the nose turret. According to records in the Ford Research Center,

> Colonel Unruh and his bombardier group had modified their B-24's by moving the tail turret to the front and setting some individual guns on a make-shift, wooden platform in the tail. He brought one of these modified ships back from Guadalcanal for observation by army authorities. It was a strange looking Liberator indeed! Instead of the usual round, plexiglas nose, there was a blunt plexiglas domed turret jutting out in front. After experimentation, Air Force Officials decided that the tail turret should be retained, and a fourth turret added in the nose of the plane.[17]

In February 1943, the U.S. Army Air Force asked for official changes. They wanted fifty nose turret models for a special mission over Berlin in July, and sent a telegram to Consolidated Aircraft, ordering them to make the changes. The telegram to Consolidated began:

> It is a requirement that B-24 airplanes incorporating the following described armament installation be delivered to the Army Air Force starting June 1, 1943.
> Contractor required to accomplish installation complete in not less than 50 B-24-E airplanes to be delivered not later than June 20, 1943.[18]

The armament included a Martin top gun turret, an Emerson tail turret, a Van Orman type belly turret, a Bendix chin turret* and the standard waist guns.

ENGINEERING CHANGES

Consolidated was directed by Wright Field to give the job top priority and to furnish 100 percent of the engineering information for making the change to Ford at Willow Run, "not later than February 28, 1943." Consolidated's reply to the Army Air Force expressed belief that a change of this magnitude could not be produced in fifty airplanes before July or August. A copy of this telegram, received at Willow Run on February 11, was the first information of the change to arrive at Willow Run.

Telegrams were exchanged daily between Wright Field, San Diego, and Willow Run, but no engineering information from Consolidated was ever received at Willow Run.

On March 10, Wright Field called Ford to see if they could incorporate the changes requested of Consolidated. Originally, Ford had contracted to use their experience in mass production to manufacture the B-24, not to perform developmental engineering. Now the Air Force was asking Ford to provide their own engineering. Ford officials agreed to accept the responsibility, the largest engineering change to date, without receiving engineering from Consolidated.

From the very beginning, the aircraft industry repeat-

---

*The Bendix chin turret was later changed to the Emerson turret on recommendation of Brigadier General E. L. Eubank. In a March 4, 1943 communication to Matériel Command (5-B), he referred to a February 25 meeting where, "It was decided that a B-24 tail type turret would be more feasible in the nose of the B-24 than the Bendix chin turret" that he, himself, had proposed in his communication dated November 1, 1942.[19]

edly condemned Willow Run for using too much tooling. They challenged Ford's use of hard dies, claiming that they would impede making engineering changes quickly and efficiently. Now, after manufacturing eight hundred bombers, the Air Force ordered a major reconfiguration of the aircraft's nose assembly. The story of that change provides an insight into the ingenuity of the men from Willow Run, an insight into a different level of engineering talent more attuned to handling requirements of mass production.

But a month had gone by since Wright Field had first contacted Consolidated, and now for Ford to comply with their request was impossible. Ford advised Wright Field that it was doubtful if the 50 planes requested could be manufactured by the June 20 deadline, but that they would make every effort possible.

On March 13, Willow Run received a wire from Wright Field advising them that the Army modification center at Tucson, Arizona, was testing the Emerson turret and that 50 of the turrets would be available for their use in May. Any necessary engineering information could be obtained directly from Tucson.

Backed by years of experience in automobile model changes, Ford pulled together all of its resources to make the impossible a possibility. Customary channels were bypassed. Production and engineering worked together to design a completely new nose assembly, attachable directly to the front fuselage, using the same mounting hole as the current assembly. This eliminated structural modification to the fuselage and extensive reworking of dies and fixtures.

ENGINEERING CHANGES

Using a technique familiar to the automotive industry, but not used in the manufacture of airplanes, the engineers made a half-size clay model of the airplane's front end. From this they obtained the general lines of the new nose assembly and made perspective drawings from which full scale plans and a model of the assembly were laid out. To move quickly, a full-size wooden die was made from which the experimental assembly was produced. Parts were hammered out by hand over the wooden model, by-passing the need for detail prints.

Working the design out by using the clay and wooden models was an important step in reducing engineering time. By April 6, fifty percent of the engineering was complete, and the first blueprint was released to production April 10.

The Emerson turret was wider than the original nose, requiring a corresponding increase in the size of the front assembly, and the turret moved on a circular track supported on a bucket-like support. The bombardier's compartment, with bomb sight mountings and bomb release equipment, was moved to the underneath slope of the front fuselage, providing the bombardier more space and a better view of the target below.

Production men from Willow Run built the prototype assembly with hand-made parts developed from engineering briefs and pictorials; the engineers moved into the Airframe Building in Dearborn where the experimental ship was built; and Ford pilots flight tested the new plane for changes in flight characteristics and aerodynamics. Air Force tests were approved, and orders came to start production.

The great advantage of the Ford design was its inter-
changeability with all other nose configurations. By using
the same mounting holes any B-24 could be converted to
the new model H by removing the plexiglas nose, attaching
the new bucket and fairing assembly, and putting in the
turret. An interchange of turrets was completed on a plane
at Willow Run in just 138 man hours. This was an extremely valuable war-time feature considering the thousands of
B-24's with insufficient nose armament.

Production of the nose assembly by the Enclosures
Department, made the Manufacturing Department responsible for the entire assembly. Bolting it onto the front of the
fuselage was the only function required of Final Assembly.

The first Emerson nose cone assembly was completed
on June 1,1943. By June 30, 42 had been completed, and on
July 15 nearly 100 were ready. The first ship to receive the
Emerson turrets, "801," entered Station 1 of Final Assem-
bly on May 24, and was accepted by the army on June 30.
It flew away from Willow Run on July 12.

On June 30, there were 56 model B-24-H's in production. This included 44 ships in final assembly from station
1 through 28, six ships outside on the ramp, and six more
delivered to Flight.[20]

It was reported that 16 of the B-24-H models with the
new Emerson turret guns were delivered in time for the raid
over Berlin. Sufficient numbers of turrets were also available in time for conversion of the remaining ships at the
army modification centers. According to Wiley O. Woods,
historian of the 90th Bomb Group, many of the B-24's fly-

ing in the Pacific War Zone were field-modified with nose turrets.

Willow Run's engineering change short-cut by several months the changes made by the old-line aircraft companies with their relatively small amount of tooling, and disproved the adamant charges against Willow Run's tooling as being too inflexible to make major engineering changes. Consolidated's San Diego factory did not get into production of the new nose turret until the first of September, their Fort Worth factory a couple of weeks later.

On February 11, 1943, after evaluating Colonel Unruh's field modification, Wright Field sent their first telegram to Consolidated requesting official production modification of the nose cone. (While this was going on, the "Connell's Special" that Colonel Rogers test flew on March 3, 1943, was repaired from its April 10 crash landing, and ready to fly again on May 3, 1943.) Wright Field, unable to obtain their urgent delivery requirements from Consolidated, in turn called Willow Run on March 10 to see if they could incorporate the changes requested of Consolidated.

From the time Wright Field made the Emerson turret available for engineering study on March 13, it took the men and women from Willow Run, just 79 days to design, build and flight test the prototype, and to manufacture the first production unit on June 1, 1943.

It was considered that the amount of tooling required to make this change, with its 47 completed master changes, its 53,456 engineering hours, and its 208,271 tooling hours, was greater in proportion than that required to make the normal yearly model change in an automobile. Further, it was accomplished without closing down the production line as is customary in the automotive industry.[21]

When Wright Field released the order to Willow Run, the speed at which the Emerson nose turret was adapted to production helped make up for its overdue authorization.

The speed was phenomenal.

The B-24 Nose Turret Designed And Built By Willow Run.

From Wright Field's March 13 telephone order, to Willow Run's First Production Unit, June 1, Took Just 79 days.

END NOTES

1. Research Center of Henry Ford Museum and Greenfield Village, Accessions 435, Box 1, I: 68.
2. Research Center, Box 1, I: 68.
3. Charles A. Lindbergh. *The Wartime Journals of Charles A. Lindbergh.* New York: Harcourt Brace Jovanovich, Inc., 1970: 677.
4. Lindbergh, 680.
5. Charles E. Sorensen. *My Forty Years With Ford.* New York: W. W. Norton and Company, 1956: 299.
6. Sorensen, 299.
7. Sorensen, 299.
8. Sorensen, 299.
9. *Willow Run Reference Book*, Appendix B: 11/16/42-10/20/43.
10. Lindbergh, 694.
11. Lindbergh, 714.
12. Lindbergh, 634.
13. John S. Alcorn. *The Jolly Rogers.* Temple City, CA: Historical Aviation Album, 1981: 74.
14. Alcorn, 73.
15. Lindbergh, 690.
16. General George C. Kenney. *General Kenney Reports.* New York: Duell, Sloan and Pearce, 1949:181
17. Research Center, Box 15, III: 46.
18. Research Center, Box 15, III: 47.
19. Alcorn, 74.
20. Research Center, Box 15, III: 53.
21. Research Center, Box 15, III: 54.

SHANTY TOWN - WILLOW RUN - U.S.A.

Outside toilets contaminated their shallow water supply.
Fortunately, there was no outbreak of typhoid - Spring 1943

Tents saved bomber workers from living around open campfires.
A family of eight with six children lived the winter of 1941-42 in this
shelter. Other families too, survived the cold Michigan winter in tents.

Chapter VII

THE VILLAGE OF WILLOW RUN
Transportation and Housing At Willow Run

Sorensen's proposal in San Diego was to construct a two hundred million dollar factory and manufacture B-24 bombers at the unbelievable rate of one an hour. This the Ford Motor Company accomplished with a daily average of nearly 30,000 employees. Unfortunately, Ford did not contract to build the Willow Run housing project.

Failure of federal, state and local agencies, builders, and area real estate associations to coordinate a housing program with Sorensen's schedule for building World War II bombers created a housing crisis of untold magnitude. It is impossible to estimate the deprivation to employees or loss of war-time production, high turnover and low employee morale brought about by lack of housing at Willow Run. The squalid conditions in which a large number of Willow Run employees lived became a national concern, and transformed a source of wartime inspiration into a highly publicized national disgrace.

Production at Willow Run got off to a fast start. Inside the factory, engineers were creating the wizardry of mass production. But outside, the dereliction of social responsibility and red tape was creating a housing fiasco to challenge the imagination. On December 8, 1941, Sorensen started manufacturing parts in the still unfinished factory,

165

but the hiring of an estimated 50-100,000 production workers had already started.*

These tens of thousands of people needed a place to live, and those living close enough to the factory needed a way to get to and from work.

The Michigan State Highway Department recognized the urgency of what was happening and acted quickly before the narrow roads caused a traffic problem of massive proportion. Detroit was the major population center from which Willow Run could expect to draw employees, but the highway system, though serving the needs of the population up until that time, was inadequate for the large number of people who were about to flood the area. The only highway connecting Detroit to Willow Run was M-17, Ecorse Road, a narrow two-lane highway built in the 1920's when the interurban stopped running. Michigan Avenue, U.S. 112, went north of the factory site into the city of Ypsilanti.

To connect Detroit with the factory, a four-lane divided expressway under construction between Detroit and Chicago was routed to the Willow Run factory[1] and built by the Michigan Highway Department in a record time of just eleven months. Construction of the highway began in November of 1941, while the bulldozers and hot-steel rivetmen were still cutting across the open fields of the airport

---

* Approximately 115,000 men and women were employed throughout the life of the contract. The turnover rate during the main period of production averaged nearly 10 percent per month, reaching a high of a little over 17 percent. The yearly turnover rate was about 117 percent. The average daily work force was close to 29,500 employees, reaching a high of 42,331 in June 1943.

and building the factory. When completed, the expressway had three levels of grade separations, greatly increasing the flow of traffic in and out of the factory's more than 15,000 car parking area. The highway, later to become a portion of the Interstate Highway System, I-94, was dedicated by Under-Secretary of War Robert S. Patterson on September 12, 1942.

Constructing the expressway from Detroit to Willow Run: heavy bridge construction at Southfield and Van Born.

Triple Overpass Being Constructed At Factory Site.

WILLOW RUN

Photos Courtesy Linda Bosheff,
Michigan State Highway Department.

Workmen Building The Overpass

Completed And In Use

THE VILLAGE OF WILLOW RUN

Before And After Completion Of The Overpass

North Highway Entrance Curves Around Completed B-24's
(Note the length of the factory)

Entering Main Gate From The North Side

Highway Dedication - September 12, 1942 by Robert S. Patterson.

Unfortunately, from the time Washington gave Sorensen the go-ahead to build Willow Run until the new highway was dedicated, no new housing had been constructed. Thousands of people recruited by Ford's out-of-state program and those who could not drive one to three hours a day to and from work began arriving at Willow Run, but there was no place for them to live.

The factory began hiring production workers the first of December 1941, and on December 7th Japan bomber Pearl Harbor. Two months later, in February 1942, Japan captured our nation's source of crude rubber, and President Roosevelt came under heavy pressure to develop synthetic rubber.

Now the problem of housing and transportation became critical. Tires were irreplaceable. (Sorensen offered to retread employee's tires at the Ford River Rouge tire plant.) Gasoline was purchased only after standing in long lines to qualify for gas rationing stamps. Then the gas was used in an automobile that could not be replaced. The thought of tens of thousands of employees driving 275,000 miles a day on irreplaceable rubber was frightening.

But nothing happened. Not one single house was constructed.

Newcomers, attracted by Ford's recruitment program, high wages in war time jobs, and feelings of patriotism were the hardest hit. They lived in their cars, tents, trailers, converted chicken coops, or tarpaper shacks, at times with a friend who had preceded them. Once they were processed through personnel at the factory, they could look forward to their first pay day; an advance against their first pay was also available, if they requested it. That took some of the pressure off, and they could start looking for a place to live.

But there were no houses.

Feelings at the time were mixed. Critics were not in favor of a permanent Bomber City that could turn into a Bomber Ghost Town when the war was over, and materials vital to the war effort were scarce. But the need for housing was also urgent. The thousands of people required to build the bombers needed a place to live, and permanent housing would take too long.

The local residents were afraid temporary housing would turn into slums and lower their property values. They just didn't want outsiders in their community overcrowding their stores and schools, and housing for the workers became a political football.

The United Auto Workers union (UAW) went to Washington to propose a model city of permanent homes. The Federal Public Housing Administration in Detroit started making plans of their own. They sent government engineers into the field to survey land that belonged to the Ford Farms without Ford's knowledge, and Harry Bennett got tough with the "trespassers." They were evicted and he pulled 500-1000 survey stakes they had used to lay out Ford property. Bennett's move supported the small farmers and private land owners, who couldn't stop the government surveyors on their own, and they too started evicting the Federal Public Housing Administration from their land.

A general revolt against federal housing and the way it

was being handled began to take place. Organized real estate agencies in the area, as well as the Ypsilanti Chamber
of Commerce and the Washtenaw County Board of Supervisors, began to fight against federal housing. The politi-
cians of Washtenaw County, overwhelmingly Republican
since the days of the Civil War, were beginning to apply
their forces against government housing and the concentra-
tion of UAW workers, primarily Democrats, who would be
residing in their county. Ford too had an interest in maintaining stable Republican control in the county. His Starter
and Generator factory located in Ypsilanti employed nearly
a thousand workers.

The Federal Public Housing Authority and the Harry
Truman Senate Committee continued to battle with the
Ypsilanti Chamber of Commerce, the Washtenaw County
Board of Supervisors, the area real estate associations, the
UAW, the Office of Price administration, and the Ford
Motor Company.

In 1942 a statement was submitted to the Truman
Committee in Washington, D. C. by the Ann Arbor Real
Estate Board, Ypsilanti Real Estate Board, and the Ann
Arbor Builder's Association reflecting their position on the
erection of permanent housing at Cherry Hill near Willow
Run. The preamble read as follows:

> The combined membership of the Ann Arbor
> Real Estate Board, the Ann Arbor Builders Associa-
> tion, and the Ypsilanti Real Estate Board feel obli-
> gated to oppose the "permanent housing" policy now
> being projected for the Cherry Hill area of the Willow

173

Run Bomber Plant.... We believe that as Real Estate Brokers and Home Builders, we have an honest "selfish reason" to fight for the continuance of our business. We believe that it is the duty of the Government to allow any business to maintain itself unless that business clearly conflicts with the war effort. It is our contention that, we, as Builders and Brokers could be a definite help to the war housing movement under proper Government leadership.

We are firmly convinced that if the housing situation had been carefully thought out and properly managed by ONE Government Agency that this confusion and delay could have been avoided. We repeat, there has been too many agencies and too much bureaucratic red tape, which, combined with the political pressure of labor groups has led to the present confusion.[2]

The workers who had come to build airplanes for the war effort were caught in the middle of a political mess. They were left to find housing on their own. Stores for food, clothing and medical services were too far away for easy access. Husbands and wives were packed together with other men and women in cattle cars converted to buses and herded off to work, their homes torn by the tension.

Also lacking was an adequate school system for their children. In the beginning only the small Spencer school serviced the area. Ruth (Kidder) Clemens was one of the early teachers who taught there, and it wasn't until the summer of 1943 that three new schools were built, Foster, Ross and Simmonds.

According to Carr and Stermer, "The No.1 Gripe:[was] No Place To Stay!"[3] Several of the letters published in their book, *Willow Run: A Study of Industrialization and Cultural Inadequacy,* are transcribed here. The letters are presumed to be from Ford's followed-up on why many who came to work as a result of their recruitment program, did not stay.

> I could not get no place to stay when I sined up. here they said I would have a place Ready fore me to stay. When I got there was no place to go, so I had to come back when you have a place fore me I would be glad to come Back as I am not Working no place. - Rosa M., Morehead, Ky., Sept. 30, 1943.

> There wasn't anything that prevented Me from going to Work i Was Just a Stranger up there and didn't have any place to Stay at that time. - George H., Pikeville, Ky., Sept. 28, 1943.

> I am verry sorry I dident get to work in your plant. Because I belive I would have liked my work. But Sir I was up their alone and dident know no one. And dident have eny Place to stay. Even for one night I was up their, so I dident know what else to do. So I came back home. I am verry sorry I caused you all so much trouble. - Rose H., Owensboro, Ky., October, 1943.

> i will reply to your letter i resined yesterday i was very Well Pleased to here from you my failure was i couldent get no room i romed around until i give up i was afraid my money wood give out and

idident no what to do But come home i wood Beeglad
to Work if i could get a Bording Place if you can in
shure a room, i will Bee more than glad to come back
and Work Work is What i want Pleas let me no soun
and ill Bee there in a few days. - J.D.G., Phelps, Ky.,
October, 1943.[4]

Regardless, when the political conflicts were resolved,
it was Henry Ford who, in October 1942, sold a portion of
his Ford Farm land to the government for the Willow Run
housing project.

The first government housing to become available at
Willow Lodge, in February 1943, consisted of dormitories
to house single men and women. By the time the factory
reached peak employment of 42,331 employees, in June of
1943, all the government could provide was 15 dormitories
for 3,000 people. They consisted of very small bedrooms
without a toilet or a bath (see p. 179). That was two-and-a-
half years after the project was begun, and although the
airport was finished, the mile-long assembly line enclosed,
and the work force expanded to over 40,000 employees,
there still was no family housing.

It wasn't until six months later, after the work force had
already peaked and started downward, that "Willow Village" belatedly opened 2,500 temporary units of family
housing. That was down from the 6,000 permanent homes
originally proposed by the UAW for an area around the
village of Cherry Hills. Community stores and services for
the residents did not open for still another seven months, in
February 1944.

Five months after the opening of Willow Village, factory employment had decreased to the point where housing

176

was no longer needed.

During the original construction Albert Kahn had designed and built a commissary at Gate 10 of the factory. One of Ford's employees who operated the commissary was Marilyn Owens. She sold candy bars, cosmetics, and supplies to the workers as they entered and left the factory, and she provided a service and a convenience to employees that helped reduce Willow Run's high absentee rate. But when the Ypsilanti store keepers discovered what was going on at Gate 10, it is claimed they blocked the gate at the commissary. Another effort to reduce absenteeism and help improve employee relations and morale was lost.

Residents in the secure atmosphere of their established homes in Ypsilanti could not relate to the problems encountered by the newcomers in their community. They did not realize the horrors of the living conditions in the village just outside of their city limits. They could not feel the crisis, the urgent need for sanitary housing, for removing the outhouses polluting the shallow wells, and for the need to boil the drinking water to prevent typhoid germs from breaking into an epidemic.

They simply could not believe the rumors they were hearing. Except for the local residents displaced by rights of eminent domain and a disgruntled neighbor or two putting up with overcrowded stores, everything seemed pretty much in order. One of the comments frequently heard was that workers were making good money at the bomber plant, and if they didn't like the living conditions, they could go back to the mountains of Kentucky or Tennessee where they came from, and live with the rest of the "hillbillies."

The residents of Ypsilanti were not aware that the

177

Michigan Department of Health was investigating their own water supply. Built just two years earlier, in 1939, their water plant had been required to exceed its design capacity. In addition, due to the population increase, "the sewage flow [had also] increased to an amount in excess of the designed capacity of the plant"[5]

In 1940, the area around Willow Run had a population of 331 people living in 94 homes, and there was no community sewer or water. While the B-24 was being built some 10,000 people lived there.

A baby was born in this tar-paper shack during the spring of 1944. When Sister Margaret Fry visited this "home" a few days after birth of the baby, she found the infant wrapped in newspaper.

THE VILLAGE OF WILLOW RUN

WILLOW LODGE
ALL THE GOVERNMENT COULD PROVIDE

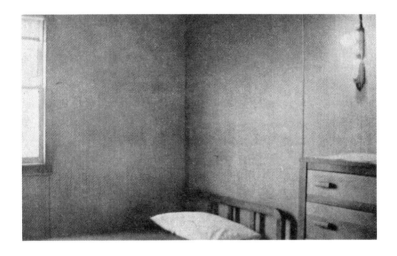

Typical Bedroom in Willow Lodge Dormitory.

Scant furnishings in a cubicle. Hot air duct for heating
is above the door, cold air return is the space under the door.

179

WILLOW LODGE

"A Day Late And A Dollar Short"

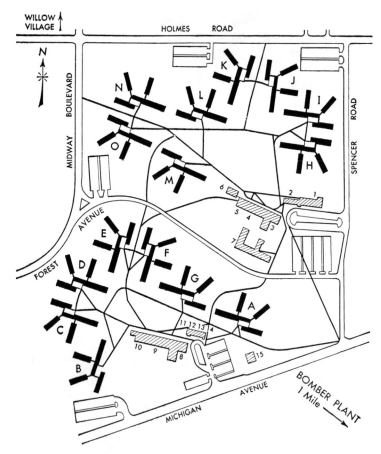

Dormitory buildings A-O as indicated.

1. Administration building—management, rental, accounting, housekeeping, maintenance.
2. Post office.
3. Cafeteria and bus stop.
4. Coffee shop and soda fountain.
5. Recreation rooms—North Community building.
6. Auditorium—gymnasium—Willow Run Theater.
7. Infirmary.
8. Recreation rooms—South Community building.
9. Canteen.
10. Library.
11. Cleaners.
12. Laundry.
13. Beauty shop.
14. Barber shop.
15. Sheriff's office, later moved to Village.

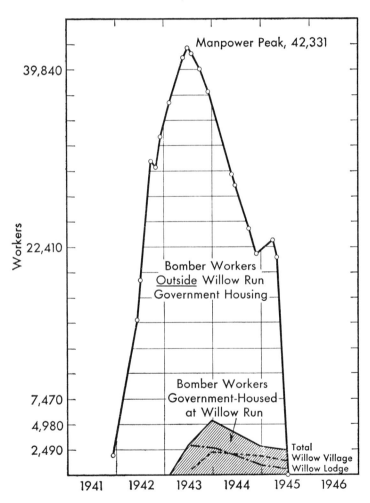

Bomber Plant Employment and Government Housing At
Willow Run, 1941 - 1945

WILLOW RUN

Month	Workers Employed			Government-Built Dwelling Units		Total Pop. Housed	Estimated Workers Housed	% of Total Workers
	On Construction of Plant	On Bombers[a]	Total	Willow Lodge (Individuals)	Willow Village (Families)			
Apr., 1941	111	None	111	0	0	0	0	0
Sept., 1941	3,362	None	3,362	0	0	0	0	0
Dec., 1941	4,554	2,052	6,606	0	0	0	0	0
June, 1942	3,140	19,295	22,435	0	0	0	0	0
Dec., 1942	550	33,589	34,139	0	0	0	0	0
Feb., 1943	460	36,673	37,133	275	0	275	275	0.7
June, 1943	175	42,331	42,506	3,014	0	3,014	3,014	7.0
Jul., 1943	453	41,795	42,248	3,014	321	4,389	3,463	8.2
Dec., 1943	652	36,833	37,485	2,700	1,728	9,799	5,119	13.4
June, 1944	0	28,411	28,411	1,381	1,571	8,029	3,580	12.6
Dec., 1944	0	23,000	23,000	699	1,420	6,518	2,687	11.6
Apr., 1945	0	20,200	20,200	639	1,497	6,718	2,735	13.5

[a] Estimated population dependent on 42,331 bomber workers at man-power peak in June, 1943, 84,662.
Total bomber population, therefore, 126,993.
Total bomber population housed by government at Willow Run in June, 1943 = 3,014, or 2.4 percent of estimated total bomber population.
At peak of government-housing occupancy, December, 1943, the 9,799 in government-housing projects at Willow Run constituted *less than 9.0 percent*
(8.8) of the estimated 110,499 bomber population at the time.

Employment and Government Housing At Willow Run
April 1941 - April 1945

THE VILLAGE OF WILLOW RUN

The sanctity of private property! Having purchased a small lot, for a few dollars, in a meadow off Holmes Road, the owner of this combination tent and trailer dwelling is shown discussing with coauthor Stermer [*Willow Run: A Study of Industrialization and Cultural Inadequacy*] (in hat and overcoat) the advantages of living beyond the control of the state law regulating trailer camps. On his "own property" in unzoned rural territory, he could thumb his nose at the trailer-camp law and the Washtenaw County Health Department. This private-property dodge was used by a score or more trailerites.... The effect on the quality of housing in the area is shown in this and in the other pictures. It was in this dwelling that the only serious crime committed in the Area occurred. A death over wine, a woman, and a card game in 1944.[6]

TRAILER LIVING

Trailers transformed living for many middle-class bomber workers. For Mr. and Mrs. Johnson who lived in St. Johns, Michigan, over a hundred miles away it changed it,

From This To This

Trailer shown in Bomber Plant Trailer Camp. Mrs. Johnson holds a sample of her rug-hooking.

A major problem of cramped trailer living was keeping clean. Unless the husband had built a vestibule - prohibited in government camps - muddy shoes and rubbers tracked good old Michigan mud into the living room after every rain - Spring, Summer, Fall, or Winter - It was always wash day for trailer wives and mothers.

WILLOW VILLAGE

Before it was finished employment had peaked and started down.
Not until four months after it was finished did it have a chain
grocery and drug store.

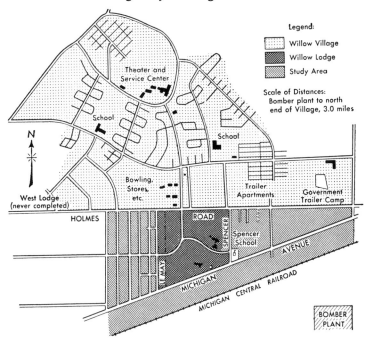

Sodas - Cigars - Candy

The Cunningham Chain Drugstore arrived seven months after peak
employment. Far right: Finally - A New School.

Typical streets In Willow Village *after improved* construction.

Greyhound "Cattle Car." The interurban trailer-bus used to transport workers to and from the factory at shift time,

THE VILLAGE OF WILLOW RUN

"What a flimsy flue did to a flimsy house"[7] Fire starting from a defective chimney burned out three families and jeopardized a fourth, December 17, 1943. Between 1943 and July 1947, seven persons died in fires like this.

END NOTES

1. Harold W. Sherman. Reminiscences. Librarian, Yankee Air Force Museum, Belleville, Michigan.
2. Lowell Juilliard Carr and James Edson Stermer. *Willow Run: A Study of Industrialization and Cultural Inadequacy.* New York: Harper and Brother, 1952: 391.
3 Carr and Stermer, 214.
4. Carr and Stermer, 214.
5. Michigan Department of Health. *Seventh Annual Report of the Commissioner of the Michigan Department of Health for Fiscal year ending June 30, 1942.* Lansing, Michigan.
6. Carr and Stermer, 75.
7. Carr and Stermer, 79.

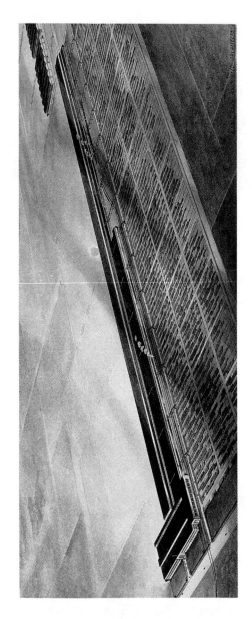

An Albert Kahn Original
"The Longest Room In The History Of Mankind."

(Sorensen's mile long factory)
Redesigned into an "L" to avoid building the factory across county lines.

Chapter VIII

BUILDING A BOMBER AN HOUR

When Sorensen conceived the idea of mass producing the B-24, he catapulted the men and women from the Ford Motor Company into the aircraft industry and told them, "Your schedule is to build a bomber an hour."

Their challenge was to build the airplane by using the reservoir of experience they had accumulated over the years in the automobile industry; their starting point was the concepts and ideas they could create in their own minds, because there was no other aircraft assembly line in the world they could use as a model; and their achievement during the month of April 1944, after overcoming all of the many obstacles, was to manufacture 455 airplanes in 450 hours. An airplane every 59.34 minutes.*

As the men from Willow Run began to suggest their ideas, they were looked upon as dreamers throughout the aircraft industry. When the word got around that Ford's goal was to produce a bomber an hour, companies building just a few large aircraft a month ridiculed their goal as preposterous. Others, cautiously respectful of Ford's mass production took a more watchful attitude.

---

*During the month of April 1944 Willow Run produced 455 airplanes in 25 working days using two nine-hour shifts.

WILLOW RUN

Albert Kahn had designed Willow Run to manufacture the B-24 in a straight, mile-long assembly operation, which allowed the fastest, most direct routing of all parts and sub-assemblies. He designed two 150-foot wide assembly bays with an overhead crane to assist in the movement of large and heavy parts. The two bays provided four assembly lines where the 55-foot center wing was mated with the fore and aft sections of the fuselage. These four lines are shown on the Factory Layout as stations 1 through 14 in Final Assembly Lines (947). To help smooth out production these stations were originally set up as "eight-hour stations," and controlled by the Final Assembly Office from the balcony. (See Appendix B, Movement Of Assembly Lines.)

Each of these two lines fed partially assembled ships into the center of the bay at station 15, and the remainder of the work stations, 15 through 28, became known as "four-hour-stations." The 150 foot bays then provided the space for attaching the outer wings, which made a total wing span of 110 feet. The ailerons and flaps were added, and engines and propellers installed; the ship was camouflaged, and fuel taken on board as it moved through the remaining stations of final assembly. Later, as efficiency increased the time for moving the eight hour stations was reduced to under four hours and the four hour stations became two.

In March 1941, the Ford engineers, working in San Diego, had divided the airplane into sections more accessible for mass production than those used by Consolidated. After determining the "cleavage lines," the next job was where, on each assembly, to install the numerous pieces of equipment. These included the wiring, hydraulic, fuel and oxygen lines, heating units, and all the other items to be installed.

From the standpoint of tooling, these divisions were more important than Ford's decision to use metal dies. They were essential in determining which work would be performed in the manufacturing departments, and which would be performed on the assembly line. They were also essential in determining the flow of material for the 465,472 parts that went into the airplane. After several attempts, 73 different sub-assemblies were approved, of which numbers 10, 24, 52, and 71 were eventually eliminated.

By using the item numbers and names of the parts listed on the Ford B-24-M Breakdown it is possible to follow the airplane as it moved its way through the factory. The parts installed at the different work stations are shown on the Factory Layout, numbered in the circles with arrows which point to the station where the parts were installed.

For example, the Emerson Turret described in Chapter VI is Item No. 61 on the parts list. The department supplying the part is "GFE" (Government Furnished Equipment). The Factory Layout shows it was installed at station 11 in Final Assembly. Another part of the Nose Turret Assembly was the Nose Enclosure. It is the first item on the parts list, Item 1A, and comes from Small Part Assemblies, Department 932F. It was installed at station 4. The Plexiglas Nose, that provided visibility for the bombardier on the underside of the new Emerson nose turret, is Item 1B. It was installed at station 16.

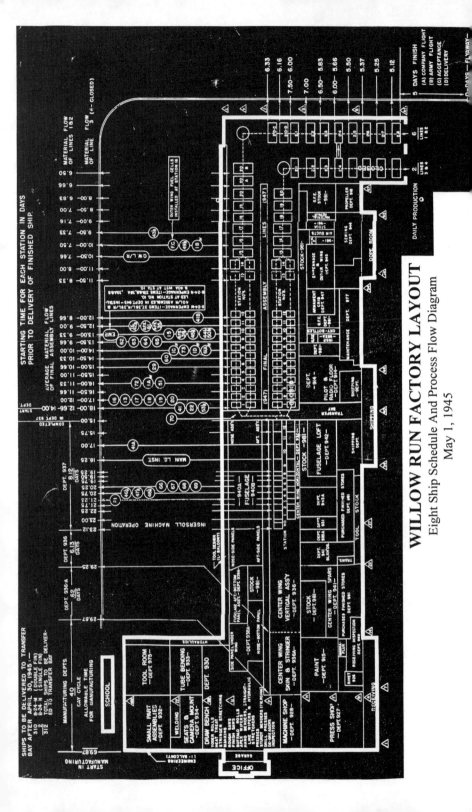

WILLOW RUN FACTORY LAYOUT

Eight Ship Schedule And Process Flow Diagram

May 1, 1945

FORD B-24-M BREAKDOWN

DEPT	ITEM	PART NUMBER	NAME

The marked difference between the Consolidated and Ford breakdown was in the fuselage. The Ford engineers divided the fuselage in to 33 different sections. The main sections, separated by the center wing, were the nose and tail fuselage, and to facilitate mass production, the fuselage was divided into panels which allowed greater access. Items one and four, the Nose Enclosure and the Pilot's Enclosure, were natural breakdowns of the nose fuselage. They were broken into twelve pieces (called the merry-go-round) that fitted around the pilot's floor. It included the two top decks, side panels and a bottom panel.

The long tail fuselage provided an easier subdivision. It was divided into four components, a tail cone, a bottom panel, and two side panels, which provided greater accessibility for more employees to work side by side, and for easier installation of electrical and hydraulic equipment.

The wing was divided into three main sections, the 55 foot center wing, which extended from one outboard motor to the other, and the two Outer Wing panels. The leading and trailing edges and the wing tips were assembled separately and attached later. Connecting the nose and tail fuselages across the wing were the canopy on top and the bomb bay side panels under the center wing.

MANUFACTURING AREA

The Factory Layout shows the manufacturing area on the west end of the factory close to the Center Wing Skin and Stringer, and Nose-Bottom Panel Departments, the first two assembly departments.

The large Press Shop, Department 927, manufactured 120,000 pieces every day on 345 presses. Fifty-six of the heavy presses ranged in capacity from 150 to 1000 ton. Thirteen were hydraulic, ranging in size from 100 to 1000 ton capacity, and required the use of 1500 gallons of oil as a hydraulic agent. The weight of the 1000 ton presses was 350 tons, 330 tons more than the weight of the bomber itself. There were 109 Ferracutes, Niagaras, and Cleveland punch presses which ranged from 30 to 750 ton capacity.

The Machine Shop, Department 928, occupied half an acre of floor space in the southwest corner of the factory and produced 25,000 pieces of 500 different parts every day. Combined with the lathes, milling machines, drill presses, and screw machines, there were a total of 220 different types of equipment in the machine shop. The first part manufactured at Willow Run was made on a horizontal milling machine in this department on December 8, 1941.

The Draw Bench, Department 930, where stringers for the wings were manufactured, employed 300 workers to maintain a work force for 250 jobs. They used 265 machines to manufacture 3700 different parts, 185,000 of which were produced daily. Later, 6228 of those parts went into every ship. They also rolled 260,000 feet of "Y"stock every day, and approximately 5,000,000 parts were formed, stretched, or pierced each month. A list of the equipment they used is itemized on the Factory Layout diagram.

Small Parts Assemblies, Department 932, where the Emerson nose turret was manufactured, along with other

Six-foot Radial Drill and Workman In Tool and Die Shop.

The men are drilling holes for punches in a large blanking and piercing die that will stamp out parts with hundreds of rivet holes at one time.

Willow Run machine shop manufacturing B-24 Bomber parts.

numerous small parts, occupied more than an acre of floor space in the northwest corner of the manufacturing area.

Equipment for the Tool Room, Department 975, which also occupied an acre of floor space, was set up in the northeast corner of the manufacturing area as soon as factory construction permitted - in January 1942. By summer, 350 tool and die makers had moved from Dearborn into Willow Run, and most of the 200 pieces of equipment ranging from the simplest of drill presses to a near-human engraving machine had been installed.

It is difficult to imagine the time and effort required to join together the fabricated parts of the B-24 bomber until one realizes that in 1944 the Willow Run Rivet Department, 926, manufactured nearly two billion rivets. To be exact 1,921,922,810 of them were made. Of all the parts that went into the airplane the rivet was, by far, the most numerous of all. There were 242,752 rivets required to build the major sections of the airplane: 78,606 were used in the center wing; 22,844 in the outer panel; 126,651 in the fuselage; and 14,651 in the tail assembly. The total number of rivets used, as given by the Material Controls Department, was 313,237.

There were 520 different kinds of rivets weighing 530 pounds used in each B-24. They ranged in sizes from 1/16 of an inch long (weighing .00005 pounds) to 3 1/4 inches long (weighing .05 pounds). Approximately 7,000,000 of them were made each day.

ASSEMBLY AREA

It took Consolidated thirteen days to set up their center wing fixture, assemble the wing with its large aluminum skins, and remove it. The fixture they used required dismantling each time a wing was completed, and before they could make another wing it had to be reassembled by sighting it in with a transit for alignment.

The problem facing Ford's production men was how to reduce from thirteen days to one hour the time required to build the wing and still insure its accuracy.

Riveting the skin and stringers together at a location other than where they were joined to the bulkhead and spar was considered by aircraft manufacturers to be impossible. They did not believe large surfaces of the skin could be made to fit accurately unless all of the matching and riveting were done on the same fixture. Ford's experience with mass production, however, told them that if the preliminary operations were properly oriented and fitted in relation to those that followed, the resulting parts should fit wherever they were assembled. They proceeded to divided the wing and skin surfaces into sections, which allowed more employees throughout the factory to work on the their assembly.

Center Wing Skin and Stringer Assembly
Department 936A

The first fixtures seen on entering the Assembly Area from the west were those in this department. They were used to hold the long skin segments for both the upper and lower surfaces of the wing while they were riveted together. (See Appendix B, Materials In Plane, for flat sheet sizes.)

The long stringers, made in the Draw Bench, Department 930, were laid out on steel benches constructed of thick metal tops mounted on heavy cast iron legs with jigs to hold the individual stringers firmly positioned. Because the wings tapered from the center of the wing outward, the stringers also tapered, and the thickness of the B-24 skin varied from .125 inches at the center to .025 inches at the wing tips. Locating points and jigs on the tables allowed workers to readily follow the different angles and junctions for supporting the stringers.

Since the upper surface of the wing applies Bernoulli's principle of lifting forces for an airplane, it differs greatly from the lower surface, and so did the assembly operations. One of those differences was the countersinking of rivet holes to provide a smooth surface for the air to pass over the upper surface.

The upper skin sections were formed of large pieces of rectangular aluminum trimmed to the correct measurement on the routing machines, and curved on Farnham rollers to conform to the contour of the wing. These skins were later blanked and pierced by dies at the Ford River Rouge plant and delivered back to Willow Run ready for the assembly. Ten of these sections comprised the upper wing surface and were riveted together on special curved fixtures before being moved and assembled to the stringers.

The skin on the lower wing surface differed from the

upper because of the wheel wells into which the wheels were retracted during flight. Directly below and above the wells, the skin had be to made much thicker than elsewhere to carried the stress of the load at these points. There were also a number of small access doors in the under-surface that were routed in the Press Shop until the skins were blanked and pierced at River Rouge. A total of 44 pieces of skin were required for the bottom surface of the wing, compared to ten for the upper surface.

After the skin surfaces had been joined together and the stringers properly prepared, they were placed in a fixture specially designed to hold the skin and stringers while they were riveted together. Through holes already pierced in the stringers, workers drilled from the stringer side through the upper skin surface while another crew working on the opposite side countersank the holes for rivets. Riveters then completed the operation. While performing these operations the workers stood on the electrically controlled platforms, serving as elevators, that paralleled the sides of the fixtures.

Upon completion of this operation, the skin/stringer sub-assembly was lifted from its fixture by one of the big cranes and moved forward.

Center Wing Vertical Assembly
Department 936

The vertical center wing fixtures that where used when joining the stringer and skin sub-assembly to the spars and bulkheads, were one of Willow Run's outstanding features.

Skin segments being riveted together in specially designed fixtures.

Center Wing Vertical Assembly.

203

The fixtures were 70 feet long, 18 feet high and 13 feet wide and installed, in groups of five, for a distance of 468 feet. The deafening roar that came from the area was produced by the driving of 78,606 rivets into each center wing and the installation of 6,439 other different parts and 1000 bolts.

The fixtures were so complex that no outside company would attempt to make them, and they were made in Ford's own machine shop at River Rouge. Each fixture weighed 28.44 tons and rested on individual foundations which kept them from being affected by heat or cold fluctuations of the plant's floor. Across the bottom ran a flat base on which locating pins and brackets were used to align the front spar in the same position each time. The top carriage located the rear spar.

While the center wings were in these vertical fixtures, four reference blocks were bolted onto the bottom of the front and rear spar. These blocks were used later to locate the wing in the mating fixture when it was joined with the fuselage. Upon completion of the center wing assembly, the end plates were moved back and a motor-driven carriage, on tracks above the fixture, would move its top bridge structure to one side. While the bridge was out of position, an overhead crane lifted the wing from its cradle, freeing it for the next one to be installed. Because this bridge structure was required to locate the spars in exactly the same position each time, it was designed not to sag more than .005 of an inch over a span of nearly 60 feet.

The design of this fixture made it unnecessary to take

it apart and set it up again after each assembly, reducing the down time from Consolidated's 250 man hours to just one man hour for Ford's operation at Willow Run. The fixture performed so well that it was estimated the number of man hours to build the center wing would be reduced from 5,500 to 1,728, which Willow Run far exceeded. The efficiency of this operation also reduced the number of fixtures used from an original estimate of 98 to only 35.

The success of the vertical center wing assembly fixture is illustrated in the following chart.

Center Wing	Cycle Time	Man Hours
145	39.5 hrs.	1,619
178	34.0	1,394
600	19.5	800
4,200	15.0	500
February 1945	8.7	357

When the center wings were removed from the vertical fixtures, their ends were within .010 of an inch of being perfect. This eliminated the need for two milling machines to trim their ends, which Pioch noted was required at Consolidated before they could attach the outer wing.

Machining The Wing

The Ingersoll machining operation, which came after the assembly of the center wing, more than justified the expectations of Pioch and the men who designed it.

The big fixture designed for machining the wing rested

on a ten-piece cast steel base which was set on a concrete foundation 18 inches deep, 20 feet wide, 70 feet long. Each of the ten castings were 7x13 feet, weighed 12,500 pounds, and rested on four leveling jacks. The castings were keyed and bolted to each other, and then fastened to hold them in place. The individual castings for the 70x13 foot foundation were so expertly cast and finished at the Rouge plant that after assembly there was only .005" variation on the surface of the entire block.

When the center wing was lifted from the vertical fixture where the skin and stringer sub-assembly had been joined with the spar and bulkheads, it was carried by overhead crane to the vertical machining and boring fixture. It was then lowered on its edge into the fixture with the front spar resting on its locator blocks. The wing itself was held in place by four towers located on the corners of the machine, which were swung out of the way while the wing was positioned.

Six men, supervised by one foreman, performed the following operations on the final machining fixture:

1. Position the wing in the machining fixture.
2. Mill eight upper engine mounting pads. Eight operations.
3. Mill eight lower engine mounting pads. Eight operations.
4. Drill four 3/8" holes in each of the eight lower engine pads. Eight operations.
5. Drill one 13/16" hole in each of the upper engine mounting pads. Eight operations.
6. Bore and spotface four landing gear needle bearings, two on each side. Four operations.

7.   Bore and spotface six main landing gear bearings, three on each side. Six operations.
8.   Remove the wing from the machining fixture.

A total of 42 operations were completed in 35 minutes or 3 1/2 man hours. The operations and time on the final machining operation consisted of the following:

	Minutes
Removing wing from Repair Bay and locking it in the fixture.	5
Setting up machine, milling and drilling the upper and lower motor mount forging.	10
Locating machine, boring and spotfacing needle bearing and main landing gear forging.	15
Unlocking and removing wing from fixture.	5

The following chart shows the progress at which adjustments in machine tools, horsepower of the tool driving motors, adjustments in bearing and material size, and efficiency of operations took place.

WING NO .	DATE	MACHINING TIME
100	11/12/42	3 hrs. 45 min.
500	4/21/43	2 "
1000	7/12/43	1 "
1500	9/22/43	40 min.
1600	10/2/43	40 "
1700	10/13/43	40 "
1800	10/23/43	40 "
1900	11/1/43	40 "
2000	11/9/43	35 "

Later on, a production record of 17 minutes was established for machining a wing section from start to finish, but the average time was about 35 minutes.

As the wing was taken out of the Ingersoll machining unit, it was turned and moved forward to the Center Wing Horizontal Department. Turning of the wing was accomplished by the use of one crane equipped with two hooks. One hook held the wing by a lifting strap bolted to the center of the wing, near the trailing edge, and another strap was attached near the leading edge. While the first hook remained stationary, the second was raised and the wing turned. This method eliminated a second crane and the job was done more quickly and with greater efficiency.

Center Wing Horizontal
Department 937

From the vertical machining operation, the engineers became convinced they could develop a faster production line if the center wings moved horizontally through the next twelve stations of the Center Wing Horizontal, Department 937, and developed a trolley conveyor for moving the wing in that position.

Installations in this department included the rear bomb rack trusses, the nacelle connection studs and access panel, and the inboard and outboard nacelle to wing fairings. At Station 6 the turbo dress-up for both the inboard and outboard engines were installed. At station ten the main landing gear was installed, and at station 11, just before leaving

Center Wing being machined in the Ingersoll Machining Fixture.
Horizontal Trolley Conveyor, Stations 1 to 12 in the background

the horizontal conveyor, 12 fuel cells, item 41A, were installed in the center wing.

While the center wing was being assembled, the people in the parallel bay along the north wall of the factory were assembling the fuselage and its component sub assemblies. The side panel under the wing, and the nose bottom panel were put together in Department 938A, while the aft bottom panel of the fuselage was assembled in Department 939A. The nose side panels, and the aft side panels went together in the Fuselage Departments 940A, and 940B.

At the end of the Fuselage area and station 12 of the Center Wing Horizontal there was a transfer bay where these two major sub-assemblies crossed over into the Final Assembly Lines, Department 947.

FINAL ASSEMBLY LINE
Stations 1 through 14

After the Center Wing was transferred by heavy crane into Final Assembly, Department 947, other parts and assemblies were added to it. At Station 1 the top fuselage deck above the wing was installed, along with items 41 and 53 and other loose parts. At Station 2 the front and rear bomb racks, catwalk, and side panels were added; at Station 4 the forward fuselage; at Station 6, item 29, the hydraulic reservoir tank; and at Station 7, item 60, the nose landing gear. The aft section of the fuselage was installed in Station 8; in Station 9, the engine power plant dress-up units were added, and in Station 11 the Emerson Nose Turret was installed. (See assembly pictures.)

The People Who Made It Happen

Fuselage, Turret, and Canopy Sections Awaiting Final Assembly

Center Wing coming off the horizontal conveyors
being readied for transport to Final Assembly

At station 8, when the fuselage was mated with the center wing it began to take on the configuration of an airplane and started to move forward on its own wheels.

Mating of the fuselage sections with the center wing was spread over several work stations, which required a means of distributing the fuselage to the proper work stations. A large bridge type conveyor system across the entire work area, designed by Albert Kahn, fed the fuselage sections into the assembly line much like automobile bodies were lowered into the assembly line at the Rouge automobile factory. Those destined for Fort Worth and Tulsa were shunted off to the Shipping Department.

Developing a fixture where the bulky fuselage section could be quickly and accurately assembled, or "mated," with the 55 foot center wing was the biggest challenge faced by the engineers. It was essential they eliminate Consolidate's time consuming problem of sighting through a transit to obtain accurate alignments, a process not feasible in mass production. They needed to find a way to automatically align these giant sections just by placing them in the fixture, a fixture that could be used reliably in high production without constantly having to check for accuracy.

Consolidated, remembering the problem they had with floor movement caused by the tide, believed it would not be possible, in Michigan's seasonal climates, to develop such a fixture. But when they saw how the men from Willow Run solved the problem they were so impressed they ordered the fixture for their own new factory.

The engineers designed and built a sturdy heavy duty

fixture consisting of a set of four large cast iron pillars or "leveling towers" about seven feet high. They were arranged in pairs, and set far enough apart to permit the fuselage to pass between them and low enough so the center wing could pass over their tops. The first operation in positioning the 55 foot wing was to set it on top of two additional towers that were used as hydraulic jacks. It was then lowered onto the leveling towers where it engage the reference blocks bolted onto the front and rear spars in Vertical Assembly. The wings were then adjusted up or down and when this operation was completed the wing was automatically leveled in flight position at 3^0-26' angle of incidence. It was also located at right angles to the center line of the fixture used to carry the fuselage.

The four leveling towers were mounted on a block of reinforced concrete 18 feet deep that rested on solid hardpan. This foundation provided the best possible support for the mating fixture and there was little danger the towers would move out of alignment.

When the method of locating the center wing had been resolved, it remained to design a means of handling the bulky fore and aft sections of the fuselage. The engineers designed two cast iron mating cars, onto which each section of the fuselage would be lowered, leveled and aligned by the use of mating straps. The straps, each with four feet-like projections, lowered the fuselage onto four machined surfaces located in each corner of the mating car, and when they were positioned the fuselage was ready for mating with the wing.

WILLOW RUN

The Little People of Willow Run

Somewhere, hidden throughout the roar of the rivets and the hammering of presses, were ten of the biggest "little people" working at Willow Run. You could find them in a tight narrow space on the inside of a wing tip bucking rivets or insulating a fuel cell against the bullets of enemy gun fire. Or, making an inspection in a space so small no other inspector could put a gauge on the part. (See Appendix A, Midgets.)

They were a highly specialized group of employees, respected by other employees, not just for their size, or lack of it, but for the dangerous work they performed while crawling around inside a wing or fuel tank where only the dwarf could fit. At shift-time, because of Ford's rule that everyone must punch their own time card, you could see them being lifted up to the time clock by one of their larger buddies.

On several occasions they were banged around and injured when a plane was moved while they were still working. The foreman, not seeing them, had forgotten they were working inside of a wing and not on its outside.

They came from the entertainment world and the fringes of American industry, but at Willow Run they were in the center ring of the world's largest industrial operation.

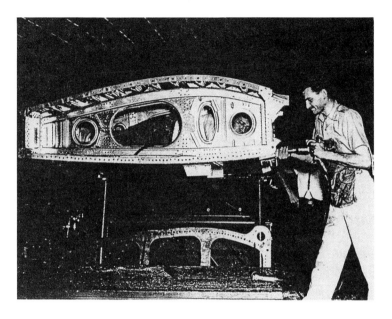

Bucking Rivets, Sealing Fuel Cells, And Inspecting Tight Places,
They Worked Where No Other Person Could.

Four-Hour Stations - Final Assembly

When the ships left station 14 they arrived at what was called the "Four-Hour Station." Here the ships were moved into the center of the 150 foot bay which provided the width needed to install the right and left outer wings at Station 15. The outer wing fuel tanks were installed at Station 16, and at Station 17 the right and left flaps were installed.

Between Stations 20 and 21 the ships were turned ninety degrees as they passed over the turntable that Albert Kahn designed into the assembly line (see photograph). It was this turntable that changed the shape of the factory from a straight mile-long assembly line into an "L" shape, and prevented the factory from being built across county lines - Wayne and Washtenaw.

The ships continued through the final phases of assembly where the propellers were added, and final check-out took place. At Station 28 the planes arrived at a five day Finishing Station where they were camouflaged, and took on gasoline and oil. Their compasses were calibrated on the compass rose, and the guns of every 5th plane were checked for accuracy at the Gun Butt as they were readied for both Company and Army Flight Test, Acceptance, and Delivery.

Flyaway of the B 24s from Willow Run, for delivery to any location in the United States or any overseas theater of war, was performed by many women pilots as well as men of the Ferry Command located at Romulus, Michigan.

END NOTES

1. *Willow Run Reference Book,* Appendix A and B.
2. Research Center of Henry Ford Museum and Greenfield Village, Accessions 435, Box 1, Vol I.

Station One - Installation of Top Fuselage Section Above The Wing.

Nose fuselage upper right awaiting its turn at Station 4.
Tail fuselage on cross over heading for shipping Department

The Nose Fuselage has been installed at Station 4.
Tail Fuselage sections waiting to be lowered at Station 8

Stations 9 - 11, Empennage, Engine Dress-Up:
Tail, Top, And Nose Turret Installation.

221

Station 12 - Looking east to Station 15 cross-over to single lane.
Observe that Outer Wing Tips have already been installed.

222

Near Station 17 where right and left Wing Flaps were installed.
Men working on the engines - Ship heading for the turn.

223

Making the turn between Stations 20 and 21 - Note the turntable used to reconfigure Willow Run, lower right.

Ford's Two Final Assembly Lines At Willow Run
They Produced A Bomber An Hour

Vestibule - Note the large row of doors on the left. Width 143'9" - Height 33'1 7/8" - Weighed 35 tons each.

The Compass Rose where the B-24 compasses were adjusted.
Left: Hangar 1 - Right: The short leg of Final Assembly

227

The Gun Butt for sighting-in and testing guns of the B-24.

Willow Run's Last B-24 "Liberator" Bomber - Number 8685.
Signed By All The Employees, June 28, 1945.
Lloyd Freeman On The Tow.

EPILOGUE

After World War II, the Kaiser-Frazer Corporation purchased the famous Willow Run bomber plant from the government for fifteen million dollars. They built the Kaiser, the Frazer, and the Henry J. automobiles, and during the Korean conflict they built the C-123 and the Fairchild C-119 flying boxcar. In 1953, when the war was over, Kaiser's airplane contracts were canceled by the government. The Kaiser-Frazer Corporation, which had accumulated large deficits from their automobile business, then disbanded operations at Willow Run. They sold their automotive equipment to Argentina, and merged with Willys-Overland in Toledo, Ohio to manufacture the Jeep.

On August 12, 1953, a crippling fire destroyed General Motor's Hydra-matic production facility in Livonia, Michigan, and within days they had made arrangements with Kaiser to take over Willow Run. By November 4 Hydra-matic transmissions were coming off the assembly line. The speed and efficiency with which General Motors was able to get manufacturing underway was truly remarkable, and served as a reminder of the early days of Willow Run.

Since that time General Motors has provided Willow Run with more than 40 years of maturation in production of automobiles and hydra-matic transmissions. Over the years, they purchased the land that lies between Rawsonville and Beck Roads on the north side of Ecorse Road to the Michigan Central Railroad (now Conrail), some of which they use as a warehouse staging area for shipping. Several years ago, General Motors moved their automobile production to another location, and today there are over 7000 hydra-matic transmissions being manufactured in the main Willow Run factory where the B-24s were made.

EPILOGUE

An International Trade Port, which would make use of Willow Run's large centrally-located airport, is currently under consideration by the Michigan Legislature, and the additional land, needed to re-route Ecorse Road for an extension of runways, has been purchased for its development.

The colossus of world industry awaits her next generation of entrepreneurs. People who think like Sorensen when he said, "The only thing we can't make is something we can't think about."

The Headquarters of the Yankee Air Force, with its library and museum of historical aircraft occupy the original buildings of the 3509th Army Air Base Unit, and Special B-24 Airplane and Engine Mechanics Training School. It is located on the Beck Road side of the Willow Run Airport.

Fifty years ago, on June 28, 1945, the last B-24 "Liberator" bomber, bearing the signatures of those who built it, came off the assembly line at Willow Run. More than 18,000 were manufactured in the United States. Today, there are only one or two that fly. The house that Louis Schlossstein worked to save during the great depression is gone and his land grows wild, as in the days of de Tocqueville.

Along the highway where H. H. Henning and C. W. Thomas made their first landing at Willow Run the sweetest tasting wild strawberries cover the ground where the old patch used to grow. The asparagus too grows wild, and the creek where the muskrats played has started to reshape itself. A gentle breeze and the thought of Mr. Fogarty's centenarian maple trees are reminders of how beautiful it used to be.

The Single Tail B-24-N

Developed by Ford under the direction of William Pioch.
Seven are estimated to have been manufactured.

APPENDIX A

CHRONOLOGICAL DATA

January 1941 - December 1944

Information presented in this Appendix comes from the only known record of Willow Run daily activities. It was compiled and used by the Willow Run Plant Guide Service under the direction of William A. Simonds. Never made available to the general public, few, if any, copies of this information would now exist. This transcription is presented here to preserve for history and the interested reader one of the best sources of information during the first four years of Willow Run.

January - 1941

4   Mr. Edsel B. Ford and other Ford officials leave to visit Consolidated Plant at San Diego to determine if Ford could build the B-24 Bomber in quantity.

7   Mr. Ford on West Coast to "study aircraft industry." Meets with Logan Miller, W. F. Pioch, Ed Scott, Ernie Walters, Wm. Taylor [also with Charles Sorensen].

8   Mr. Ford announces that Company will begin immediately with plans to use its mass production facilities in construction of B-24 bomber parts. Ford said entirely new type of plant would be constructed to handle the job.

12   Ford officials visited Wright Field and notified Air Corps that Ford could start as soon as ordered by the Government.

233

February

5 OPM declines Ford offer to build complete bomber, "at least for the present." War Department officials said they would adhere to a plan for Ford to make bomber parts only, to be assembled elsewhere.

19 Knudsen announces Ford will build bomber plant at Ypsilanti to produce subassemblies.

21 Ford received letter of intent to build air frames for 1,200 bombers to be shipped to assembly plants at Tulsa and Fort Worth.

22 Ford has plans and drawings for plant virtually completed.

March

4 Party of company officials leaves for San Diego. They rent offices and prepare to set up drafting room and other equipment. They also set up tool room at the Consolidated Plant.

11 Crew of 200 Ford engineers and production experts reach San Diego from Dearborn.

13 Ford receives educational contract on the B-24, amounting to $3,418,000.

24 Work order request filed for 1st die.

28 First work done on site of plant as crews began clearing away woodlands to make room for airfield.

31 Bomber Educational Contract W535-ac18061 signed.

April

18 Ground-breaking and excavation work started on Bomber Plant.

20   First concrete poured in foundation footings.

May

1   Company begins plans for enlarging Willow Run Plant on verbal assurance from the Government that it will build complete B-24 bombers as well as B-24 subassemblies.

3   Railroad spur from New York Central Railroad main line reached Bomber Plant site. First piece of structural steel framework erected.

20   Ford receives sub-contracts from Douglas and Consolidated to build airframes (590 K. D. [knocked down] and 10 B. U. [built up] on each).

June

5   Air Corps sent letter of intent for 800 complete planes. Willow Run plant dedicated.

18   First orders placed for tools to be used in bomber construction.

25   First concrete floor poured. Defense Plant Corporation Lease (Plancor 151) signed by E. B. Ford.

July

14   Designing of Center Wing Vertical Fixture started.

26   Production and engineering staff return from San Diego to set up airframe division at Ford Airport.

August

12   First machinery installed at Willow Run.

13   First sewer laid in airfield.

15   First brick walls under construction at Willow Run Plant.

22   First concrete poured on runways in airfield.

September

1   First piece of machinery arrives at Bomber Plant.

7   First group of men transferred from Dearborn Airframe to Willow Run.

26   Ford becomes a primary contractor on the Consolidated B-24 with a Government contact for 795 complete bombers (W535-ac21216).

27   Machines in Tool Room started for first time [perhaps referring to electrical power].

October

15   First bomber part produced in Press Shop, Rouge.

21   First fixture completed. First landing at Willow Run Airport on radio beacon by H. P. Henning and C. W. Thomas.

22   First official Airport landing made by Major Doolittle.

November

6   First assembly Fixture arrived at Willow Run (Wing Flap).

19   Aft fuselage for #1 ship started at Dearborn Airframe.

December

3   Last sewer in airfield completed.

4   Last concrete poured in runways.

8   First horizontal milling machine put in operation and first part produced at Willow Run

24   Started setting up first Center Wing Fixture.

January - 1942

4   Nose fuselage for #1 ship started at Dearborn.

13   Letter of intent for 700 complete planes and spare parts received.

14   Ground broken for Trade School at Willow Run.

15   Center Wing fixture ready for production. The first part was also placed in the fixture on this day. Change order #1 to prime contract W353-ac21216 was signed increasing order for spare parts for 795 complete B-24E bombers from $19,870,000 to $27,375,000.

23   Pilot's Floor for #1 ship started.

February

10   Rudder for #1 ship started.

11   Miss Agnes Menzies, first woman employee, started work as nurse in the First Aid Department.

16   Ford Motor Company entered into special facilities contract No. W535-ac26564 with War Department covering facilities for transportation by truck of component assemblies to Tulsa and Fort Worth.

18   Center Wing Leading Edge for #1 ship started.

21   L.H. Outer Wing Panel for #1 Ship started.

24   Bomber sub-assembly trucking contract between Ford Motor Company and E & L Transportation Company was signed whereby E & L were engaged to transport certain materials and component assemblies between Willow Run, Tulsa and Fort Worth.

25   Government contracts increased to a total of 4,495 ships to be built.

March

18   Elevator for #1 ship started.

19   Pilot's Floor for #1 ship completed.

21   Rudder for #1 ship completed.

23   Charles A. Lindbergh engaged as engineering research consultant.

31   First shipment of subassemblies left Bomber Plant, consigned to Douglas Aircraft Corp.,Tulsa, Oklahoma.

April

1   L.H. Outer Wing Panel for #1 ship removed from vertical fixture. Ford Motor Company started training in First Aid.

7   Elevator for #1 ship completed.

8   Second shipment of subassemblies left Bomber Plant for Tulsa.

9   Aft fuselage for #1 ship completed at Dearborn.

10   Center Wing Leading Edge for #1 ship completed.

11   Supplement #1 signed with Douglas providing for 1000 additional K. D. and spare parts for 1600 planes.

14   Supplemental #1 signed with C.A.C. [Consolidated Aircraft Corporation] providing for 800 additional K.D., and spare parts for 1400 planes.

15   No. 1 Center Wing taken out of vertical fixture.

16   No.1 Center Wing complete.

18   Nose fuselage for #1 ship completed at Dearborn.

20   Ratio established between Douglas, C.A.C. and Ford on K.D. shipments.

May

15   First Ford-assembled bomber (ship .01) completed and turned over to Flight Department. [Ford's educational unit assembled from parts delivered from Consolidated.]

19   M. L. Bricker assigned to Willow Run full time.

June

6   Donald Nelson, Head of War Production Board, Sir Oliver Lyttleton, British Minister of Production, and Averill Harriman of Lend-Lease Administration visit Willow Run.

8   Pilot line of assembly fixtures completed.

12   1st ship # (.01) to hangar from factory.

19   First Ford-assembled bomber flight tested this day (3:45 to 4:20 p.m.).

22   First contingent of Air Corps ground crew trainees, 6 in number, reported for school.

24   Contract W-2119ac11 for training enlisted personnel signed. First class held in new Airplane School Building.

July

1   King Peter II of Jugoslavia visits plant and talks with workers of Jugoslavian descent.

2   Hanger hospital occupied.

12   First K.D. set shipped to Douglas.

13   Central unit of hangar occupied.

14   No. 4 wing, first to be placed in Final Machining Unit. [This is the unit created by Wm. Pioch and designed by John Mistele.]

21   Construction of Barracks for Air Corps Ground Crew students started. Wing #4 completed in Final Machining unit.

25   New State Highway Road System to south parking lot opened to traffic.

31   Lt. Gen. H. H. Arnold, Chief of Army Air Force, inspects Willow Run.

August

17   On contract W535ac Supplement Agt. #5, Ford was allowed an additional 900 B.U. ships making a total of 5,395.

September

1   First ship [.01] accepted.

8   Contract DAW 525-ac2820 (Bombardment Squadron Service) signed.

10   Ship #1 completed on Final Line.

12   New highway with triple overpasses dedicated by Under-Secretary of War Robert S. Patterson.

18   President and Mrs. Franklin D. Roosevelt, accompanied by Donald Nelson, inspected plant.

25   Lt. Col. Bradley Saunders, Resident Representative, AAF, succeeded by Capt. Frank Moonert.

30   Ship #1 accepted by Army.

October

3   Center Wing #59 assembled in 93 1/4 hours.

29   Conference with General Wolfe, Consolidated, Douglas, North American and Ford representatives.

31   Seventh ship delivered to flight (including .01). Ground broken on Federal project east of airfield.

November

4   First Ford-made set of superchargers installed in ship #28.

6   Paving started on apron of Federal project.

7   First shipment to North American leaves Willow Run.

8   First ship delivered to Fort Worth.

10   100th Center Wing assembled in vertical fixture.

15   San Diego offices closed and Ford representatives return to Willow Run.

16   B-24 Engineering Sub-committee at Willow Run [1942 investigation of how to handle the massive amount of engineering change orders that was delaying production. See entry dated October 20, 1943].

27   Center Wing #145 assembled in 37 hours 50 minutes, or 1619 man-hours. Average of 41 men on fixture.

28   Ships #1 and 2 flown away by Ferry Command 3:35 P.M.

December

1   Gas rationing started.

9   W535-ac18061 merged with 21216.

17   Center wing #178 assembled in 19 hours 10 minutes, or 933 man-hours.

18   Left-hand Outer Wing #160 assembled in 3 hours 55 minutes, or 44.25 man-hours.

23   Center Wing #200 commenced on assembly fixture.

January 1943

7   Ship #100 entered Final Assembly Line.

11   First class in Production Training School began training.

15   On first anniversary of commencement of first Center Wing, #237 was started in fixture.

22   Col. Eddie Rickenbacher visits the plant and writes name on ship # 99.

241

WILLOW RUN

February

15 First unit of Willow Run housing facilities opened, "Willow Lodge."

19 Senate Committee headed by Senator H. S. Truman visits Willow Run.

March

3 Approval for manufacture of stabilizers at River Rouge Plant.

8 Approval for manufacture of Landing Light Doors and Island Doors at Ford Motor, Hamilton, Ohio.

12 Outboard and Fuel Access Doors approved for manufacture at Hamilton.

15 Plant water system supplied 100% by Rawsonville Wells. Ship #99 flown away.

16 Ship #100 delivered to Flight.

19 Oleo Doors approved for manufacture at Hamilton, Ohio.

April

2 Willow Run Plant awarded "Bulls-Eye" flag for high war bond subscription. Herbert Gaston, Assistant to Secretary of Treasury, made presentation.

6 C. E. Wilson, Executive Vice-Chairman of WPB, visited plant.

12 First Landing Light Door and Island Door assemblies received from Ford Motor, Hamilton, Ohio.

13 Pattern Shop moved to Airframe at Dearborn.

14 500th Center Wing Section commenced in vertical fixture. Received approval for manufacture of Pilot's Enclosure by Pittsburgh Plate Glass Company. First finished Oleo Doors

received from Hamilton. Island Door Assemblies released to Hamilton Plant.

15   First finished Outboard Fuel Access Doors received from Hamilton.

22   Radio Operator's Floors and Truss Bulkhead approved for manufacture at the "B" Bldg., Rouge Plant. Landing Light Door Assemblies released to Ford Hamilton Plant.

24   Ship #200 delivered to Flight.

26   Center Wing Flap approved for manufacture at Gibson Refrigerator Co. Trailing edges approved for manufacture at Reynolds Spring. Construction started on Warm Up Hangars.

27   Engine Cowling, Nose Ring, and Engine Dress-Up approved for manufacture at Lincoln Plant.

28   Ship #300 entered Final Assembly Line.

29   Brake and Pedal Control Assembly approved for manufacture at the Oakes Products.

30   Fixtures (rudder) sent to Rouge Tire Plant. Air Ducts approved for manufacture at Lincoln Plant. Flyaways for the month reached 100 for the first time.

May

4   Fins approved for manufacture at Rouge Tire Plant.

5   Aileron and Elevator approved for manufacture at Rouge Tire Plant. Side Gunner's Door approved for manufacture at Hamilton, Ohio.

7   First finished parts (Nose Ring and Engine Cowling) received from Lincoln Plant.

10   General Enrique Penaranda, President of Bolivia, visits

Plant. Wing # 600 completed in vertical fixture.

11   First finished parts (Truss Bulkhead) 4.1 and Radio Operator's Floor received from Rouge "B" Building.

14   Wing Tips approved for manufacture at E. G. Budd Co.

15   First finished parts (stabilized) received from Rouge Tire Plant. Bomb Doors approved for manufacture by Budd Manufacturing Co.

18   Brake Pedal Control Assemblies released to Oakes Products. Purchasing Department moved offices to Willow Run.

21   First Finished parts (rudder) received from Rouge Tire Plant. Ship #300 delivered to Flight.

22   Fixtures (Bomb Rack) sent to Metal Moulding, Detroit. First finished parts (Pilot's Enclosure) received from Pittsburgh Plate Glass Company. Ship #400 entered Final Assembly Line.

24   Ship K. D. 801 (B.D. 489) entered the Final Assembly Line. Bomb Rack approved for manufacture by Metal Molding.

25   Wing #700 completed in vertical fixture.

26   Mr. Edsel B. Ford, President of the Ford Motor Company died.

June

1   Mr. Henry Ford resumed presidency of Company. Army Air Base School opened in new quarters east of the airfield. Transferred from MM 11 Balcony.

2   First finished parts (Side Gunner's Doors) received from Hamilton. Wing #700 sold and sent to Douglas. Dr. Edward Benes, President of Czechoslovakia, visits Plant.

3 First finished parts (Bomb Rack) received from Metal Molding Co., Detroit.

4 First finished parts (Fin) received from Rouge Tires plant. First finished parts (Brake and Pedal) received from Oakes Products, Decatur, Illinois.

7 Wing #800 commenced in vertical fixture.

8 Electrical Assembly approved for manufacture by National Totalizator.

9 Wing #800 completed in vertical fixture. Ship #500 entered Final Assembly Line.

11 Canopy approved for manufacture by Rouge Tire Plant.

12 Compass Rose tested for the first time. First finished parts (Center Wing Flap) received from Gibson Refrigerator Company. Ship #400 delivered to Flight.

15 First of Sewing Department approved for manufacture by Allen Industries, Detroit, Michigan.

17 Wing #800 sold to Ford.

19 First finished parts (Center Wing and Outer Wing Trailing Edge) received from Reynolds Spring Co. First finished parts (Aileron Assembly) received from tire Plant.

21 Wing #900 started in vertical fixture.

24 K.D. Ship #801 (B.D. 489 delivered to Flight. Construction began on New Materials Building.

26 Wing #900 completed in vertical fixture.

30 First Wing Tip Assembly received from E. G. Budd company. Catwalk Assembly approved for manufacture by Glendale Products.

WILLOW RUN

July

1   Loft boards moved to MM-11 Balcony. First finished parts (Trim) received from Allen Industries.

2   First Canopy Assemblies received from Tire Plant.

3   First Elevator Assemblies received from Tire Plant.

7   Wing #1000 started in vertical fixture. First concrete poured for New Materials Building.

8   North line of Outer Wing horizontal conveyor moved out. First application of new U. S. Army insignia on B-24s in assembly lines.

10 Wing #1000 completed in vertical fixture. First finished parts (Air Ducts) received from Lincoln Plant.

13 Ship #500 delivered to Flight.

15 Nose Ring Assemblies released to Lincoln Plant. Gen. Henri Giraud inspects Willow Run.

19 Ship #600 entered assembly line. Wing #1100 started in vertical fixture. Air Duct released to Lincoln Plant. First finished parts (Bomb Doors) received from E. G. Budd. Oleo Doors released to Hamilton Plant.

24 Vice-President Henry Wallace made tour of plant.

25 Lt. Col. H. S. Jones replaces Lt. Col. Gordon as U. S. Army Air Forces Resident Representative.

26 Wing #1100 completed in vertical fixture.

28 First electrical assemblies received from National Totalizator. Anniversary of first graduation of Army Ground School.

30 Mr. Henry Ford's 80th birthday.

APPENDIX A - YEAR 1943

August

5   Ground broken for #2 Hangar in southwest corner of airfield. Outer Wing (25%) approved for manufacture by Bechtel, McCone & Parsons Co. Wing #1200 started in vertical fixture.

6   Outboard Fuel Access Doors and Side Gunner's Door released to Hamilton Plant.

7   Ship #600 delivered to Flight.

9   Truss Bulkhead released to Ford Rouge Plant, "B" Building.

13   Outer Wing (75%) for manufacture by Highland Park Plant.

14   Pilot's Enclosure released to Pittsburgh Plate Glass Company. Ship #700 started in Final Assembly Line.

21   K. D. Ship #1201 (B.U. 742) started in Final Assembly Line. Outer Wing Trailing Edge released to Reynolds Springs Co.

23   Wing #1300 started in vertical fixture.

25   Motor Cowling Assemblies released to Lincoln Plant.

26   Engine Dress-up Assemblies released to Lincoln Plant.

27   Work order issued to move Plexiglas Department to Pittsburgh Plate Glass Company at Creighton, Pa. Work Order issued to move Tail cone fixture to Highland Park.

31   Door Bulkhead (Sta. 6.0) approved for manufacture by W. B. Deyo.

September

1   Ship #700 delivered to Flight. Bomb Door Assemblies released to E. G. Bud Co.

4   First Catwalk Assembly (Item 16) received from Glenvale

247

WILLOW RUN

Products. Major Moonert transferred to Central District. Bomb Rack Assemblies released to Metal Molding.

6   Wing #1400 in vertical assembly fixture. Side Panels (items 5 & 6) approved for manufacture by Ford Highland Park. 1st Wing on 2nd contract entered Final Assembly. Commence replacement of Station 15 by transverse conveyor. Secretary of Treasury, Henry Morgenthau Jr., in spected plant.

7   2000 lb. Bomb Rack approved for manufacture by Metal Molding. Rudder Assembly released to Tire Plant.

8   Final Line 2A started to close down. Rear Bottom Panel (Item 32) approved for manufacture by Highland Park.

9   Ship 800 begun in Final Assembly Line. Electrical Assemblies released to National Totalizator. "Aft" Fuselage Side Panels (Items 30 & 31) approved for manufacture at Highland Park.

13   Center Wing Bulkheads approved for manufacture at Lincoln Plant.

17   Wing #1500 in vertical assembly fixture.

22   Ship # 95 last on original contract delivered to Flight.

23   Ship #800 delivered to Flight. Hydraulic tubing (27 assemblies) approved for manufacture by Highland Park.

25   Wing #1801 started in vertical assembly fixture.

28   1st ship on 2nd contract flown away. First finished parts (Outer Wing) received from Highland Park.

30   Monthly schedule of 250 exceeded by four ships giving a total of 254 for month.

October

4   Elevator Assembly released to Tire Plant, Rouge.

5   Miscellaneous Assemblies (932) approved for manufacture at Ford Highland Park.

6   Forward Upper Deck (Item 3) approved for manufacture by Lloyd Mfg. Co.

8   Center Wing Trailing edge released to Reynolds Spring.

9   Wing #1700 started in vertical fixture.

10 Miscellaneous Electrical Assemblies approved for assemby Highland Park.

12 First Nose Wheel Doors received from Hamilton, Ohio.

14 First Upper Rear Deck (Item 12) received from Tire Plant.

15 Department 981 (Shipping), 977 (Maintenance), 913 (Clean-up), 989 (Heating and Power) and 979 (Plant Protection) occupy space in the New Materials Building.

    Ship #900 delivered to Flight. Machine shop work approved by Highland Park Plant.

16 K. D. 1801 entered Final Line (BU 1020) (line 2). First rear Side Panels (Items 30 & 31) received from Highland Park.

18 Lowell Thomas broadcasts from School Auditorium.

19 First Forward Upper Deck (Item 3) received from Lloyd M.G. Co.

20 Wing #1800 in vertical assembly fixture. 2000 lb. Bomb Rack Assembly released to Metal Molding. First Door Bulkhead (Station 6.0) received from Deco Co. Engineer in changes in B-24 halted except those authorized by prior approval of the Chief Material Command, Wright Field.

21 Nose enclosure approved for manufacture by Highland Park. Life Raft and Emergency Hatch Door approved for manufacture at Hamilton, Ohio.

22 Rear Upper Deck (Item 12) approved for manufacture at Rouge Tire Plant.

24 Final Line #2 reopened with ships Nos. 1020, 1022, 1023 (1801 series).

25 Excavating for drain tile for new apron started.

26 Wing Tip Assembly released to E. G. Budd Co. First Rear Bottom Panel Assemblies received from "B" Bldg., Rouge.

27 Aileron Assemblies released to Tire Plant, Ford Motor Company. Ship # 1000 enters 8-hour stations at Final Line. Grading preparatory to pouring of concrete for new apron started.

30 Catwalk assemblies released to Glenvale Products.

31 Monthly schedule of 302 exceeded by 5 ships giving a total of 307 for October.

November

3 Broadcasting Station B-24 opened for business at Willow Run. Ship #1000 delivered to Flight.

4 First Nose Side Panels (Items 5 & 6) received from Highland Park. First Miscellaneous Assemblies (Dept. 932) received from Highland Park.

5 Hydraulic Tubing Assemblies released to Highland Park and first ones received.

6 Wing #2000 started in vertical Fixture. First 2000 lb. Bomb Rack received from Highland Park. Departments 981E (Rough Stock and Sheet Stock), 976 (Transportation),

981 (Receiving) and 981 (Salvage) moved into New Materials Bld..

8   Worked commenced on construction of Gun Butt. Canopy Assembly released to Tire Plant. Machine Shop Assemblies released to Highland Park and first ones received.

10   Nose Wheel Door Assemblies released to Hamilton plant.

12   Door Bulkhead Assemblies (station 6.9) released to Deco.

15   Wing #2100 started in vertical fixture.

17   Master Change Ship #1176 (K.D. 2101) entered 8-hour stations of Final Line. Miscellaneous Electrical Assemblies released to Highland Park

18   Department 927 (Shears) set up in New Materials Building.

19   Miscellaneous Assemblies (Department 932) released to Highland Park Plant.

20   Center Wing Flap Assembly released to Gibson Refrigerator. Record set for Flyaways and Army delivery when twenty planes were delivered in one day.

21   Department 981 (Spare Parts Crib) set up in the New Materials Bld..

22   Stabilizer Assembly released to Rouge Tire Plant.

24   Wing #2200 entered the vertical fixture. Ship #1176 (K.D. 2101) removed from assembly line and delivered to Flight.

25   Master Change Ship #1020 (K.D. 1801) removed from Line 2.

27   Department 981 (Barrel Stock) moved to New Materials Building.

30   Monthly schedule of 307 exceeded by 28 ships, total 335.

December

2   Center Wing #2300 started in vertical fixture.

4   Orders issued at Wright Field to discontinue camouflage of B-24s.

5   Carpenter Shop moved to the New Materials Building.

8   Master Change Ship (K.D. 2401) entered 8-hour stations of Final Line.

9   Center Wing #2400 started in vertical fixture.

10   Upper Rear Deck (Item 12) released to Tire Plant.

11   Center wing #2400 completed in vertical fixture.

13   "Shop Coat" of zinc chromate on skin sections discontinued.

17   Center Wing #2500 started in vertical fixture.

18   BU Ship #1300 completed in the Final Assembly Line.

23   BU Ship #1200 completed in Final Assembly Line.

7   Ship No. K. D. #3201 designated as effective ship for deletion of exterior camouflage.

29   Poured last of concrete for Gun Butt. Center Wing #2600 started in vertical fixture.

31   At 12:00 o'clock east end of the new hanger was occupied by Flight Department. At 3:15 o'clock the first ship was moved into the new south hanger. Monthly schedule of 352 exceeded by 13 ships giving a total of 365 ships.

January 1944

1   1272 BU ships completed during 1943. 1300 ships flown away from Willow Run during 1943. 1106 K.D. ships shipped to Douglas and Consolidated during 1943.

3   Master Change Ship K. D. 2801 entered 8-hour stations of Final Line.

6   BU Ship #1400 completed in Final Assembly Line. Center Wing #2700 started in vertical fixture.

8   New Record for Flyaways established when 29 ships were flown from Willow Run Airport.

12 A Center Wing was sent to Airframe Bldg. at Dearborn for experiment on engine removal. Fourth War Bond Drive started at Willow Run A. M. Krech in charge.

14 BU Ship #1500 entered the 8-hour stations of Final Line today. Center Wing #2800 started in vertical fixture.

20 Center Wing #2900 started in vertical fixture.

21 BU Ship #1500 completed in Final Assembly Line.

25 New Willow Run Gun Butt used for the first time.

28 Center Wing #3000 started in vertical fixture.

29 Installation of cascade oxygen supply system complete.

31 Equipment moved from Ypsilanti Stove Works to New Materials Bld..

February

4   Ship No. 1600 completed in Final Assembly Line.

5   Master Change Ship K.D. No. 3201 entered #1 Final Assembly Line. Wing #3100 started in vertical fixture.

12 Master Change Ship K.D. No.3201 complete in assembly line. First ship to be assembled at Willow Run without camouflage paint.

14 Wing #3200 started in vertical fixture.

15 Willow Run went over the top in the 4th War Loan Drive.

16   Ship No. 1700 completed in Final Assembly Line.

19   Wing #3300 started in vertical fixture.

20   Open House for Willow Run employees and their families.

24   Willow Run Inspection Department received Class "A" rating. 10,000th student graduated from AAFTTC School at Willow Run Base.

26   Wing #3400 started in vertical fixture.

27   Ship #1800 completed in Final Line. Open House for employees.

29   To date 1824 ships have been assembled at Willow Run. In addition 657 K.D.'s have been shipped to Douglas at Tulsa and 809 to Consolidated at Fort Worth.

March

2   BU. Ship #1900 entered line No. 4 of Primary Assembly.

4   Master Change Ship No. K.D. 3601 entered Line No. 1. Wing #3500 started in vertical fixture.

10   Master Change Ship No. K.D. 3601 completed in Final Assembly.

11   Wing #3600 started in vertical fixture.

12   Parking Lot for 150 cars built at Salvage Yard.

13   BU. ship #2000 entered #1 Assembly Line.

14   Highest number of initial flights released (19).

15   Master Change Ship No. K.D. 3901 entered Line No. 2.

17   BU. Ship #1900 completed in Final Assembly.

18   Ship No. 2000 completed in Final Assembly. Prototype B-24-K [single tail] started at Willow Run. Highest No. of initials flown (42). 50 acceptances in one day.

APPENDIX A - YEAR 1944

21   Master Change Ship No. K.D. 3901 complete in Final Assembly. BU. 2285).

24   Record set from factory to delivery (44hrs.).

25   Wing #3800 started in vertical fixture.

31   462 K.D. sets have been produced at Willow Run, 62 to Consolidated, 78 to Douglas and 322 to Final Assembly. Total produced at Willow Run to date is 3752 - 735 to Douglas, 871 to Consolidated, 2146 to Ford final assembly lines. 57 over Army schedule for March.

April

1   Center Wing #3900 started in vertical fixture.

5   Ship No. 2100 completed in Final Assembly.

7   Ship No. 2200 completed in Final Assembly.
      Wing #4000 started in vertical fixture.

14   Wing #4100 started in vertical fixture.

18   Last of Outer Wing fixtures removed from Assembly Building.

20   Wing #4200 started in vertical fixture.

21   Ship No. 2300 completed in Final Assembly.

24   Ship No. 2400 completed in Final Assembly. Master Change Ship #4401 started in Line No.2 of Primary Assemby. Record for Flyaways established when 42 ships were flown away. Production flights set new record (94).

27   Wing #4300 started in vertical fixture.

30   Total production to date - Ford 2483 - Douglas 801- Consolidated 923 - Grand Total 4207.

May

3   Wing #4400 entered vertical fixture.

8   Ship #2500 left Final Line.

10   Wing #4500 entered vertical fixture. Last K.D. shipment to Consolidated, closing sub-contract.

12   Ship #2600 left Final Assembly Line.

17   Wing #4600 entered vertical fixture.

23   Ship #2800 entered Primary Assembly.

24   Ship #2700 left Final Assembly Line. Wing # 4700 entered vertical assembly.

25   K.D. #5001 (3142) entered Primary Assembly Line.

31   Ship #2800 left Final Assembly Line.

June

1   Commencement of the 5th War Loan Drive at the Bomber Plant.

2   Center Wing #4800 started in vertical fixture.

3   BU Ship #2900 entered #3 Primary Line.

6   D-Day. Plant observed silence for 1 minute.

8   Center Wing #4800 ready for Final Line.

9   Center Wing #4900 started in vertical fixture.

12   BU Ship # 3000 entered Primary Line No. 2.

13   BU Ship # 2900 completed in Final Line.

15   Athletic field used for first time for ball game between Dept. 935 A and 938 A.

16   Wing #5000 started in Center Wing vertical department. BU Ship #3000 completed in Final Line.

19   BU Ship # 3100 entered Primary Line No. 1.

21   Wing #5100 started in Center Wing vertical department.

22   Wing #5000 entered Primary Line # 1.

24   BU Ship #3100 completed in Final Line.

26   BU Ship #3200 entered Primary Line No. 4.

28   5000th Ship (BU 3154 - K.D. 5016) completed in Final Line. Wing #5200 started in Center Wing vertical department.

30   Total Shipments to date - Ford 3204, Douglas 937, Consolidated 939. Total for June - Ford 387, Douglas 66.

July

5   BU Ship No. 3300 entered Line No. 2. Wing # 5300 entered vertical fixture.

6   Master Change Ship K.D. 5251 removed from Final Assembly.

7   Last knock-down shipment to Douglas (K.D. 5224). Total shipped 954. BU Ship #3200 removed from Final Line.

10   Ship No. 3300 completed in Final Assembly Line.

11   Wing #5400 entered vertical fixture.

12   BU Ship No. 3400 entered line. Master Change Ship K.D. 5501 entered line.

13   Gen. H. H. Arnold at Willow Run.

17   BU Ship #3400 completed in Final Line.

18   Wing #5500 entered vertical fixture.

19   Master Change Ship No. K.D. 5501 completed in Final Assembly.

22   Master Change Ship No. K.D. 5751 entered Final Line.

25   Wing #5600 entered vertical fixture.

26   Ship #3600 entered Final Line.

29   Master Change Ship # K.D. 5751 removed from Final Line.

31   BU Ship #3600 completed in Final Line.

August

1   Wing #5700 started in vertical fixture. Single tail ship fixture and tool design begun [Model B-24-N].

2   Ship BU 3700 entered Primary Line No. 2.

7   Wing #5800 started in vertical fixture.

8   Ship # 3700 removed from Final Line.

10   Ship #3800 entered Line No. 2.

14   Wing #5900 started in vertical fixture.

15   Ship #3800 finished in Final Line. Master Change Ship # 6001 entered Line No. 2.

16   BU Ship #3900 entered Line No. 1.

19   First Ford Bomber (BU 3655) crashed near Almont, Michigan. Master Change Ship No. K.D. 6001 (BU 4107) completed in Final Line.

21   Wing #6000 started in vertical fixture.

22   BU Ship #3900 completed in Final Assembly.

24   Ship BU No. 4000 entered Line No. 1.

28   Wing #6100 started in vertical fixture.

29   Ship #4000 completed in Final Line.

31   BU Ship No. 4100 entered Line No. 2 of Primary Assembly. BU 4106 6000th Ship entered Line No. 4 of Primary Assembly. Total BU's for August - 432; Total to

date 4013. Grand Total (K.D.'s & BU'S) - 5906.

September

1   Five 9-hour days per week. 1st log run of altitude chamber.

7   Ship B.U/ 4100 completed in Final Assembly. Wing #6200 entered vertical fixture.

8   Master Change Ship BU 4357 (K.D. 6251) entered Line No. 2.

11   6000th ship off the Line.

14   Master Change Ship K.D. 6251 (BU 4357) removed from Final Line.

15   Employee's service garage in northwest corner of New Materials Bld.. started.

18   Wing #6300 entered vertical fixture.

19   BU Ship #4300 entered Line No. 1.

22   Master Change Ship K.D. 6501 (BU 4607) entered Line No. 3.

25   B.U 4400 entered Line No. 2.

26   Wing #6400 entered vertical fixture.

29   Total to date - Ford 4388, Douglas 954, CAC 939, Grand Total 6281; Monthly Total 375 Army Accept, 4357; Flyaways 4304.

October

2   Master Change Ship 4607 (K.D. 6501) completed in Final Line. Employee's service garage completed.

4   Ship #4500 entered Line 2 today. Wing #6500 started in vertical fixture.

6   Wing #6500 completed in vertical fixture.

10   Ship #4500 completed in Final Assembly.

11   Wing #6600 started in vertical fixture.

12   Ship #4600 entered Line No. 1.

13   Wing #6600 completed in vertical fixture.

18   Ship #4600 completed in Final Assembly.

20   Fixtures for Items 8 and 11 (radio operator's floor and truss bulkhead, Sta. 4.1) returned to Willow Run. Wing #6700 started vertical fixture. Ship #4700 entered Line No. 2.

21   Prototype ship fueled [Single tail].

22   First running of engines on Prototype.

23   Master Change Ship 4857 (K.D. 6751) entered Line No. 2. Work begun on construction of single tail cone fixture in Willow Run Pipe Shop.

24   Wing #6700 completed in vertical fixture.

27   Master Change Ship 4857 (K.D. 6751) completed in Final Assembly.

30   Installation work begun on tail cone fixture for prototype at K-20.

31   Ship #4800 entered Line No. 1. Wing #6800 started in vertical fixture. Production for October - 348; 23 ships over schedule. Total production to date including K.D.'s 6629. U.S. Ferrying Command set up offices in Winter Warm up Hangars.

November

2   Wing #6800 completed in vertical fixture.

3   BU ship #4800 completed in Final Assembly.

5   First flight of single tailed prototype of B-24.

8   Production schedule increased from 275 to 308 for month. Wing #6900 started in vertical fixture.

9   Ship BU #4900 entered Line No. 1 of Primary assembly. Lt. Col. H. S. Jones, Resident Officer, USAAF promoted to full Colonel.

10   Wing #6900 completed in vertical fixture.

13   Departments 940 A and B [fuselage] placed on one shift (days).

14   Master Change Ship BU #5107 (K.D. 7001 model B-24-M entered Line No. 1. BU Ship #4900 completed Final Assembly.

15   Prototype design [of single tail] accepted.

16   Wing #7000 started in vertical fixture.

17   B.U Ship #5000 entered Line No. 1.

19   First of four Sundays plant opened for public inspection.

20   Sixth War Loan Bond Drive started. First of fixtures for Item 8 and 11 returned to Willow Run.

21   Wing #7000 completed in vertical fixture.

24   Fixtures for Items 8 and 11 completely moved to Willow Run. Master Change Ship #5107 (K.D. 7001) completed in Final Assembly. BU Ship #5000 completed in Final Assemble.

27   Wing #7100 started in vertical fixture. George Hayes [badge #] *5172, General Shift Foreman, Dept 934 was first blood donor at Willow Run Blood Bank. Miss Helen Manchester, BK [badge #] 4206, Tubing Inspector was the first woman.

29   Wing #7100 completed in vertical fixture.

261

30   Production for November - 318. Total BU's to date, 5054. Total K.D. sets to date, 6982.

December

5   Master Change Ship K.D. 7201 (BU 5307) entered Line No. 1.

7   Col. H. S. Jones left to take up duties at Boeing Aircraft. Wing #7200 started in vertical fixture. #7000 ship compelted.

8   First B-29 to land at Willow Run Airfield. Ship #450233 first to enter experimental 7-station assembly line in Hangar #1.

9   BU Ship #5200 entered Line No. 1.

10   23,568 visitors attended Open House.

11   Wing #7200 completed in vertical fixture.

13   Master Change Ship K.D. 7201 (B.U 5307) completed in Final Assembly.

15   Property (33.279 acres) upon which Army cantonment stands was returned to Ford Motor Company together with buildings. Wing #7300 started in vertical fixture.

16   6th War Loan Drive oversubscribed 40.2%

18   Master Change Ship K.D. 7401 (BU 5507) entered Line No. 1. BU Ship No. 5300 entered Line No. 2. Wing #7300 completed in vertical fixture.

22   Master Change Ship K.D. 7401 (BU 5507) completed in Final Assembly.

26   Directive received from Wright Field requesting 206 ships without ball turrets by January 30, 1945. Also 55 ships without tail turrets to be delivered by Jan 30, 1945. Wing

#7400 started in vertical fixture.

29 Ship BU 5400 started in Line 2. Wing #7400 completed in vertical department.

30 Production for December - 296; 2 over schedule. Army acceptance - 296; Total BU's to date 5350; Total K.D. to date - 7242.

. . . . End of Chronological Data . . . .

On June 28, 1945 production ceased. The last bomber built was a B-24M, serial No. 44-51928. There were 8685 B-24s manufactured at Willow Run - 6792 were assembled by Ford, and 1893 were knock-downs (939 for Consolidated and 954 for Douglas).

On October 31, 1945, The Ford News Bureau, Administration Building, Dearborn, Michigan published the following notice.

The Ford Motor Wednesday concluded its maintenance operations at Willow Run, ending an occupancy that started with construction of the huge bomber plant in 1941.

Company officials said that on the final day there were approximately 1,400 persons on the payroll, but that after today there would be approximately 100. These employees will complete inventory, and handle property records. The remainder either will be transferred to other Ford plants, or their services terminated.

Production of B-24 bombers was started at Willow Run in 1942 and when the Air Force ordered output stopped 8685 of the four-engined bombers had been produced.

APPENDIX B

WILLOW RUN ENCYCLOPEDIA

The information presented here, as in Appendix A, is transcribed to preserve for Willow Run a nearly lost segment of its history.

-A-

ADMINISTRATION BLDG:
   242 feet long; 53 feet wide. Floor space (with garage) 36,730 square feet. Occupied in March, 1942.

AILERON: SEE "CONTROL SURFACE"
   Total area (each) 41.55 sq. ft.; Area aft of hinge, 64.3 sq. ft.; Covered with grade A Cotton; 6 coats of dope. Travel up 20° & down 20°.

AIR BASE, ARMY:
   Accommodations for 3700 men. Area - 270 acres. 12,000 men trained up until 7/1/44. Runways - 4,817 ft. long. Apron - 3325 ft. long x 416 ft. wide. 50 foot taxiways connect apron to runways 27R & 27L.

   School: At peak graduation 240 men every 4 days. Training in 4 echelons of aircraft maintenance. B-24 familiarization school under S. D. Mullikin. 1st & 2nd echelon trains crew chiefs, flight engineers & mechanic, largest of 3 schools. Peak enrollment -1500 students last summer [1944]. 3rd echelon, R-2800 School; maintenance & repair 2000 HP Pratt & Whitney engines. 4th echelon (supervision of Chevrolet) trains men to tear down and overhaul 1250 HP Pratt

& Whitney engines.

AIRPORT: SEE "LIGHTS, AIRFIELD"
Size - 1,434 acres. No. runways - 6. Length of longest run way 7,286 ft.; Length of shortest runway - 6,363 ft.; Runways 160 ft. wide; 7.7 miles long. Taxiways 80 ft. wide; 2.3 miles long. Area of runways & taxiways - 828,000 sq. yds. Area of aprons 320,000 sq. yds. Runways within Bomber Plant Airport total 35,830 ft. Army Air Base runways 4,817 ft.; Total 40,647 ft. Paving completed in 94 working days. Drain tile - 58 miles; sewer 16 miles; total 74 mi. Thickness of run-ways 8 inches in center; 6 inches on each side.

ALROK:
Coat good for 950 hours of exposure before corrosion. Operations: 1-Loading, 2-Cleaner, 3-Rinse tank, 4-Acid tank, 5-Rinse tank, 6-Alrok tank (Time 14 min.), 7-Rinse tank, 8-Rinse tank, 9-Alrok seal (Time 14 min.), 10 Rinse tank, 11-Hot water rinse, 12-Drier, 13-unloading. Baskets remain in dip approximately 3 min. ½ minute required for change (except 6 and 9 as indicated). Complete cycle approx. 1 hr. & 20 min. Overall length - 33 ft.; distance travelled - 66 ft. (Ford designed).

ALTIMETER:
Tested in airtight chamber. Dial measures heights in 20-ft. graduations. A diaphragm in the altimeter expands only 3/16 of an inch to move dial pointer a total of 21 ft. when registering height from sea level to 50,000 ft.

ALTITUDE CHAMBER:
(Hanger #1) From 70^0 above to 70^0 below in 8 min. From ground level to 40,000 ft. in 6 min. Dimensions 21x9 ft. Air lock 5 ft. Doors weigh 1 ton each. 500 HP cooling system.

WILLOW RUN

ANTI-ICING FLUID:

Consists of 85% Isopropyl-alcohol and 15% glycerine. Fluid piped from 1000 gal. tank near first overpass to gashouse. Distributed by slinger rings to leading edge of propeller blades. 22 gal. tank located in Bomb bay area of ship.

APRON:

(In Front of Hanger #1), 1500 ft. long. North end is 480 ft. wide. South end is 720 ft. wide. (In front of Hangar #2), 1200 ft. long & 740 ft. wide. Area - 320,000 sq. yds. (At Army Air Base), 3325 ft. long x 416 ft. wide.

AREA:

Plant & Flying Field, 1878 acres. Factory floor - 3,503,016 sq. ft. (80.25 acres). 1st floor area - 2,764,836 sq. ft. Mezzanine - 297,380 sq. ft Second floors, 440,800 sq. ft. Total floor area including hangars 4,734,617 sq. ft. (109 acres).

Adm. Bldg. & Garage, 36,730 sq. ft.; Personnel Bldg, 24,234 sq. ft; Hangar #1, 268,570 sq. ft; Hangar #2 235,174 sq. ft.; Winter Hangar, 38,822 sq ft.; New Mtls. Bldg., 577,120 sq. ft.; Airplane School, 49,494 sq. ft.; Sewage Disposal, 20,900 sq. ft.; Paint and Oil Storage, 12,000 sq. ft.; Transportation Garage, 9,900 sq. ft.; Dope and Paint Storage, 8,800 sq. ft.; Commissary, 13,398 sq. ft.; Gas House, 1500 sq. ft.; Incinerator, 1,420 sq. ft.; Power House, 47,409 sq. ft.; Total stock areas, 593,502 sq. ft. For a total of 17%. (not including New Mtls. Bldg.).

Summary of Stock: Tool Cribs & Stations, 38,982 sq. ft.; Purchased Finish Stores, 54,728 sq. ft.; Prod. Finished Parts, 143,796 sq. ft.; Component Items, 60,799 sq. ft.; G. F. E. Storage, 31,754 sq. ft.; Mtl. Review Cribs, 7,725 sq.

ft.; Shipping, 58,316 sq. ft.; Power, Mill-Wright & Misc, 61,687 sq. ft.; Total (ground Floor) 457,787 sq. ft.

Stock Areas - Mezzanine & 2nd Floors. #1: Abrasive Stk, 2240 sq. ft.; Area #4 Office 760 sq. ft.; Bbl Stk, 2785 sq. ft.; Elec. Stk. 5780 sq. ft.; Elec. Stk, 2000 sq. ft.; Elec. Drill Stk, 1280 sq. ft.; Electric Motor Storage, 1360 sq. ft.; Final Assembly Stk, 7200 sq. ft.; Fin. Pts. Storage, 7200 sq. ft.; Furniture Stk, 1210 sq. ft.; G.F.E. 2800 sq. ft.; G.F.E. 1395 sq. ft.; G.F.E. Office 780 sq. ft.; IBM Offices, 3900 sq. ft.; Mtl. Conservation Crib, 9040 sq. ft.; Mtl. Office, 19,040 sq. ft.; Millwright Stk, 990 sq. ft.; Misc. Stk, 9530 sq. ft.; Pneumatic Tool Stk, 950 sq. ft.; Prod Rubber Stk, 7480 sq. ft.; Purch. Pts. Stores, 2400 sq. ft; Purch. Pts. Stores, 3000 sq. ft; Purchased Pts. Store, 2430 sq. ft. Purch. Fin. Pts. 1280 sq. ft; Purch. Fin. Pts. 1500 sq. ft., Purch. Fin. Pts. 385 sq. ft.; Purch. Fin. Pts. 3000 sq. ft.; Purch. Fin. Pts. 900 sq. ft.; Purch. Fin. Pts. 440 sq. ft.; Purch. Fin. P.s. 900 sq. ft.; Purch. Fin. P.s.. 900 sq. ft. Stat. Stores, 3265 & 2880 sq. ft.; Stk. D. Crib, 680 sq. ft.; Stock Office, 1040 sq. ft.; Surplus Rough Stk, 4125 sq. ft.; Tool Crib, 250 sq. ft.; Tool Crib 510 sq. ft.; Tool Crib 510 sq. ft.; Trim Stk., 13,280 sq. ft.: Wire Stk, 810 sq. ft.

Total - 132,715 sq. ft.

Total Incl. Bal: . . . . 593,502 sq. ft.
New Mtls Bldg: . . . . 481,770 sq. ft.
Grand Total: . . . . 1,075,272 sq. ft.

ARMAMENT: SEE "TURRETS"

ASSEMBLY LINES: SEE "MOVEMENT OF"
Total length of all, 5,450 ft. Width of each bay 150 ft; height of bays 36 ft. Length of Primary Line, 720 ft. Distance from Transfer bay to east end of plant, 1440 ft. Dist-

267

ance from L-40 to exit doors - North bay, 2,185 ft., center bay, 1825 ft.; 4 primary lines of 14 stations each. When line between L-40 and station 15 regarded double, 680 ft. is to be added to ass'y line. North wall to plant exit 930 ft. Transfer Bay 16 ft. high, 40 ft .wide. Mezzanine between lines 15 ft. wide.

AUTOSYN:
Self-synchronous instrument to measure engine functions. Transmitted electrically from moving parts of engine, thus eliminating use of rigid and semi-rigid connections.

-B-

B-24 STUDIO:
Opened for broadcasting Nov. 3, 1943. Broadcast to 44 lunch rooms and eating places in plant and hangars, besides cafeterias, dining rooms and special outlets.

BATTERY:
Two 24-volt batteries in each ship. Wt. 75 lbs. ea. Electric needs supplied from 4 - 200 amp. generators. Batteries serve as emergency supply. Aux generator in each ship - 70 amp cap. driven by 3 HP motor.
Laboratory: 50 charging panels charge 50 batteries at one time. 500-gallon lead-lined acid tank. Carried in ship in rubber-lined, aluminum containers near bombardier's sta tion.

BOMBS:
The number of demolition bombs to be carried is interchangeable, & varies with the fuel load: 2-4,000 lb; 4-2000 lb; 8-1000 lb; 8-500 lb; 12-300 lb; 20-100 lb. Max. load to be carried by plane should not exceed 8,600 lbs. and is

determined by the amount of fuel carried.

BOTTOM TURRET: SEE "TURRETS"

BOXES:

Between 500 and 1200 assembled every month in carpenter shop.

BUILDINGS IN PROJECT:

Bomber Plant, New Mils. Bldg, Pump Hse #1. Scale House, Oil & Gas, Power Hse, Service Garage, Gas Station, Commissary, Pump Hse #2, Aviation Service, Dope and Paint, Hangar 1, Hangar 2, Warm-up Hangar, Apprentice School Personnel Bldg, Incinerators, Sewage Disposal, Sanitary Pump House, Compass Rose. Other facilities include: Sub-station #1 & 2, Cooling towers & buildings in the south yard used by contractors, warehouse etc.

-C-

CABLES IN SHIP:

226 cable assemblies per ship. Longest piece 53'3". Short 8". Seven types used.

CABLE:

Amt. required for cranes, conveyors, elevators, etc. 124,200 ft, ranging in size from 3/16" to 1'-1/8" in dia. Over 6000 ft. used for replacement every two wks. At this rate the total footage of cable, 124,200 ft., will be replaced every 344 working days. Daily use of rope - approx. 375 ft., or 4500 ft. every 2 weeks. The length of various slings on the equipment ranges from 6" to 200 ft.

CAFETERIA:

No. of people served: Breakfast, 800; Dinner, 1500; supper, 500. 23 cooks and bakers employed; 110 waiters. Dining

WILLOW RUN

Room: 250 served daily, 146 at one time.

CAMOUFLAGE:
Weight of paint per ship was between 90 and 120 lbs.
Increase in speed of non-camouflaged from 8-12 m.p.h.
No longer considered essential for effective ship protection.

CARBURETOR AIR TEMP. GAUGE:
Tells temperature of air.

CARGO BINS:
Made at Iron Mountain, [Michigan]. Load cap. - 1200 lb.
Assembled and used bins reconditioned in carpenter shop
at Willow Run.

CENTER WING SECTION: SEE ALSO "WING"
No. of diff. bulkheads, 27; No. of rivets, 78,606; No. of
bolts, 1,000; No. of individual pts. exclusive of rivets &
bolts 6,439. Furnished on two parallel lines, 468 ft. long.
Painting: Fuel cell area sprayed with spark inhibiting var-
nigh. Weight of entire wing group, 6652 lbs. When center
wing leaves vertical fixtures, ends are less than .010" of
being perfect.

CENTER WING FIXTURE: (Weight in pounds)

Overhead Det 30	R&L	(W&K)		12,023
Overhead Det 1	R&L	(W&K)		7,124
Overhead Det 2	R&L	(W&K)		5,015
Overhead Patt A	R&L			14,000
Overhead Patt B	R&L			2,984
Overhead Patt C	R&L			1,150
Overhead Patt D	R&L			1,294
Overhead Patt E	R&L			3,750

Overhead Patt G R&L	170
Overhead Patt H R&L	170
Center Beam	200
Center Post	200
Center Det	300
End "A" plates R&L	2,000
End Carriages	1,000
Center Carriages	200
Risers R&L	2,000
120 ft Drill Flaps	800
Patt E Plates & risers R&L	1,000
Other Details	1,500

TOTAL - Pound 56,880

28.44 Tons. Deduct approx. 2 tons for machining. No. of Fixtures - 40. Width of fixture - 60 ft. Time of assembly (Oct, 1944) 433 man hours.

CENTER WING MILLING MACHINE:

Operations:(1) Set up wing (2) Mill eight upper engine mount pads - 8 op. [operations] (3) Mill eight lower engine mount pads - 8 op. (4) Drill four 3/8" holes in ea. of the eight lower engine mount pads - 8 op. (5) Drill one 13/16" hole in ea. of the upper engine mount pads - 8 op. (6) Bore & spotface 4 landing gear needle bearings (2 on each side) 4 op. (7) Bore & spotface 6 landing gear bearings (3 on each side) 6 op. (8) Remove wing from machine. Total 42 operations. No. of men: 6 and 1 foreman. *Accuracy of:* Motor mount forgings vary from .003 of and inch to .020. Landing gear bearings are within 5 minutes of required angle.

Construction: Cast iron base made at Rouge Plant in

271

10 PCs, each weighing 12,500 lbs. Total wt. 125,000 lbs. Base resting on concrete slab 18" deep, 20' wide 70' long. Machine weighs 27 tons; cost $168,500. Designed by Ford engineers. [W. F. Pioch and John Mistele] Built by Ingersoll Milling Machine Co. Only one of its kind in existence. Record time for (machining) wing - 17 minutes.

CERROBEND: (Wood's Metal)
Used in Tube Bending department to keep tubing from crimping while being formed. 800 lbs. used ea. wk. Of this 720 lbs reclaimed. Melting point 160 degrees. Temperature kept at 200°.

CLEAN-UP: SEE ALSO "PAPER & SCRAP PAPER"
Staff -750. Amt. of soap used - 2 bbls liquid, 1-1/2 bbls powdered per wk. Also 1 bbl "Flux" (2 lbs dissolved in 14 qts. of water.) 20 men wash windows daily.

COLD HEADING: SEE "RIVETS"

COMMISSARY:
174 ft. long, 77 ft. wide. 13,398 sq. ft. area.

COMPASS ROSE:
Non-magnetic construction. Dia. 52' 2". Wt. 85 tons. Power unit - 30 H.P. motor. Only one of its kind in the country.

COMPRESSED AIR:
8 compressors in Power House - Capacity of ea. 1665 cu. ft. of air per min. 9,000,000 cu. ft. used daily. Highest used in one day - approx. 13,000,000 cu. ft.

CONTRACT ORDERS:
With Douglas (W 535-ac-18722), number of planes-

954, with Consolidated-Vultee (W535-ac-18723), 939 planes. With Government (W535-ac-21216) 8709 planes. Total 10,602.

CONTROL SURFACES: SEE "EMPENNAGE," "AILERONS," "RUDDER"

(Movable - ailerons, rudders, elevators) cloth-covered with grade "A" cotton to dampened vibration. Given 6 coats of dope (4 to 5 oz. per sq. yd.).

CONVEYORS:

136 separate conveyors in plant. 75 drive units Approx.- 5,000 feet of chain. 425 ft. in Press Shop, 260' in Cold Heading Dept. (Alrok). Approximately 4000 ft. interplant conveyors. 2-4 links removed in hot weather because of expansion of chain. Not replaced in winter because of wear on pins.

COST:

Of building & equipment - $103,000,000.

CRANEWAYS:

68 traveling units. 5 & 15 ton cap. Total length 29 mi. service walk used to repair craneways - 1½ mi., 309 lifts made in building bomber. Combined lifting capacity 520 tons.

CRASH TRUCKS:

Equipped with ten 100 lb. cylinders of CO_2 under 850 lbs. pressure. Also 200 gal. per minute water pump. Equipped with 2-way radio.

CREW OF B-24:

Crew composed of 10 men: Pilot, co-pilot, bombardier, navigator, radio operator, 5 gunners.

WILLOW RUN

CRIBS:

Main Floor-Assembly area: 7 Mtl. Review Cribs ranging from 6x19 to 20x50 ft. Total area - 3,975 sq. ft. 4 Purch. Fin. Stores Cribs ranging from 40x80 ft. to 90x340 ft. Total area - 63,303 sq. ft. 11 G.F.E. Stk areas and cribs ranging from 15x15 to 135x140 ft. Total area of 30,342 sq. ft. 79 Stk Cribs and areas ranging from 7x18 to 75x180 ft. Total area of 186,530 sq. ft. 46 Tool cribs ranging from 5x15 to 30x200 ft. Total area of 24,447 sq. ft. Millwright & Power stk area - 4,910 sq. ft.

Main floor - Manufacturing area: 4 Mtl Review cribs ranging from 6x9 ft. to 14x41 ft. Total area - 35,144 sq. ft. 18 Tool cribs ranging from 7x7 ft. to 40x49 ft. Total area - 11,879 sq. ft.

Balconies & 2nd Floors (both areas)

Stock (Rough Finished)	75,624 sq. ft.
Tool Cribs	7,830 sq. ft.
G.F.E.	840 sq. ft.
Stationery Stock	10,520 sq. ft.
Misc & Abrasive	11,660 sq. ft.
Office Space	18,568 sq. ft.
(Subtotal)	125,042 sq. ft.

Grand total area cribs in main building: 487,186 sq. ft.

CYANIDE PLANT:

Average daily flow - 263,633 gals. 3 reaction tanks, 26,000 gal. capacity. Only one of its kind in country.

-D-

DEGREASER:

Detrex Solvent Machine (Press Shop) Trichlorethylene or "Peracolor" used. Washes stock up to 10 ft. in length.

APPENDIX B

15 degreasing units in plant consisted of 13 vapor spray units, 1 vapor slush unit, 1 conveyor type unit. Also, 3 stills to reclaim solvent. Temp. of solvent 188° F.

DECENTRALIZATION:
To Jan 1944, 3,477 sub-assemblies & parts moved outside W.R.

DIES:
Total made since plant started - 29,124. Request for work order for first die filed March 24, 1941. Dies in production at Willow Run 8,721; outside plants 6,536; Salvaged or in storage 13,867. (12-14-44)

DOORS: SEE ALSO "HANGAR"
Pre-flight lines - Wt. 35 tons ea. 400 lbs. added to counter weights when painted. Width - 143'9". Height 33' 1 7/8". Same dimensions apply to emergency doors at east end of [Ships] Hospital area.

DOPE ROOM: SEE ALSO "CONTROL SURFACES"
Temp. of 80° F. and relative humidity of 50% plus or minus 10% required at all times. Ten air changes per hour for entire room. Three 100-ton refrigeration units to dehumidify the air.

DRAW BENCH:
265 machines. 185,000 pieces delivered to inspection daily. 6228 pieces per ship. 3700 separate parts formed. Active rolls -300 for approx. 250 jobs. 260,000 ft. of "Y" stock rolled daily. About 5,000,000 pieces rolled, formed, stretched or pierced each month.

DUAL TACHOMATER INDICATOR:
Indicates RPM of each engine by means of autosyn., and

aids in Synchronizing the engines.

-E-

ELECTRIC EYE:

Used for opening doors. Also on X-ray machine in Metallurgical Lab to shut off machine when foreign object gets in way.

ELECTRIC WIRING:

Approx 5 mi. in each ship. Wire cut in approx 3,000 pieces varying in length from 8" to 32'. 500 sets of harness. Inside ringout: 2 girls, 33 circuits, time 2 hours. Circuit Code Prefix Letters: A-Heater, B-Bomb, C-Propeller, D-Hydraulic, E-External Lights, G-instruments, K-Automatic Pilot. L-Lights (Internal), M-landing Gear, P-Power, R-Radio, S-Started, T-Engine, H-Ignition , V-Misc.

EMPENNAGE: SEE "CONTROL SURFACES"

Height 12 ft. Width tail fin to tail fin, 26'. Area of elevator, 67.06 sq. ft. Area of fin, 123 sq. ft. Area of Rudder aft of hinge, 64.3 sq. ft. Wt. of tail group, 906 lbs. No. Rivets, 14,651. In landing, tail may whip down from 2-4 in. Built to withstand 25 times force of gravity (25Gs). Perfect landing takes 1 or 2 Gs. The highest known was 22 Gs on landing.

ENGINES:

1250-HP Pratt & Whitney; air-cooled; 14 cylinders. Held in place by 4, 5/8 inch, nickel steel bolts. Ring-out, 15 circuits on each engine. Wt. of 4 engines (accessories), 1559 lbs. Weight of engine nacelles - 1745 lbs. Before dress-up each engine weighs about 1500 lbs. Wt. of engine installed, 6050 lbs.

Gasoline consumption at cruising speed per engine, 45 gal/hr At max. speed, 95 gal/hr. At take-off, 110 gal/hr. cruising speed 180 mph at 10,000 ft. Max. speed 260 mph. Landing speed 96 mph.

Bolts: The four aircraft bolts are std. p.s.. and are referred to by engineers as AN 10-71 (upper-5/8"dia. by 7-1/8" length) and AN 10-47 (lower 5/8" dia. by 4 & 7/8" length). They are tested for tensile strength and rated 29,670 lbs. The yield strength is 23,740. Made of Cadmium plated nickel steel.

Mounts: Made of chrome-moly steel. Inside of tubing flushed with linseed oil to prevent corrosion caused by oxidation.

ENGINE "DRESS-UP": SEE "WEIGHT OF SHIP"
At Lincoln plant. Wt. - 780 lbs. includes accessories and cowling, flaps, nose ring, air duct, etc.

ENGINE FUNCTION:
#1 Engine - Air pressure & vacuum; #2 engine - supply gasoline vapor, alternate for air pressure and vacuum; #3 engine - supercharger to 6 heaters in ship. Operated hydraulic system; #4 engine - no extra functions.

-F-

FABRIC:
Over 380 yards of 1850 different cuttings used in each ship. Amt. waterproofed, 57 yds. Curtains of coated sateen, 47 yds. 35 pads over protruding pts. Kapok replaced by "Fiber-glass" and later "milkweed". 59 strap assemblies. Fiber-glass also used for protective plates on which fuel cells rest to keep them off stringers. (Ford developed).

WILLOW RUN

FIN: SEE ALSO "EMPENNAGE"
Area, total - 139 sq. ft.

FIRE EXTINGUISHER (Ship):

For engine protection. consisted of two 11 lb. steel cylinders containing CO_2 gas under 1800 lbs. pressure PSI.

FIRE PROTECTION: SEE ALSO "CRASH TRUCKS"
51,212 sprinkler heads; 128 sprinkling systems; 135 trained men; 1200 auxiliary; (sub-station - airport, 17 men). No. fire extinguishes, 2,182; fire hydrants, 91; fire alarm boxes, 183; standing pipes, 126; hose, 21,825 ft.; deluge sprinkling system, 16 gal/min over 10 sq. ft. under 75 lbs pressure. Water supply - east tank (407,000 gals).

FIRST AID:
25 full time first aid men; 110 emergency stretchers. 6 First Aid Stations in plant.

FIXTURES:
Total fixtures ordered, 19,002; in production, 10,915; at Willow Run, 5,867. Salvage or in storage, 8,067 (12-14-44).

FLAPS:
Raised at 750 lbs pressure. Travel of flaps (Max) - 40°. Lowered at 450 lbs pressure. Cannot be lowered if ship is flying above 155 mph. When extended, lift of wing is increased 55%, drag 70%. Wt. - 125 lbs. each. Area, total - 144.1 sq. ft.

FLIGHT: (Dec 25, 1944)
Est number of miles flown 3,747,400. No. of hours flown

18,737. Initial flights 4,149. Army acceptance 4147. Deliveries 4113. Shortest time ship completed through process from factory to delivery - 44 hours, March 21 - 24, 1944. 73,669 flights without field mishaps.

FLOORS:
Area all buildings (total) 4,734,617 sq. ft. (109 acres). Maintenance - one carload of [wooden] blocks installed every month. Blocks rest over an 8 inch layer of reinforced concrete.

FLUORESCENT LAMPS: SEE "LIGHTS"

FREE AIR TEMP GAUGE:
Tell pilot when ice is likely to form.

FUEL CELLS:
No. in ship - 12 in center wing section. Cap. 2,372 gal. 3 in ea. of two outer wing panels. Cap 348 gals. Total cap all cells, 2720 gals. Wt. of fuel appx. 16,320 lbs. Total weight of cells (empty) 2468 lbs. Cap. of cells in outer wing panels - 58 gals. ea. 160 cells installed in center wing panels every 18 hour working day. Three-layer self sealing construction, built around plaster of Paris mold. Access Doors: two on under side of C. W. section to install and repair fuel cells. Ea. held in place by 750 screws.

FUEL FOR SHIPS: SEE ALSO "WEIGHT"
Approx 30,000 gal of 100 octane gasoline and 1100 gal of oil put in ships every day before deliver to Flight. Stored in 6 - 25,000 gal. underground tanks. Oil & Gas House: 162 ft. long 67 ft. wide. 10,080 sq. ft. Gas Handling System: 60,000 gals. oil and 150,000 gals of

gas. 20 min to gas ship and 41 other operations in gassing area. Said to be world's largest gas station.

FURNACES:
9 nitrate furnaces. 7 heat treat furnaces.

FUSELAGE:
Dimensions: Length 67'4". Height 10'5". Width 7'5". No. Rivets, 126,651. Top fuselage to ground, 12'1". Top of tail to ground, 17'11". Distance between inboard propellers tips and fuselage, 23'1/2". Wt. of fuselage group 3,407 lbs. NOTE: Fuselage length as given is from actual measurements of ship on ass'y line. Loft measurement is 805.54 inches. (Furnishing Aft Panels): Length of conveyor, approx. 400 ft'. Travel time, 1.8 ft per. min. capacity 42 panels in 9 hour shift.

(Nose Panels): Conveyor length, 480 ft. Rate of travel, 1.97 ft. per min. Maximum tolerance of 1/16" for mating center wing section.

-G-

GARAGE (ADMINISTRATION):
223 ft. long, 57 wide.

GAS (Heating):
Consumption - 10,000 cu. ft. daily.

GASOLINE & OIL: SEE "FUEL"

GASOLINE CONSUMPTION OF B-24: SEE "ENGINES"

GAUGES: (INSPECTION)
15,000 used on ship.

APPENDIX B

GENERATORS: (PLANE)

4 - 200 amp generators on ea ship. Enough electricity can be generated by these 4 generators to supply electricity for four average homes Auxiliary: Driven by a 3 HP gasoline motor. Wt. - 122 lbs. RPM's 25,000. Capacity, 70 amperes, and 27 volts.

GROUND MAINTENANCE:

9442 scrubs, 274 trees planted, 53 tons grass seed.

GUNS: SEE "MACHINE GUNS"

GUN BUTT:

400 cu. ft. of cement used for construction. Walls 20" thick. 65,000 rounds of ammunition fired every mo. Approx size - 30x40 ft; 30 ft. high; (310 cu. yds. of sand). Every 50th ship, guns fired while ship is in air. Every 300th ship-bomb drop test. Guns of every 5th ship test-fired at gun butt. Spent bullets recovered from sand by electro-magnet.

GYRO HORIZON INDICATOR:

Tells pilot whether ship is level.

-H-

HANGAR NO I:

Length, 1,255 feet 8 inches. Depth, 162 feet. Height 79 feet. 268,570 sq. ft. Eight (8) bays. Doors, 144 ft. wide by 42 ft. high, moved by motors of 10 HP. Wt. 45 tons.

Dormitory: 36 beds, 4 private beds. Function: Ships prepared for delivery and delivered from here.

HANGAR NO II:

Length 1203 ft. Depth, 161 ft. 8 bays. Doors, 144 ft.

281

wide by 42 ft. high moved by motors of 10 HP. Wt. 45
tons. Function: Inspection and preparation for initial
flight. Heating: 4 heating plants at rear of building.

HEATERS IN SHIP:
Number of 6.

HEATING & VENTILATION; SEE ALSO "POWER HOUSE":
"REFRIGERATION", "TOWERS, COOLING"
Fan capacity. 5,500,000 cu. ft. (Equal to heating 3600 - 5
room houses). No. of supply fans 201 - Capacity 7,500,000
cu. ft/min. No. of exhaust fans, 637. Capacity 6,000,000
CFM. No. of condensate pumps 50. No. air washers, 10.
Hot water piping ranges in size from 18" in dia. to 3/4" and
pressure from 250 lbs. Three 100-ton refrigeration units to
dehumidify the air. 1700 radiators, 2500 steam traps.

HEAT TREAT:
No. of parts treated daily 12,800 lbs of rivets. 250,000
ft. drawn sections. 55,500 misc. parts. Press shop
heated to 925° av. Range between 910 &1010 depending on
type of material. Recirculated hot air furnace - electric,
Ford - Holcraft. Only one of kind in aircraft industry.

HOSPITAL:
8 doctors, 1 dentist, 44 registered nurses, 25 First Aid
men Area, 8560 sq. ft. No. of cases handled in
1943, 819,779. Men's ward, 6 beds, 4 cots. Women's
ward, 10 beds, 6 cots. First Aid Stations located at: #1-J-7,
#2-B-12, #3-G-18, #4-L-38, #5-G55, #6-L-66.

HYDRAULIC ASSEMBLY:
97 assemblies in each ship. 1800 made daily. 43,200 per
mo. Cap. of system in ship 18 gals. 850 PCs. in system
Wt. 466 lbs. Accumulators: 10" dia. press, 900-1050

lbs. PSI. Fluid circulated by 7 piston displacement pump driven by #3 engine. Output Approx. 7 gals per min. If it fails, electrically operated pump is mounted on right bomb bay side panel for use. If it fails, hand pump is mounted on floor beside co-pilot.

HYDRO PLANT:
Constructed in Spring, 1940 to make car locks and keys. Now 80 different parts machined for bomber. 640 casting made each day. 55 employees. Power: 60.3% water wheel, 29.1% steam, 10.6% generator set.

-I-

I.B.M.: (INTERNATIONAL BUSINESS MACHINES)
Located at B-18, 2nd balcony. 56 employed on 2nd shifts. Equipment includes: three, 405 alphabetic printers; 3 summary reproducers, 5 sorters, 2 collators, 3 multipliers, 20 key punches, and 2 interpreters. Daily production report for Time office, Production Inspection and area offices. Report gives totals of production by part no., by departments and by division. Also handles all monthly scheduling for production and C.M.P. on six month basis for Material Department, showing production figures and balance to be built. Material Review Report, daily for material Control, Salvage and Time office.

ICEBOXES: SEE ALSO "RIVETS"
No. in plant approx., 100. Temp 10° to 20° below zero. 2 days supply of rivets kept on hand (Press Shop). Temperature 10 to 20 degrees below zero. Large Iceboxes 20 degrees below zero. To keep rivets from age hardening.

INGERSOL MACHINE: SEE ALSO "CENTER WING MILL-
ING MACHINE" & "FINAL MACHINING UNIT"

INSPECTION:
Inspection Plates: No. on ship, 120. Inspectors: No. of
(company), 1805, Army 109 (1-1-45). 15,000 inspection
gauges used in building bomber. No. of inspectors (August
1944), 1956.

INSTRUMENTS:
No. on instrument panel only 54. (Does not include
switches or levers).

INTERVALOMETER:
Releases bombs from racks in sequence. Operates
through solenoid in bomb selector panel. Bombs can be
spaced to drop from 7 to 750 feet apart. Can release
from 1 to 20 bombs per second.

-K-

"KD" SHIPS: SEE ALSO "SHIPPING"
Douglas 954; Consolidated 939

-L-

LABORATORY: (Metallurgical)
2 General Electric X-Ray machines used to detect flaws
in castings. 3000 ft. of X-Ray film can be developed daily
in dark room. Apparatus for testing tensile strength -
200,000 lbs. capacity. Has complete chemical
laboratory. Special research.

LANDING GEAR:

(Main) - Each main strut weights approx ½ ton 4 ways to lower: hydraulic, electric motor to drive pump, hand operated pump, emergency gear box. Can be retracted in 22 seconds under pressure of 1,000 lbs. PSI and lowered and locked in 44 seconds under 800 lbs. pressure. Total landing gear wt. 3002 lbs. Oleo strut max. extension, 13". Operative extension - 10 ½". Operative compression 2 ½.

LANDSCAPING:

No. of trees, 274. No. shrubs, 9,442.

LAYOUT, PLANT:

Plant layout board, 36" x 48", painted black. 1/4" inch-to-the-foot scale. 157 boards comprise main floor layout for plant, 23 for balconies, 11 for hangar, 7 for school, 1 for Personnel Building.

LIGHTS, AIRFIELD:

1 airport substation; 1 hangar sub-station; 1 control panel (control Tower) for airport lighting; 1 rotating beacon; 1 code beacon (flashes WR in code); 1 ceiling projector; 1 portable traffic signal; 2 search lights (in control tower); 143 building obstruction lights; 64 field obstructions; 113 boundary lights (outline the field); 37 taxi lights (flush & cone-mounted); 12 blue flasher lights; 56 hangar floodlights; 84 field floodlights; 379 contact lights (outline runways); 36 green flush type range lights (installed on concrete and end of each runway); 55 yellow range lights (mounted on conical bases); 12 "Green Arrow & Red Cross" landing signals; 2 wind "tees"; 12 field vaults (miniature substations,

housing transformers, relays, etc for field lighting); 1 pedestal vault; 12 ground traffic signals (a 3-light signal at tend of each runway).

LIGHTS, LANDING:
Two 600 watt retractable lamps.

LIGHTS, PLANT:
Fluorescent, 104,000 units, 76,000 fixtures; 152,000 tubes, 4' long.

LIGHTS, SHIP
Ultraviolet type used to eliminate glare. Instruments made very sensitive to this type of light by use of special radium paint on dials. 6 ultraviolet type and 16 regular (including recognition lights) in each ship. Does not include bulbs behind instrument panel.

LOCKERS:
No. in plant 54,000.

LOFTING:
Done on 16'x64', 16 gauge steel surfaced tables. Surface painted with white paint. Deviated limits caused by atmospheric conditions reduced to one 1/100th of an inch by using steel rather than wood-surfaced tables. Division area, 340'x30'.

LUNCH ROOMS:
No. in plant and hangars, 24. Does no include tables set up between lockers.

-M-

MACHINE GUNS:
Ten .50 caliber, M2 Browning. Air-cooled, recoil operated,

belt fed. Ammunition fed to guns by metallic link disintegrating belt. Ammunition can be fed from either side by repositioning block ass'y. Dimensions: 56 ½ x 5; 7/8 x 3 & 7/8 inches. Wt: approx. 65 lbs. Fires 700-850 rounds per minute 15 to 20 rounds bursts with one min. interval between bursts. Muzzle velocity - 2800 ft./sec. Has recoil buffer to help absorb shock. Manufactured by Frigidaire & Colt Fire Arms Co. Shipped in individual boxes from Army depot.

MACHINE SHOP:

500 different parts machined. Almost 25,000 parts per day. ½ acre; 220 machines (lathes, drill presses, screw machines etc.). First part produced at Willow Run in Machine Shop - 12/8/41.

MAGNYSN RADIO COMPASS:

Operates from transformer located in wing. Makes possible following radio beam.

MAIL:

1943 avg. of 10 2/3 mail sacks received each day. Outgoing Aug: 13 1/3 sacks daily.

MARKINGS:

Total number on ships - 1,233.

MATERIAL IN PLANE:

Aluminum alloys - 85%; Steel - 13%; magnesium - .33%; Brass-copper-bronze -66% Rubber-glass-plastic - 1.01%; Total 100 %. Flat sheets 48"x144" or 36"x144". Special size 48"x 234".

WILLOW RUN

MATERIAL CONSERVATION:(Started W. R. June 28, 1943)

Month	Engineering Changes	Reclaim	Total	Men
July	63,894	13,450	77,344	35
Aug.	107,545	4,048	111,593	42
Sept.	114,588	7,882	122,470	45
Oct.	58,306	24,539	82,845	48
Nov.	78,360	8,726	87,086	49
Dec.	145,253	14,510	159,763	53

MATERIAL IN ONE BOMBER:

To build bomber takes enough aluminum for 55,000 coffee percolators; enough alloy steel to make 6,800 electric irons; and steel in 160 washing machines; enough rubber to recap 800 automobile tires; and enough copper for 550 radio receivers. (From "Flying", October, 1943).

MATERIAL FLOW:

Main Assembly: Shortages occur when float is below 200 ships. Small Parts shortages occur when float is below 600 ships. Rough stock shortage below 600.

"MERRY-GO-ROUND": (Pilot's Floor)

No. of cars, 30. Length of circuit, 400 ft. No. of stations, 30; Time to complete circuit - approx. 18 to 36 hours. (2½" to 6" per min.). Number of installations approx. 190. Driven by 1 hp electric motor. Ratio geared from 1800 to 1 to 900 to 1.

METALLURGICAL LABORATORY: SEE "LABORATORY"

APPENDIX B

MIDGETS:
Number employed at Willow Run, 10. Install stiffener rods in auxiliary fuel cells. Also serve as inspectors and to attach outer wing assembly to center wing at splice joint.

MONORAILS:
Length in Manufacturing Building, 12 miles. All buildings 18 miles.

MOVEMENT OF ASSEMBLY LINES:
Line originally planned as 8 hour station, 1-12 inclusive. 4 hour stations 13-28 inclusive. Time reduced to under 4 hours in stations 1-14 inclusive, and 2 hours in stations 15-28. Master control panel located at east end of balcony at K-54 and H-54. Schedule of movement regulated by Final Assembly Office. Based on production requirements.

-N-

NACCANOL:
Trade name for solution used to determine leaks around oxygen line connections. Foams when leak is present.

NOSE TURRET: SEE "TURRETS"

NEW MATERIALS BUILDING:
520x1028 ft., floor space - 577,120 sq. ft. Started June, 1943. Completed December 1943. 9 furnaces to heat building. 5 stock departments; Shearing Department; Shipping; Salvage; Material Conservation; Carpenter Shop; Employee's Garage; Receiving Inspection; Maintenance; Blueprint Crib. All component items, such as outer wings, stabilizers, rudders, fins, trailing edges, bomb bay doors, and bottom panels are shipped. 703

boxes ranging from a gross weight of 475 lbs. to 4000 pounds are export packed to Army specifications. More than 31 carloads shipped each month. Emergency kits packed for overseas shipment, average 2-10 boxes daily. Rough stock in the form of sheet aluminum, coils, extrusions, wire, bar steel, and sheet steel shipped to Ford plants, outside aircraft plants and South America. The Material Conservation department ships out surplus stock that is available to other aircraft plants.

-O-

OIL:

Amount used for tool maintenance per week, 3745 gallons; 300 pounds of grease. *In ship* 142 gallon tank for each engine.

OIL SEPARATORS:

No. at Willow Run, 2 (located at east and west ends of factory). Used to separate oil from water before latter is emptied into Willow Creek. Water entering detention basin contains 16.3 P.P.M. (parts per million). When it leaves the basin its content is 2.4 P.P.M. The oil removed equals approx. 85% of original reading. Water kept in detention basin for 1½ hrs. Capacity of oil separator - 1000 gals. per minute, in dry weather about 400.

OUTER WING PANELS: SEE ALSO "WING"

Length, 27½'. Wt. 725 lbs. No. of rivets, 22,844. No. of bolts to attach to center wing section, 120. 15 bulk heads. 13 skin sections. Manufactured at Highland Park.

OXYGEN:

Lines - 450 lbs. pressure in tanks. 50 lbs while on lines

to keep out moisture. 45,000 - 50,000 cu. ft. used daily in testing equipment in ship under 425 lbs. pressure. Valves in lines freeze if more than .0002% moisture in oxygen. System at plant: 24 thirty-foot cylinders, each holding approx. 3300 cu. ft., in vault between assembly building and hangar. Piped to 21 points in plant. Tank truck brings liquid oxygen; temperature -183°F. Warning signal when pressure drops 450 to 110 lbs. PSI in tanks on ship.

-P-

PAINT:

Paint dries in 3 minutes by use of infrared lamps. 30 diff. kinds of paint; 95% made at Highland Park. 8 spray booths plus main and camouflage booth. 3000 signs and decals per ship. Last camouflaged ship #3844 (KD-3190). Paint & Dope Room: 324 ft. long x 19 ft. wide. Spray booth 150 x 80 ft. with 36 ft. ceiling.

PAINT MAINTENANCE:

Area to cover equal to 5 foot fence 236 miles long. Approx. 4,859,000 sq. ft. covered.

PAPER TOWELING: "SEE SCRAP PAPER"

3½ carloads every month. Wrapping 1 carload. Tissue, 176 cartons of 50 rolls each , per month.

PARKING LOTS

Capacity all lots - 15,300 cars.

PARTS: B-24-J (5/23/44)

	Unlike	Total
GK (ex. sp.std. pts.)	26,389	70,278
Spec Std. Pts.	310	17,840

WILLOW RUN

	Unlike	Total
Std. pts. (except rivets)	2,970	63,130
Misc. pts. not in above groups	200	987
All pts.	29,869	152,235
Rivets	519	313,237
Grand Total	30,388	465,427

(GFE & purchased assemblies counted - 1 part each.)

PARTS - ASSEMBLY
   12,000 pieces. per day (Dept. 932); 4,500 per day (Dept. 934).

PATTERN SHOP:
   Wood models made from lofting specifications. 25,000 board feet of lumber used monthly. Mahogany used for master forms, pine and spruce for others. 34 pattern makers. Shop - 200 x37 feet.

PERSONNEL BUILDING:
   46x209 ft. Floor space - 24,234.

PIPING:
   Waste & soil pipe, 17 miles. Drinking water piping (Mfg. Bldg.), 5½ miles. Process piping, 15 miles. Steam piping, 50 mi. Fiber conduit, 110 miles. Steel conduit, 580 miles. Conductor pipe, 6 miles.

PILOTS:
   At W. R. 10/15/44, 51 including Chief Pilot and Co-pilot.

PILOT'S FLOOR: SEE "MERRY-GO-ROUND"

PITOT TUBE:
   Records air speed of ship. Has self-contained electrical

heating element to prevent internal ice formation.

PLANT CONSTRUCTION QUANTITIES:

Brick - 10,000,000 pieces; Concrete - 317,000 cubic feet; Gunite - 350,000 sq. ft.; Steel-sash 120,000 sq. ft.; Paint 200,000 gal; Steel - 38,000 tons; Electric wire & cable 2,000 miles; Fibre conduit -110 miles; Steel conduit - 580 miles; Wood blocks - 16,000,000 pieces; Conductor pipe - 6 miles; Roof sumps - 6 miles; Monorails (Mfg. Bldg.) 12 miles; Monorails (All bldg.) - 18 miles; Fences - 11 miles; Sheet metal - 2,400 tons; Glass panes 28855 (30 different types).

PLANT DIMENSIONS:

Length - 3,200 ft. (east to west); Width 1,277 ft.; Area floor space (plant only) - 3,503,016 sq. ft.; Main bldg. floor space - 80 1/4 acres; Roof only - 67 acres. If west wall were held solid, east end would be shoved out 5 ft. 6 inches by hot weather. Prevented by 7 copper expansion joints; 2 across width of plant.

PLANT PROTECTION:

No. of men - 335; No. cars (with 2-way radios) - 8.

PLATING:

Cadmium - 6 plating tanks; including 4 zinc, 1 cadmium, 1 dichromate. 38 cleaning tanks.

PLEXIGLASS:

30 PCs. in ship. Temp. for forming, 250°. One-half as heavy as glass, about as hard as copper; shatterproof. Make equivalent needs of approximately 35 ships per day. Dipped in Protectokote to protect against scratches (Ford developed).

WILLOW RUN

POWER PLANT:

Requirements of entire plant approximately 13,200 KWH. Supplied by Willow Run Power Plant - 5,000 KWH (remainder furnished by Detroit Edison Co.). *Power House:* Size of 160 x130 feet. Boilers-four 870 HP each (fuel oil). Oil consumption of boilers average winter day, 35,000 gallons. Area - 47,409 sq. ft.

PRESS SHOP:

345 presses including 13 hydraulic presses ranging from 100 to 1000 ton capacity. Mechanical presses range from 30 to 750 ton capacity. 56 heavy presses 150 to 1,000 ton capacity. 109 punch presses (Ferracutes, Niagaras, Clevelands). Weight of 1,000 ton presses = 350 tons. Amount of oil used in large hydraulic presses as a hydraulic agent = 1500 gallons. 120,000 pieces processed per day.

PROPELLER:

Diameter, 11'6". Weight of including governor, (all four) = 1892 pounds. Number balanced, 65 every 18 hours. Balancing standards aligned within .003". Blades made of drop-forged aluminum alloy. Hub of steel.

-Q-

QUANTITIES: SEE "PLANT CONSTRUCTION"

-R-

RADIO:

Standard Equipment: 3 command receivers, 2 command transmitters, 1 liaison receiver and transmitter, 7 tuning units, 1 marker beacon receiver, 1 radio compass receiver,

1 inter-plane phone system, localizer receiver. 11 stations. Liaison set used between ship and base. Range to 1000 miles; 2 antennae. Localizer receiver used for blind landing. Teardrop houses loop antenna which operates automatic radio compass. In response to radio signal, loop rotates and positions itself and compass dial indicates di rection of signal.

RADIO FACILITIES: (Airfield)

1 radio Range (beacon) Station (Stony Creek and Willis Rd.); 1 Radio Marker Beacon Station (Stony Creek and Willis Rd.); 1 Radio Transmitter Station (near Hangar No. 2) which includes: 1 traffic Control transmitter (245 KC); 1 Army Acceptance transmitter; 1 U.H.F. transmitter (FM); 1 State Police transmitter (F.M.); 1 Plant Protection trans- mitter (F.M.); 2 V.H.F. Acceptance transmitters; 1 Radio Compass Calibrating transmitter (360° from compass rose & operated from it); 1 Radio Receiving station containing 14 fixed receivers.

Acceptance Control Station: Operating controls for all all transmitters and receivers; recorder for all conver- sations.

Control Tower: Operating controls for traffic dispatching and police transmitters & receivers.

RATE OF CLIMB INDICATOR:

Registers rate by change in barometric pressure.

RATE DEPARTMENT:

18 checkers.

REFRIGERATION:

Refrigeration equipment in service, 2,035 tons.

RIVETS:

Rivets required to build major sections:

Total. 242,752
Center Wing. 78,606
Outer Wing. 22,844
Fuselage. 126,651
Tail. 14,651

Note: The foregoing does not include all the rivets on the B-24. The total as given by the Material Control Department is 313,237. Made daily at W. R., Approx. 7,000,000; 520 different rivets; 750 to the pound. From 1/16 to 2 ½ inches long. Fastest machines produce 400 per min. 313,000 rivets per ship 686 lbs. 28 cold heading machines; 8 diameters, 100-400 per min. Icebox type - 17S. Icebox rivets shear strength is 30,000 lbs. per sq. in. Non-icebox 25,000 lbs. per sq. in. Lightest rivet weight .00005 lbs. Heaviest Rivet weights .05 lbs. No. rivets made in 1944 was, 1,921,962,810.

Riveting Equipment: No. squeeze guns at W. R., 2,889. Loaned out, 1838. Total = 4,719 [?]. *Rivet Time to Drive:* Two teams of riveters drove 6,975 rivets in 9 hours.

ROADS:

Length of plant roads, 8-1/2 miles (concrete) Length of patrol roads around airport 3 miles. Length of gravel roads in salvage yards, 3/4 mile Area of concrete roads and pavement, 229,000 sq. yds.

ROOF AREA:

Total for all bldgs. - 2,750,000 sq. ft.

ROPE: SEE "CABLE"

RUDDER: SEE ALSO "CONTROL SURFACES"
Total area both - 65 sq. ft. Travel each way 20°.

RUNWAYS:
Number - six (6). Length of longest ((L9) - 7,366 ft. Length of shortest (L4) - 6,510 ft. Width - 160 ft. Center of SW & NE runways on radio beam from airport range station. Runways numbered according to compass head ings. Last digit is dropped from figure. Numerals in con crete 50 ft. long at end of each runway with a circle of concrete around each. At intersection of runways are 10 acres of concrete. Area runways & taxiways 828,000 sq. yds. Inside W. R. airport area - 35,830 ft. Army Air Base 4,817 ft. (7.7 Mi). Thickness of 8" tapered to 6". If runways of airfield were placed end to end, they would make a highway (2 lanes) 40' wide 31 mi. long or a single highway 62 miles long.

-S-

SALVAGE: SEE "SCRAP"

SAWS:
Average 200 circle saws and 30 hand saws a day sharp-ened. 25,000 ft. of band saw blades used every month. Two plants, Manchester and Highland Park send saws to Willow Run for sharpening.

SCALES:
134 scales ranging in size from 100 lbs. to 60 ton capacity.

SCHOOL, AIRPLANE:
Trained 50,000 students up to November 1944. No. of classroom instructors - 18; on production - 11. Area

of school building 49,494 sq. ft. 410 ft long, 58 feet wide. Laboratories include electrical, radio, hydraulics, chemistry, instrument and research. Facilities included library, auditorium (seats 325), small furnace, small machine shop. Classrooms included engine, blueprint reading, drafting and rivet theory.

SCHOOL, APPRENTICE:
Length of time to complete - 6,000 to 8,000 hours. Length of classes 2-4 hours per week. Average age 18-21. At Willow Run-December, 1942 - 385 apprentices.

SCHOOL, ARMY AIR BASE: SEE "AIR BASE"

SCHOOL, PRODUCTION TRAINING:
Operated in departments.

SCHOOL RIVET:
Up to October 26, 1944 - 21,785 riveters completed rivet training. Now confined to department's on floor as shop training "on the Job".

SCRAP:
1400-1800 cans emptied daily. Saving in paper toweling from 50 cases to 90 over 24 hour period; 187,500 sheets used. Salvage at Willow Run will represent a daily total of 206,000 pounds, a large part of total is in aluminum, which reaches the figure of 84,312 lbs., 90% of which is type segregated. Waste paper will run 35,560 lbs. daily. Solids and turnings which include steel, cast iron, copper, bronze, brass and zinc will total 76,995 pounds daily. Plexiglas - 953 lbs., old files - 54 lbs., grinding wheels - 173 pounds, material from sewing shop total 557 lbs. About 171 gallons of oil are also salvaged daily. The Salvage Department returns many items to production. The daily average

amounts to 69,699 pieces.

SELECTIVE SERVICE:
In 1943, 15.18% of total quits were employees entering military service. Number of men called in January 1943, 888; The number of men called in January 1944, 178.

SERVICE GARAGE:
(New Materials Bldg.) For plant employees. Open 19 hours daily starting at 7 A.M. Towing & service all makes [of automobiles]. Phone 8757 Russ Dawson.

SEWERS:
Manufacturing Building - 18 miles; parking lots - 9 miles; parking lots (drain tile) - 6 miles; waste and soil pipe - 17 miles; airport storm sewers - 72 miles; airport drain tile - 85 miles. *Sewage Disposal*: Approximately 1&1/2 million gallons treated daily. Plant - 27 ft. long, 27 ft. wide. Area; 3,300 sq. ft.

SEWING: SEE "FABRIC"

SHEARING: (New Materials Bldg.)

14 shears: 3 - 20 foot, 3 - 8 foot, 7 - 6 foot, 1 Allegheny scrap cutter. 7000 pieces sheared per ship. 50 diff. metals from .012 - .25". 14,000 pieces daily. 2 shifts, 61 men.

SHIELDED RADIO TEST ROOM:

Copper-walled room built inside copper-walled room. Said to be only one in existence. Effective as high as 500 megacycles.

SHIPPING:

Shipments from Willow Run, New Materials Bldg., Salvage yards, and Defense Plant Corp average 935 daily under inter-plant transfers, direct sales & shipment of government materials. Shipment of regular spares average 10% of total B-24 parts list. To date parts to cover 7,000 bombers have been shipped. Expedite shipments are sent by Air Freight or Railway Express, covering every request of Air Service Command.

SHOWERS: 56 in plant.

SKIN:
Thickness of, from .128" to .025".

STABILIZER, HORIZONTAL: SEE "CONTROL SURFACES"
Total area: 140.54 sq. ft.

STAGGER BALANCING:
Leading edges of rudder and elevators flared to permit slip stream of air to pass through to assist pilot in moving control surfaces.

STATIC DISCHARGERS:
On vertical fins and wing tips. Metal arms with self-contained wick saturated with glycerine. Used to discharge static electricity that builds up in ship while in flight.

STRINGERS: SEE "DRAW BENCH"

STOCK: SEE "AREA" & "CRIBS"

SILICA-GEL:
Moisture absorbent and dehydrating agent kept with precision-made parts while in storage. Indicates amount of moisture by changing color from original shade of blue to red.

APPENDIX B

-T-

TABS, CONTROL:
Manufactured at Rouge Tire Plant. Area of elevator tabs (both) 2.40 sq. feet. Used to "trim" ship while in flight. All metal construction.

TABULATING: SEE "I. B. M."

TANKS: SEE "WATER:"

TAXIWAYS:
Width - 80 ft. Two lead from Apron 1 to Apron 2. Eastern taxiway leads to runways 4L, 4R, 9R. 50-ft. taxiways connected apron at Army Air Base & runways 27R & 27L. Total length - 12,081 ft. (2.3 mi.). Area of runways & taxi ways - 828,000 sq. yds.

TELAUTOGRAPH:
Issues general orders from main office of Material Control to 22 stations. Relieves traffic on trunk telephone lines. Furnishes written evidence of each request for stock or shortage in all Material Control areas.

TENSIOMETER: Used to check tension on cables in ship.

THERMOCOUPLE INSTRUMENT:
Registers heat of engines. Coupled to number five (5) cylinder of each engine.

THIMBLES, SAFETY:
350 in use by operators of squeeze rivet machine operators.

TIME DEPARTMENT:
140 employees; 8 field offices. Number of clocks = 220

WILLOW RUN

TIRES: (Main Strut)

Size: 56" diameter; 16 ply. Weight = 250 pounds. Weight of tube = 37½ pounds. Weight of Complete wheel assemby = 562 pounds. Construction: Natural Rubber side walls, synthetic tread. Ground contact area 345 sq. in. Nose Wheel: Size 36" diameter, 10 ply. Designed to carry load of 8,200 lbs. Tubes: All tubes are made from natural rubber. Must support 27,000 pounds. Will support (as set) over 200,000 lbs.

TOLERANCES:

Maximum allowed in mating fuselage sections to center wing = 1/16". Engine mounts = .02" to .003"; C.W. ends = .010".

TOWERS, COOLING:

Three towers constructed of sheet metal, lined with red wood. Cool air for Administration Bldg., dope room and decompression chamber.

TOWER, CONTROL:

5 transmitters, 16 radio receivers, 1 radio range station, 2-35 mm film recorders, 1 teletype. Over 500 pair electric wires enter control panel; 436 switches. 73,669 flights (to 12/1/44) without field mishaps. First used: June 24, 1942.

TRAILERS:

(For "KD" Ships) Original fleet = 114 trailers. 85 since transferred to other aircraft plants. Since August 1, 1944, no assemblies shipped from Willow Run as "KD". Comparing shipment of a B-24 by railroad car & trailer discloses that 4 railroad cars were needed as against 2½ trailers. A trip to San Diego and back made by trailers made in 9½ days. While on the road, drivers changed every 5 hours. At some points along the route, overhead bridges had to be cleared; a three inch clearance was aver age. Maximum weight that a trailer could carry was 27,000 lbs. Averaged 250 round trips a month, the highest number ever made was 375. Trailers transferred: Consolidated, 42; Curtiss-Wright, Buffalo, 30; North American, Dallas, 4; North American, Kansas City, 4; Douglas, Oklahoma City, 4; Douglas, Tulsa, 1; Ford, 6.

TRAIN: (For Visitors)

Powered by 18-plate Philco storage battery, weighing 1358 lbs. (Type 19XV)

TRANSPORTATION:

(Automotive equipment) 56 passenger cars, 12 station wagons, 47 stake trucks, 16 truck tractors, 31 pickups, 78 dump trucks, 51 misc. trucks 72 scooters, 14 Ferguson-Sherman tractors, 45 Moto-tugs, 50 four- wheel stake trail ers, 24 semi-trailer, 10 gravity dump trucks, 28 shop trucks, and 9 Mercury Banty tugs. (Does not include units used by contractors & serviced by Transportation Department).

TRANSPORTATION BUREAU:

Number of cars registered, 12,885; Drive about 274,960 miles per day. Use about 18,331 gals. per of day. Approx. 49 tire certificates used daily. Averaged 3.1 riders per car. Detroit - 201 zones; 50 surrounding townships. 35 bus trips daily by DSR; 150 trips daily by private lines. Average bus count per day - 2,854.

TUBING:

Amount used, 278 feet rubber; 3,300 feet metal. 1800 tubes in ship; 12 systems; 36 hand-benders; 4 power-drive Parkomartic. Hydraulic systems - 2 on each ship. Approximately 25,000 tubes bent and marked with identification tape daily.

Identification Colors:

SMOKE-SCREEN - brown-white; HYDRAULIC - blue-yellow-light blue; COMPRESSED AIR (pressure-25 psi) yellow-green; STEAM - light blue-black; PURGING - light blue - yellow; EXHAUST - light blue-brown; ANTI-ICING - white-red; OXYGEN - green; PITOT PRESSURE - black; AIR SPEED STATIC PRESSURE - green-blue; MANIFOLD - light blue-white; VACUUM - light green-white; AIR PRESSURE, COMPRESSED (20 PSI) - light blue-green; FUEL LINE - red; FUEL AND OIL VENT - red-black; LUBRICATING OIL - yellow; COOLANT AND PRESTONE - white-black - white; FIRE EXTINGUISHER - brown; WATER - white; FLOAT-ATIONS - light blue. Master form blocks made in carpenter shop.

TURRET, BOTTOM: (Sperry Retractable)
Local control (Gunner inside). Power-Vicker electro-hydraulic unit. Voltage - 40 volts. Sight - Sperry Automatic computing type. Guns are charged individually by manual chargers. Diameter of turret - 44"; diameter of turret ring - 47½"; Heights of hangar assembly (retracted) 104 1/8". Heights of turret & hanger assembly (extended) - 131 5/8". Rotation in azimuth - 360 degrees; elevation of guns-85° from vertical. Ammunition stored in containers attached to hanger assembly outside of turret. Ammunition storage - 650 rounds per gun. Weight of turret - 780 pounds.

Operation: Side pressure on hand grips gives azimuth rotation; forward or back pressure moves turret up or down.

APPENDIX B

TURRET, NOSE: (Emerson Electric-Type A-3D)
Local control (gunner inside). Electrically operated; voltage - 27.5 volts. Guns are charged individually by manual chargers. Sight: ring reticle reflector type. Protection: bullet-proof glass and armor plate in front of the gunner. Diameter of turret - 42"; heights-69"; weight - 720 lbs; Azimuth rotation - 150 degrees; elevation of guns - 60° above horizontal; depression of guns - 50° below low horizontal. Ammunition storage - 700 rounds per gun, stored in boxes located outside of turret on each side of nose fuselage.

TURRET, TAIL:
Type - Army A-6-C. Manufactured by Southern Aircraft Corp. Hydraulically operated; no armor protection. Equipped with K-10 compensating sight. Diameter - 40"; height - 58"; weight approximately 550 lbs. 500 rounds of ammunition per gun stored in bins located in aft section of fuselage. Azimuth rotation 122°. Depression of guns - 40° below horizontal; elevation 71° above horizontal.

Operation: Side pressure on gun grips actuates a rack & pinion (located under the gunner's seat) which rotatoes the turret. Forward or backward pressure actuates hydraulic jack (in front center of turret) which moves the guns in a vertical plane.

TURRET, TOP: (Glenn L. Martin - Type A-3D)
Local control (gunner inside turret). Power-electrical. Volt age - 27.5 volts D.C. Sight: reflector ring reticle compensating type. Guns are charged individually by manual charger. Protection: armor plate below ring in front of gunner. Diameter of turret - 42". Heights - 60"; Weight - 564 pounds. Azimuth rotation - 360°; elevation of guns

from 3° to plus 85°; depression of guns 8° below horizontal. Ammunition storage - 480 rounds per gun stored in containers suspended from turret ring in front of gunner.

TURRET INTERRUPTERS:
Used to prevent gunner from accidentally firing into his own ship during combat.

TURBO SUPERCHARGER:
Inventor Dr. Sanford Moss, General Electric. Horse Power generated - 180 each. Temperature of super charger air 400°F. Lubrication - Jet and splash system. Each engine requires 135 pounds of air per minute at sea level. Speeds up to 28,000 RPMs; Ford built at River Rouge Plant until October 1944. 52,244 produced.

TYLER LAKE:
Surface area: 640,000 square feet. Contents: approximately 30,000,000 gallons. Depth: average 9 feet.

TYPEWRITERS:
734 at Willow Run, including 250 Electromatics (1/5/45).

V

VISITORS:
(Sunday, December 10, 1944) Passed the 200,000 mark.

W

WATER: SEE ALSO "TOWER, COOLING"
Approximately 5,000,000 gallons daily. Two water tanks hold 400,000 gallons each. Supplied by three Rawsonville wells; pumped through two 24" mains at rate of 270,000 gallons per hour.

WATER TREATMENT PLANT:

Capacity - 6,000,000 - gallons per day; 700 gallons per min. Average treated - 4,500,000 gallons per day. Amount of lime used - approximately 1,600 pounds per million gallons of water. Soda ash averaged 250 pounds daily. Size: 71 feet long; 70 feet wide. Area 18,000 square feet.

WEIGHT OF BOMBER: (From Engineering)

	Wt. In Lbs.
Wing Group	6,652
Tail Group	906
Fuselage Group	3,407
Landing Gear	3,002
Engine Nacelles	1,745
4 Engine (Installed)	6,050
4 Engine (access)	1,559
Power Plant Control	288
Propellers & Government	1,892
Starting System	212
Lubricating System	682
Fuel System (SS tank)	2,468
Instruments	179
Surface Control	594
Furnishings	1,146
Communications	773
Electric Equipment	1,064
Anti-icing	208
Aux. Power Plant	119
Hydraulic	466
Armament	2,819

Designed Load	36,231
Crew & Parachutes	2,000
Fuel (2087 gals.)	12,946
Oil (120 gals.)	870
Flex guns & instal.	2,370
Bombs (4 - 500 lbs)	2,006
Useful Load	19,769
Max Wt. Allowable	56,000

Plane weighs 37,205 lbs. as it enters Gas House, 47,255 when it leaves. In hangar added 500 lbs. stowage, 1,600 gal. gas, 120 gal oil. Wt. on delivery 49,900 lbs. 50 lb. variation in ships.

WEIGHING THE B-24:
15% of all ships are weighed. Scales located in Gas House are only ones of kind in aircraft. Ships leveled and weighed in 5 minutes. Each of three weighing platforms has 52,000 pound capacity.

WELDING:
Welding Spot: 8500 pieces per day; 60,000 welds; 25 welds per minute. 700 assemblies are spot welded. 63 machines at W. R. 66 proposals accepted, with 46 in production. 90.55 man hours saved per ship or 37,668 per month; replacing 5,620 rivets. Total of 7181 spot welds per ship. In front bomb doors are 1992 welds; in aft, 1176. Roller welders capacity - 300 welds per minute. Arc and gas - 2500 pieces per day.

WELDING, ACETYLENE:
85 unlike aluminum duct and tubing assemblies welded with acetylene gas. 10 chemical cleaning tanks.

APPENDIX B

WINDOWS:
No. in plant - 28,855. 30 different types of glass used.

WING: SEE ALSO "CENTER WING", "OUTER WING" AND "FUEL CELLS"
Dimensions: Length - 110 feet. Area - 1048 sq. ft. Wt. of wing group - 6652 lbs. When plane climbs, wing tips are higher than normal. Limit of wing deflection 45", but safety margin permits up to 6 ft. Tail may whip down 3/4". Built to withstand 25Gs (25 times force of gravity). In perfect landings might be 1 to 2 Gs. Known record is 22 Gs.

WING TIPS:
Mf'd. by E. G. Budd Co., contains 1,650 rivets. Built separately from outer wing panel.

ADDENDA

ALROKING:
52,115 pieces and 9,000 pounds of rivets alroked daily.

AMMUNITION LOAD: (Weight in pounds from engineering)

Nose turret	1200 rounds,	349 lbs.
Top Turret	800 rounds,	233 "
Bottom Turret	1016 rounds,	296 "
Tail turret	632 rounds,	184 "
Waist Guns	1000 rounds,	292 "
TOTAL	4648 rounds,	1354 "

309

WILLOW RUN

AREA, SHIP:
>   Skin surface: Wing - 2200 sq. ft.; Fuselage - 1200 sq. ft.;
>   Empennage - 500 sq. ft.; Engine Nacelle - 300 sq. ft.
>   Total - 4200 sq. ft.

ENGINE INSTALLATION:
>   10 minutes to lower and secure with four bolts. 1 1/2 hour
>   per engine for complete installation.

HEAT TREAT: (Draw Bench)
>   Four Holcroft electric furnaces and quenching chambers.
>   Temperature of furnaces 935° F. Time approx. 2 hrs. de-
>   pending on gauge of material. Capacity - 1800 lbs. per hour
>   per furnace.

NOSE WHEEL:
>   Weight of assembly - 358 lbs.; tire 51 lbs.; tube 20 lbs.;
>   wheel 38 lbs.

STURDYBENDERS;
>   Used to punch holes in stringers for aluminum skin rivet
>   ing. 312 holes can be punched in a 28-ft. strip at one time.

SUPERCHARGER:
>   Each weighs 140 pounds.

TUBING:
>   1726 tubing assemblies in ship.

YODER ROLLS:
>   250 different rolls used. 11 machines.

APPENDIX B

CHRONOLOGY ADDENDA

CONTRACTORS' MANCOUNT

January 1,	1941 0
July 1,	1941 183
January 1,	1942 3762
January 30,	1942 4500
July 1,	1942 3163
January 1,	1943 614
July 1,	1943. 181
January 1,	1944 646
July 1,	1944 885
January 1,	1945 43

APPENDIX C

WILLOW RUN TELEPHONE DIRECTORY
January 1941 - December 1944

-A-

Abbott, L.F.		8128 - 8667
Abrasive Stock		8217
Adams, Jack		8441- 2
Adm. Bldg. Garage		8203
Aero Medical		8183 - 8611
Aft Bottom Fuselage		8675
Aft Fuselage		8378
Airplane School		8550
Air Transport Command		8727
Albertson, W		8695
Alexander, Capt. C. G.		8676 - 77
Area 1 (Material)		8294
Area 2 (Material)		8528
Area 3 (Material)		8527
Area 4 (Material)		8043
Area 5 (Material)		8700
Area 6 (Material)		8145
Area 7 (Material)		8554
Area 8 (Material)		8092 - 8314
Area 9 (Material)		8641
Area 10 (Material)		8731
Area Sup't. Office	(1-A)	8135
Area Sup't. Office	(1-B)	8245
Area Sup't. Office	(2)	8209
Area Sup't. Office	(3-A)	8159
Area Sup't Office	(3-B)	8725
Area Sup't. Office	(5)	8536

APPENDIX C

Armament Crib	8601
Armament (Engr.)	8283
Army Operations	8614 - 8623
Assembly (Sup't.)	8516 - 7

-B-

B-24 Studio (Adm.)	8291 - 8132
Badge Crib (GG-11)	8010
Badge Crib (J-33)	8389
Baker, D.	8158
Banks, Capt. Wm.	8409 - 8614 - 8623
Bannasch, I	8175
Barnabee, J. I.	8186
Barth, C.	8626
Bass, C.	8068
Bastian, D.	8242
Battery Lab.	8608
Bell, A	8329
Bennett, H. H. (Office)	8486 -7
Bernard, C.	8140
Bibb, E. W.	8325
Blaess, W.	8393 - 8635
Bldg. Grounds & Airport Maint.	8107
Bloomburg, P. (Adm.)	8332
Blott, Jack	8458
Blue Print Machines	8188
B/P & Releases (Engr.)	8286 - 8549
Boelter, L.	8037
Bond, Ed. J.	8260 - 8459
Bonis, J.	8470
Bomber Lunch	8048
Bounds, C.	8079

313

Bradley, G.	8188
Branion, H.	8203
Breest, E. (Export Shipping)	8463
Breest, L.	8217
Bricker, M. L.	8441 - 2
Briggs, R. H.	8584
Britton, Dr. H. H.	8183 - 8611
Brown, Ernest	8230
Bullock, F. D.	8415
Burkhard, C.	8605 - 8606
Bush, J. V.	8608
Butterfield, C. D.	8049 - 8109

-C-

Cadaret, John	8518 - 8532
Cafe (Hangar)	8693
Cain, W.	8037
Cannon, S. K.	8159
Carlton, C. J.	8344
Carpenter Shop	8184
Cecil, T.	8785
Chamberlain, F. L.	8521-2
Champion, J.	8793
Chief Engineer (Power House)	8365
Chief Flight Engineer	8612 - 8755
Church, M.	8415
Ciupak, J.	8281
Clark, Dr. C. J.	1883 - 8611
Clean-up	8569
Clifton, N.	8045
Cline, M.	8356 - 8578
Coff, Joe	8707

APPENDIX   C

|---|---|
Coker, Capt. T. W.	8054 - 8148
Cold Heading	8082
Collins, Gil J.	8441 - 2
Compensation	8268 - 9
Conant, A.	8003
Cooke, G.	8060 - 2
Cooley, Don	8348
Contract (Adm. Bldg)	8518 - 8532
Controls (Engr.)	8274
Controls Surface (Engr.)	8283
Control Tower	8396
Corpin, D. P.	8276 - 8587
Cortesi, J.	8284
Couch, M.	8110 - 8685
Coultier,J.	8362
Conveyors	8127
Crane Operators	8386
Crane Repair	8386
Cromwell, F.	8129
Cullimore, J.	8159
Cummings, E. H.	8156
Cummings, E. (Engr.)	8186
Cummings, W. W.	8154
Cummins, M.	8157 - 8650
CVAC (Engr)	8161 - 8177
CVAC Rep. (Hangar	8360 - 8713
CW Bulkhead & Spars	8159
CW Horizontal	8144
CW Leading Edge	8752
CW Sub-Ass'y	8249
CW Vertical	8038
Cyanide Plant	8568

315

-D-

Dahlinger, C.	8212 - 3
Dailey, R. H.	8276 - 8587 - 9
Dake, Ray	8071
Danna, J.	8302 - 3 - 4
Davis, Joe	8481- 2
Dawson, Dr. W. A.	8212 - 3
Day, E.	8563
Day, G. W.	8328
De Clerque, R.	8003
Deferments	8285
De Forest, S. A.	8564
Dempster, D.	8402
Die Storage	8566
Dispatcher (Hangar)	8682
Distribution (Outside Plants)	8251 - 8397
Doeren, H. (Traffic)	8425
Dope Room	8720
Dorrance, W. H.	8107
Draw Bench	8124
Dulmage, R.	8096 - 8430
Dyer, A.	8706
Dyke, S.	8028
Dysinger, K.	8097

E

East End (Plant Protection)	8691
Eckles, C. (Receiving)	8056
Elberth, R.	8067
Eldredge, R.	8293
Electrical	8350
Electrical (Cons't.)	8511

Electrical (Crane Rep)	8386
Electrical (Eng.)	8272 - 8771
Electrical (Maint.)	8041
Ellis, J.	8273
Ellison, C.	8023
Empennage	8664
Empson, R. J.	8724
Engineering (Control)	8783
Engineering (Illustration)	8744
Engineering (Release Sect.)	8286
Employment	8009 - 8072 - 8337
Employment (Field)	8204
Employees' Relations	8748 - 8341
"E. O." Items (Eng.)	8500
Esckilsen, Larry	8450
Esordi, S. E.	8289
Evenseon, L. H.	8135

-F-

Fabricating Shop	8200
Farley, R. J.	8415
Fenker, L. H.	8707
Ferris, C. W.	8127
Fey, A.	8232
Field Engineering	8012
Final Assembly	8238
Fire Department	8071
Fitzpatrick, D.	8278
Flight Mechanics' Office	8579
Flight Operations	8654
Flight Records	8665
Flight Refueling	8526

Flory, F. C.	8620
Folley, Walter.	8532 - 18
Forche, A.	8084 - 21
Ford, Don	8181
Ford, G.	8108
Ford, S.	8253 - 8309
Ford, Victor	8422 - 3
Foremen's Personnel	8784
Foster, T.	8707
Freitag H.	8664
Fuel Cells	8144
Fuel Station (Sta. 28)	8760
Furnishings (Eng.)	8186
Fuselage (Framework)	8329

-G-

Gauges (Design)	8266
Galasso, A.	8173 - 8181
Gas House	8760
General Shipping	8792
Gerding, S. F.	8612
G. F. E. Equipment (Adm.)	8716 - 8615
Gillespie, R. J.	8550
Gilligan, O. R.	8366
Gleason, R. J.	8672 - 8293
Goodknight, F.	8240 - 8220
Gourley, Ed	8486 - 7
Granger, D.	8050
Green, J.	8135
Grenier, E. P.	8354
Grounds Maint. (Hangar # 1)	8571
Gueldner, L.	8161

APPENDIX   C

Guides (Personnel)	8464 - 8130
Gullekson, G.	8297 - 8533

-H-

Hall, B.	8707
Hangar, Balcony (Eng.)	8622
Hangar (Eng.)	8505
Hangar, Maint. (Hangar # 1)	8679
Hanson, H. B.	8012
Harcas, M.	8050
Harrington, J. J.	8450
Harris, W.	8563
Harrold, Wm.	8715
Hart, H.	8168
Hant, Joe	8715
Hayward, R.	8283
Heales, J.	8707
Heating, & Ventilating	8097
Hefley, E. J.	8612
Helms, G.	8680
Herschler, R.	8241
Higginbotham, O.	8707
Hill, J.	8012
Heins, G.	8516 - 7
Hoadley, H.	8108
Hoisington, E. R.	8020
Holloway, P.	8046
Holloway, V.	8313
Holmes, A.	8706
Hospital	8212 - 3
Houston, Robert	8311 - 2
Hoyt, L.	8536

Hughes, Matt.   8163
Hughes, R. L.   8109 - 8049 - 8326
Hunsburry, P. E.   8122
Huston, Lt. Col. Paul. W.   8460 - 8676
Hutchinson, J.   8031 - 8252
Hydraulic (Eng.)   8604
Hydraulics   8115
Hydro Plant   8600

-I-

Inspection (Army)   8737 - 38
Inspection (Bernard)   8140
Inspeciton (Burkhard)   8140
Inspection (Fixture & Tool Gauge)   8028
Inpection (Hangar)   8258 - 8644
Inspection (Layout)   8047
Inspection (Liaison)   8026
Inspection (Mfg.)   8680
Inspection (Receiving)   8470
Inspection (Sielke)   8024
Inspection (Structural)   8346
Inspection (Young)   8258
Instruments (Eng.)   8272
Instrument Laboratory   8608
Insurance Group   8342
Iovine, Capt. G. G.   8614 - 23
I. P. T.'S   8563
Item Leaders (Tool Design)   8646
Item Serials (Material)   8370

APPENDIX C

-J-

Jannuzzi, J.	8792
Jarrchow, H.	8622
Jarvis, J.	8603
Jensen, A.	8675
Jesme, R.	8144
Johnson, A.	8044
Johnson, Maj. D. W.	8460 - 8676 - 77
Johnson, E.V.	8272 - 8771
Johnson, H.	8039
Johnson, Rodney	8003
Johnson, Walter	8453 - 4
Jones, Capt. B. F.	8614 - 8623
Joyce, John	8707

-K-

Karlovetz, Paul G.	8663
Kehn, W.	8696
Keily, E.	8781
Kennedy, J.	8707
Kenny, H.	8378
Kerbyson, E. C.	8783
Ketchman, R.	8604
Killian, T. A.	8620
Krech, Col. A. M	8341 - 8748
Kroll, R.	8358
Kujawa, Capt. L. J.	8676 - 77
Kuzara, J.	8224

-L-

Laboratory	8036
Labor Relations	8157 - 8650
Lending Gear (Eng.)	8129

Laney, B. J.	8572
Laney, B. M.	8328
La France, F.	8274
Lanning, J.	8360 - 8713
Lary, Paul	8750
Laughna, R. P.	8625 - 8723
Leaves of Absence	8011
Legal Liaison	8584
Leo, Capt. D.	8614 - 23
Levleit, Dan	8435
Library	8264
Lipinski, E.	8092 - 8314
Lobby (School)	8620
Loft (Eng.)	8507
Lucas, H. M.	8268 - 8549
Luedeman, E.	8068

-M-

Machine & Fixture Design	8175
Machine Repair (Material)	8087
Mackie, Howard	8073 - 4
Machine Shop	8006
Maintenance (Adm.)	8332
Maintenance Carpenters	8510
Maintenance (Hangar)	8679
Manufacturing Office	8707
Manson, Herbert	8095 - 8153
Master Release (Eng.)	8500
Material Conservation	8393 - 8635
Maxwell, E. G.	8189 - 8330
Mayer, J. M.	8737 - 38
Mater & Misc. Changes	8301

APPENDIX   C

Mc Clellan, J.	8060 - 2
Mc Clure, K.	8082
Mc Cutcheon, M. T.	8723
Mc Donald, Irvin	8401
Mc Dougall, J.	8181 - 8633
Mc Kenzie, C.	8716
Mc Laughlin, M.	8055
Mc Maters, A.	8177
Mc Menamy, C.	8129
Mc Niel, W.	8064
Mc Roberts, R.	8707
Mechanical Maintenance (Power House)	8365
Medberry, Maj. Ray	8460
Mida, Bert	8184
Miller, Ed.	**8003**
Miller, Logan	8411 - 2- 55
Miller, Richard	**8124**
Milligan, R.	**8008**
Misc. Stock (Material)	8085 - 8548
Moore, Robert	8486 - 7
Montonye, J.	8038
Mullen, W.	8200
Mullikin, S. D.	8030 - 8344
Mummery, G. E.	8202
Murray, W.	8707

-N-

Nestor, T. A.	8049 - 8109 - 8326
Newkirk, D.	8251 - 8397
News Bureau	8189 - 8330
Nichols, W. J.	8545
Nida, Ed.	8209

WILLOW RUN

Noll, Conrad	8584
Novak, J.	8752

-O-

Oberts, Russel	8000
Oil & Paint Stock	8079
Opperation Sheets	8256
Orr, Robert	8159
Outside Production	8613 - 8418 - 8521 - 2

-P-

Paint Dept.	8040
Paint Maint.	8238
Palmer, R.	8519
Parachute Room	8671
Parks, E.	8026
Parts & Check-Off Lists	8325
Pattern Vault	8227
Patterson, C.	8516 - 7
Patterson F.	8162
Pattison, N. K.	8722
Pay Office	8338 - 8749
Payroll	8364
Pearson, Gus	8301 - 8394
Pellerin, Ralph	8685
Personnel (Adm.)	8486 - 7
Personnel Records	8116 - 8 - 8123
Peters, W.	8707
Peterson, R. G.	8663
Petri, C.	8342
Petty, Mel	8411 - 2 - 8455
Photographic Dept.	8237
Pickels, Don	8173 - 8181 - 8633

Pilot's Floor	8160
Pilot's Seats (Mf'g)	8242
Pioch, E.	8175
Pioch, W. F. (Eng.)	8133
Pipe Shop	8163
Planning Division	8325
Plant Layout	8108
Plant Protection	8073 - 4
Plant Protection (L-26)	8229
Plant Protection Lobby (Hangar)	8666
Plant Protection (Hangar)	8164
Plating	8023
Plexiglas	8267
Power Dept.	8096 - 8430
Power House (Electrical)	8244
Power Equipment	8365
Power & Millwright	8156
Power Plant (Eng.)	8281
Powers, lst. Lt. R. E.	8614
Pre-Flight (Sta. 26)	8715
Press Shop	8068
Print Shop	8663
Production Co-ordination (J-55)	8110 - 8772
Production Control	8356 - 8578
Production Records	8049 - 8109 - 8326
Production Time Control	8695
Propeller room	8334
Pumping Station	8125 - 26
Purchasing	8432 - 3

-R-

Radio (Plant Protection)	8191

Radio (Engineering)	8206
Rainey, C. W.	8608
Rate & Deferment	8284 - 8618
Raum, C.	8110 - 8772
Receiving Dept. (Plant)	8050 - 3 - 6
Receiving Dept. (New Mtls Bldg)	8055
Refrigeration	8096
Reid, Jack	8186
Reinelt, R.	8569
Reynolds, Lee	8601
Richards, A. B.	8036
Riecks, A.	8338 - 8749
Robb, J.	8186
Rogers, L.	8061
Rough Sock	8793
Ruddiman, Edsel	8173 - 81 -8633

-S-

Safety	8362 - 8537
Salvage Yard	8061
Salvage Materials	8748
Salvage records	8313
Saws	8785 - 8115
Scarlett, G.	8255
Scheduling	8397 - 8251
Scheffler, C.	8268
Schmidt, W.	8744
Schumaker, A. J.	8281
Scott, L.	8657
Sechrest, R.	8245
Service Garage (Employees)	8757
Severson, E. M.	8755

APPENDIX C

Sewage Disposal	8134
Shear Department	8785
Shemanske, F.	8567
Sheridan, T.	8516-7
Shingler, K.	8006
Shipping Dept.	8060
Shipping (General)	8792
Shipping (New Mtls Bldg)	8137 - 8792
Ship's Records	8339
Sielke, M.	8024
Simonds, Wm. A.	8130 - 8464
Sirlin, N.	8132 - 8291
Sivy, W.	8175
Small Parts	8241
Smith, A.	8684 - 8508
Smith, R.	8227
Solverson, F.	8047
Sommerville, R.	8244
Spalding, R. D.	8720
Spares Division	8625 - 8723
Spaulding, R.	8040
Spiegel, A.	8293 - 8672
Spuhler, W.	8755
Stambaugh, Lt. R.	8117 - 8545
Standard Parts (Eng.)	8278
Stanton, C. N.	8275 - 8446
Starke, B.	8171
Starr, P. A.	8289
Station (Final Ass'y)	8520
Staudinger, Joe	8108
Steel Stock (Material	8253 - 8309
Stem, A.	8585

Stewart, Alan	8753
Stroup,T	8510
Structure (Engr.)	8500
Stokers & Fuel Oil	8365
Styles, Leo T.	8586 - 8681
Superintendent's Office	8411 - 2 - 8455
Superintendent's (Asst.)	8453 - 4 - 8481 - 2
Superintendent (Field)	8003 - 8359
Supervisory Conference Dept	8450
Sutliff, Z	8602 - 8171
Sweeton, J.	8085 - 8548
Snyder, O.	8094

-T-

Tabulating & Systems	8293 - 8672
Taylor, Frank	8396
Taylor, W. H.	8275 - 8446
Teeple, W. C.	8550
Telegraph (Adm.)	8122
Telephone repair	8100
Templet Crib	8027
Thibodeau, A.	8272
Thomas, C. W.	8275 - 8446
Time Department	8407
Time Study	8220 - 8240
Tipper, D.	8679
Tool Coordination	8255
Tool Design	8173 - 8633
Tool Room	8171
Tool Stock Cribs	8094
Tool Stock & General Stores (Mat'l)	8088 - 9
Tool Stock Ledgers	8182

APPENDIX   C

Tool Trouble	8626
Tracing Files	8188
Transportation Bureau	8349
Transportation Garage	8724
Trim (Eng.)	8186
Typewriter Repair	8100

-U-

Unruh, Ray	8521 - 2
Upchurch, E.	8752

-V-

Van Dyke, F.	8208
Vandermade, P.	8264
Van Houten, E.	8534
Van Vactor, J.	8160
Vaughan, E.	8388
Virgo, S.	8679
Visitor's Lobby (Main gate)	8075 - 8263

-W-

Wagner, Walter F.	8481 - 2
Wahl, R.	8571
Waling, J.	8087
Walter, C.	8249
Wessman, H.	8346
Weather Bureau	8755
Water Filtration Plant	8126 - 25
Webb, R.	8474
Weeks, J.	8159
Weidmann, J.	8707
Weight (Eng.)	8354

WILLOW RUN

Welding	8037
Wellock, G.	8256
Wendell, T.	8115
Wesley, D.	8266
Westerman, H.	8348
Whitney, C. E. (Air Base)	8491
Wiese, Miss Johanna	8264
Williams, R.	8350
Williams, Jerry	8049 - 8326 - 8109
Wilson, W. A.	8334
Wing (Eng.)	8129
Woodcock, I.	8566
Work Order Department	8032

-Y-

Yantins, J.	8283
Young, E.	8258

-Z-

Zielke, F. W.	8126
Zoumbaris, G.	8071

APPENDIX D

PRESTIGIOUS WILLOW RUN VISITORS

Honorable Norman Armour, Ambassador to Argentina

General H.H. Arnold, United States Army Air Force

Dr. Eduard Benes, President of Czechoslovakia

Joseph Beck, Grand Duchy of Luxembourg

Irving Berlin, Composer "This Is The Army"

Prince Bernhard, President Consort Netherlands

Attorney General, Francis J. Biddle

Joe E. Brown, Hollywood Actor

Walter Davenport, Staff Writer, Colliers

Sir John Dill, British Field Marshall

Walt Disney, Hollywood

Honorable Joseph B. Eastman, Chief Defense Transportation

James Farley, Ex-Postmaster General

Garcie Fields, Hollywood Actress

Harvey Firestone, Jr. Firestone Tire Company

Herbert Gaston, Assistant Secretary Treasury

Major General Giles, Assistant Chief of Staff USAAF

General Henri Giraud, Free French Forces

Manfred Gootfried, Managing Editor, Time

Honorable Joseph Grew, Under Secretary of State

W. Averill Harriman, Ambassador to Russia

Wm. Randolph Hearst, Jr., Newspaper Publisher

C. D. Howe, Canada's Minister of Munitions and Supplies

Paul Hunter, Publisher, Liberty

Eric Johnson, U.S. Chamber of Commerce

Gertrude Lawrence, English Actress
Walter Lippman, Commentator
Captain Oliver Lyttleton, British Supply
Dr. Carlos Martins, Ambassador of Brazil
Louis B. Mayer, M.G.M. Hollywood Studios
Sir Malcolm Mc Donald, British High Command
Adolph Menjou
Raymond Moley, Writer
Henry Morgenthau, Jr. Secretary of Treasure
Charles Murphy, Editor, Fortune
Justice Frank Murphy, Supreme Court
Honorable Walter Nash, Minister, New Zealand
Donald Nelson, War Production Board
Dr. Licenciado Ezequiel Padill, Mexico
Robert Patterson Under Secretary of War
General Enrique Penaranda, President of Bolivia
King Peter II, Jugoslavia
Walter Pidgeon, Hollywood Actor
President Manuel Prado, Republic of Peru
Honorable Sam Rayburn, Speaker US House of Represent-
atives
Colonel Eddie Rickenbacker, Aviator and World War I ace
General Alberto Romero, Ecuador
U.S. President and Mrs. Franklin D. Roosevelt
General L.G. Rudenko, Union of Soviet Socialist Republics
Beardsley Ruml, Author "Ruml Plan"
Governor General Ryckmans, Belgian Congo

APPENDIX D

Manuel de Freyre Y. Santander, Ambassador Peru
Governor Sewell, State of Maine
Chester Shaw, Managing Editor, Newsweek
C. W. Shaw. Assistant Secretary of State
Igor Sikorsky, Aircraft, Helicopters
General Brehon Sommervell, Service of Supply
Boyden Sparks, Writer
Arthur Hayes Sulzberger, New York Times
Lowell Thomas, News Commentator
Senator Harry Truman and Senate Committee
General Sir W. K. Venning, British Supply Mission
Vice-President Henry A. Wallace
C.E. Wilson, War Production Board.

BIBLIOGRAPHY

Alcorn, John S. *The Jolly Rogers*. Temple City, CA: Historical Aviation Album, 1981.

Carr, Lowell and James Stermer. *Willow Run: A Study of Industrialization and Cultural Inadequacy*. NewYork: Harper and Brothers, 1952.

de Tocqueville, Alexis. *Journey To America*. New Haven: Yale Press, 1960.

Ford, R. Bryan. *Henry's Lieutenants*. Detroit: Wayne State University Press, 1993.

Henning, William H. *Detroit, Its Trolleys and Interurbans*. Fraser, Michigan: Michigan Transit Museum, 1978.

Horst, Cathy and Diane Wilson. *Water Under the Bridge*. Belleville, Michigan: Van Buren Township Bicentennial Commission, 1972. Photos by David Carlson.

"In 100 Days Contractor Grades, Drains and Paves $3,900,000 Airport." *Construction Methods*, March 1942: 42-45+.

Kenney, General George C. *General Kenney Reports*. New York: Duell, Sloan and Pearce, 1949.

Kidder, Donald E. Reminiscence.

Lacey, Robert. *Ford, The Man and The Machine*. Boston: Little, Brown and Company, 1986.

Lindbergh, Anne Morrow. *War Within And Without*. New York: Harcourt Brace Jovanovich, Inc., 1980.

Lindbergh, Charles A. *The Wartime Journals of Charles A. Lindbergh*. New York: Harcourt Brace Jovanovich, Inc., 1970.

Pioneer Society of Michigan. *Historical Collections*.

Research Center of Henry Ford Museum and Greenfield Village, Dearborn, Michigan: Accession 435.

Schramm, Jack and William Henning. *Detroit Street Railways Vol. I: City Lines 1863-1922*. Chicago, Illinois: Central Electric Railfans' Association, 1978.

"Seven Months Schedule Completes 62-Acre Building for Ford Bomb-

BIBLIOGRAPHY

er Plant." *Construction Methods*, January, 1942: 42-47+.

Seventh Annual Report of the Commissioner of the Michigan Depart ment of Health for Fiscal Year Ending June 30, 1942. Lansing, Michigan.

Sherman, Harold W., Librarian. Reminiscence. Yankee Air Force Museum, Belleville, Michigan.

Shook, Robert L. *Turnaround.* New York: Prentice Hall, 1990.

Sorensen, Charles E. *My Forty Years With Ford.* New York: W. W. Norton, 1956.

"Will It Run?" *Flying Magazine,* May 1943: 21-3+.

Willow Run Reference Book 1941-1945. Unpublished.

Wilson, Marion. *The Story of Willow Run.* Ann Arbor: The University of Michigan Press, 1956.

INDEX

336

INDEX

INDEX

DENTON METHODIST CHURCH   DENTON, MICHIGAN

The Denton Methodist Church, pastorate of George T. Nevin for 20 years, stands in honor of all the early pioneers of Denton. Founded, by Clark and Hanna Horner, the first family to have resided on what became the Willow Run airport, its Sunday school and adult men's class were presided over by Eva and Elmer Kidder, the last family to have left. Interestingly, both families resided on the same piece of property, now within the confines of Willow Run.

This photograph is from the collection of Doretha (Youngs) and Edward Woods McKelvey who provided care and maintenance of the Denton church and its cemetery. Their home stands on the original 1827 land grant in the Willow Run area.

343

To order, call the author

1-800-754-6830
Access Code 30